## HISTORICAL DICTIONARIES OF
## U.S. HISTORICAL ERAS

### Jon Woronoff, Series Editor

*Portrait of Ronald Reagan*

*Portrait of George H. W. Bush*

*Ronald Reagan's Inauguration*

*George H. W. Bush's Inauguration*

# Historical Dictionary
# of the Reagan–Bush Era

Richard S. Conley

*Historical Dictionaries of
U.S. Historical Eras, No. 7*

The Scarecrow Press, Inc.
Lanham, Maryland • Toronto • Plymouth, UK
2007

SCARECROW PRESS, INC.

Published in the United States of America
by Scarecrow Press, Inc.
A wholly owned subsidiary of
The Rowman & Littlefield Publishing Group, Inc.
4501 Forbes Boulevard, Suite 200, Lanham, Maryland 20706
www.scarecrowpress.com

Estover Road
Plymouth PL6 7PY
United Kingdom

British Library Cataloguing in Publication Information Available

**Library of Congress Cataloging-in-Publication Data**

Conley, Richard Steven.
  Historical dictionary of the Reagan–Bush Era / Richard S. Conley.
    p. cm. — (Historical dictionaries of U.S. historical eras ; no. 7)
  Includes bibliographical references.
  ISBN-13: 978-0-8108-5064-4 (hardcover : alk. paper)
  ISBN-10: 0-8108-5064-8 (hardcover : alk. paper)
    1. United States—Politics and government—1981–1989—Dictionaries.
  2. United States—Politics and government—1989–1993—Dictionaries.
  3. United States—History—1969—Dictionaries.  I. Title.
  E876.C665 2007
  973.927—dc22                                                    2006031226

∞™  The paper used in this publication meets the minimum requirements of
American National Standard for Information Sciences—Permanence of Paper
for Printed Library Materials, ANSI/NISO Z39.48-1992.
Manufactured in the United States of America.

# Contents

# Editor's Foreword

Presidential administrations sometimes appear more successful the farther the actual events slip into the past and can be compared to the hesitations and blunders that follow. There is no question that Ronald Reagan, "the Great Communicator," was relatively popular with the general public, although his actual policies were received less well. His vice president and successor, George H. W. Bush, was not able to work such magic. There was strong resistance to the conservative revolution in many quarters, and the economy was not able to alleviate the distress of those who did not benefit from it. Foreign policy, however, took a turn for the better, going from deterrence to détente to cooperation with the toughest enemy the nation had known. After all, Reagan finally ended—some even said "won"—the Cold War, and Bush brought a stunning and quick conclusion to the Persian Gulf War. Thus it's worth taking another look at exactly what was and was not accomplished in the period from 1981 to 1993.

The chronology tracks the events of this time period, then the introduction offers a more general overview, highlighting both the key events and the major trends. The dictionary offers numerous, concise entries on crucial people, including the presidents themselves, their assistants and closest collaborators, their families, and their opponents and critics. Other entries summarize major events, significant legislation, and prominent issues of the time. The bibliography provides resources for additional reading.

This *Historical Dictionary of the Reagan–Bush Era* was written by Richard S. Conley, an associate professor of political science at the University of Florida, who teaches courses on American politics in general and the U.S. presidency in particular. He studies the postwar Republican presidents and is presently writing a book on George W. Bush. Dr. Conley has also lectured widely and published articles in leading scholarly journals, including *Congress and the Presidency*, *Presidential Studies Quarterly*, and *White House Studies*. Thus he is eminently capable of situating the crucial period of 1981 to 1993 in the broader context of what went before and what has followed and continues to affect us.

Jon Woronoff
Series Editor

# Acronyms and Abbreviations

| | |
|---|---|
| AAMA | American Automobile Manufacturers Association |
| ABC | American Broadcasting Corporation |
| ABM TREATY | Anti–Ballistic Missile Treaty |
| ADA | Americans with Disabilities Act |
| AIDS | Acquired Immune Deficiency Syndrome |
| ATF | Alcohol, Tobacco, and Firearms (Bureau of) |
| AWACS | Airborne Warning and Control System |
| CBS | Columbia Broadcasting System |
| CDU | Christian Democratic Union (German Political Party) |
| CIA | Central Intelligence Agency |
| CIS | Commonwealth of Independent States |
| CNN | Cable News Network |
| DJIA | Dow Jones Industrial Average |
| EEOC | Equal Employment Opportunity Commission |
| EOP | Executive Office of the President |
| EPA | Environmental Protection Agency |
| FBI | Federal Bureau of Investigation |
| FEMA | Federal Emergency Management Agency |
| FMLN | Farabundo Martí National Liberation Front |
| FSLN | *Frente Sandinista de Liberación Nacional* |
| GATT | General Agreement on Tariffs and Trade |
| GOP | Grand Old Party |
| HEW | Housing, Education, and Welfare (Department of) |
| HHS | Health and Human Services (Department of) |
| HIV | Human Immunodeficiency Virus |
| HUAC | House Un-American Activities Committee |
| HUD | Housing and Urban Development (Department of) |
| IBM | International Business Machines |

| | |
|---|---|
| ICBM | Intercontinental Ballistic Missile |
| INF TREATY | Intermediate-Range Nuclear Forces Treaty |
| KAL | Korean Air Lines |
| KGB | *Komitet Gosudarstvennoy Bezopasnosti* (Committee for State Security, USSR) |
| MAD | Mutually Assured Destruction |
| NAACP | National Association for the Advancement of Colored Persons |
| NAFTA | North American Free Trade Agreement |
| NASA | National Aeronautics and Space Administration |
| NATO | North Atlantic Treaty Organization |
| NSC | National Security Council |
| NSDD | National Security Decision Directive |
| OIRA | Office of Information and Regulatory Affairs |
| OMB | Office of Management and Budget |
| ONDCP | Office of National Drug Control Policy |
| PATCO | Professional Air Traffic Controllers Association |
| PAYGO | pay-as-you-go (budget) |
| PLO | Palestinian Liberation Organization |
| PNAC | Project for the New American Century |
| POW | Prisoner of War |
| PRC | People's Republic of China |
| SALT I | Strategic Arms Limitation Treaty I |
| SALT II | Strategic Arms Limitation Treaty II |
| SDI | Strategic Defense Initiative |
| START | Strategic Arms Reduction Treaty |
| SWAPO | South-West African People's Organization |
| TWA | Trans World Airlines |
| UN | United Nations |
| UNPROFOR | United Nations Protection Force |
| USS | United States Ship |
| USSR | Union of Soviet Socialist Republics |
| VISTA | Volunteers in Service to America |
| WTO | World Trade Organization |

# Chronology

**1980** **26 February:** Ronald Reagan wins the New Hampshire primary with 51 percent of the vote. **17 July:** Reagan accepts Republican nomination for president. **19 July to 3 August:** The 22nd Olympic Games in Moscow; the United States boycotts the games in protest of the Soviet invasion of Afghanistan. **28 October:** Reagan debates Jimmy Carter and turns the phrase "There you go again." **4 November:** Reagan wins the general election and 44 states; Republicans gain a majority in the Senate.

**1981** **20 January:** Reagan takes the oath of office and becomes the 40th president; Iran releases hostages taken at the U.S. embassy in Teheran and held for 444 days. **18 February:** Reagan addresses legislators at a joint session of Congress and outlines his economic program. **30 March:** John Hinckley Jr. shoots Reagan in an assassination attempt. **12 April:** The first launch of a space shuttle. *Columbia* launches on its first mission. **28 April:** Reagan goes before Congress to rally support for his economic package. **13 May:** Pope John Paul II is shot by Mehmet Ali Ağca, a Turkish gunman, as he enters St. Peter's Square in Rome. **3 August:** Air traffic controllers go on strike; Reagan fires over 11,000 who refuse to return to work within 48 hours. **19 August:** Reagan nominates Sandra Day O'Connor to the Supreme Court. In the Gulf of Sidra, two Libyan fighter jets attempt to intercept U.S. jets and are destroyed. **6 October:** Egyptian President Anwar Sadat is assassinated by army members who were part of a militant Islamist group. **12 November:** Reagan adopts "zero option" policy—the United States will deploy Pershing II missiles in Europe, but will cancel if the Soviet Union withdraws intermediate-range weapons targeted on Western Europe. **13 December:** In response to the Solidarity movement, Polish leader Wojciech Jaruzelski declares martial law.

**1982  2 April:** Argentina invades the Falkland Islands. **30 May:** Spain becomes the 16th member of the North Atlantic Treaty Organization (NATO). **6 June:** Israel invades Lebanon. **13 June:** Nuclear freeze demonstration in Central Park in New York City draws more than a million. **14 June:** Falkland Islands War between Argentina and the United Kingdom ends, with Britain reestablishing ownership. **6 July:** Reagan agrees to send a small peacekeeping force to Lebanon. **9 August:** John Hinckley Jr., Reagan's would-be assassin, is committed to a mental hospital indefinitely. **25 August:** U.S. Marines arrive in Lebanon as part of an international peacekeeping force. **2 November:** Republicans lose 26 seats in the House of Representatives in the midterm elections. **10 November:** Soviet General Secretary Leonid Brezhnev dies and is replaced by Yuri Andropov.

**1983  7 February:** Iran invades the southeast of Iraq. **8 March:** Reagan calls the Soviet Union "focus of evil in the modern world" during a speech at the National Association of Evangelicals in Orlando, Florida. **23 March:** Reagan proposes the Strategic Defense Initiative (SDI). **18 April:** Bombing of U.S. embassy in Beirut, Lebanon; 63 killed. **25 April:** Soviet leader Yuri Andropov invites American schoolgirl Samantha Smith to visit the Soviet Union after she writes a letter to him about nuclear war. **9 June:** Conservative Party leader Margaret Thatcher wins reelection in the United Kingdom as prime minister. **20 July:** Polish government ends martial law. **1 September:** Soviet jets fire on Korean Airlines (KAL) Flight 007, killing all 269 on board. **9 October:** Interior Secretary James Watt resigns. **13 October:** Reagan appoints William Clark secretary of interior. **19 October**: Prime Minister Maurice Bishop and 40 others are killed in a coup d'état in the island nation of Grenada. **23 October:** A suicide truck bomber kills 241 Marines at their barracks in Beirut, Lebanon. **25 October:** United States invades the island of Grenada and rescues medical students. **20 November:** One hundred million Americans watch *The Day After*, an account of the aftermath of a nuclear war. **23 November:** United States begins deploying Pershing II missiles in West Germany.

**1984  9 February:** Soviet leader Yuri Andropov dies and is succeeded by Konstantin Chernenko. **26 February:** U.S. Marines leave Lebanon. **3 March:** CIA agent William Buckley is kidnapped in Lebanon. **4 April:** Reagan calls for an international ban on chemical weapons. **16**

**April:** Reagan signs National Security Decision Directive 138, which outlines policy against terrorism. **6 June:** Reagan celebrates the 40th anniversary of D-Day in Pointe du Hoc, France, where he gives a speech to World War II veterans. **19 July:** Walter Mondale accepts the Democratic nomination for president. **28 July to 12 August:** Summer Olympics are held in Los Angeles, California; Soviet Union boycotts. **23 August:** Reagan's "Morning Again in America" reelection campaign commercials are unveiled. **17 September**: Tory Party leader Brian Mulroney becomes prime minister of Canada. **7 October:** Reagan debates Walter Mondale in Louisville, Kentucky, and performs poorly. **21 October:** Reagan debates Mondale a second time, and answers claims he is too old for a second term by saying, "I will not make age an issue of this campaign. I am not going to exploit, for political purposes, my opponent's youth and inexperience." **31 October:** Indian Prime Minister Indira Gandhi is assassinated. **4 November:** Reagan wins reelection with 59 percent of the popular vote and 49 states. **3 December:** Union Carbide plant in Bhopal, India, sustains a leak; more than 2,000 killed.

**1985   20 January:** At age 73, Reagan takes the oath of office for the second time. **11 March:** Soviet leader Konstantin Chernenko dies and is succeeded by Mikhail Gorbachev. **5 May:** Reagan visits the Bitburg Cemetery and Bergen–Belsen concentration camp in West Germany. **3 June:** William Buckley, the CIA agent taken hostage in Lebanon in March 1984, dies. **14 June:** TWA Flight 847 from Athens is hijacked; terrorists kill navy diver Robert Dean Stethem. **13 July:** Reagan undergoes cancer surgery on his large intestine. **2 October:** Actor Rock Hudson dies of AIDS. **7 October:** Passenger ship *Achille Lauro* is hijacked by Palestinian terrorists. **16 November:** Reagan arrives in Geneva for a summit with Soviet leader Mikhail Gorbachev. **3 December:** John Poindexter becomes national security advisor. **10 December:** The International Physicians for the Prevention of Nuclear War wins the Nobel Peace Prize.

**1986   15 January:** Reagan signs bill making Martin Luther King's birthday a federal holiday. **17 January:** Reagan undergoes surgery on his colon. **28 January:** The space shuttle *Challenger* explodes 73 seconds into its flight, killing all on board, including the first civilian in space, Christa McAuliffe. **5 April:** La Belle discotheque in West Berlin bombed by terrorists; three are killed, 230 are injured. The United

States alleges Libya is responsible. **14 April:** United States raids Tripoli and Benghazi, Libya, in retaliation for the bombing of La Belle night-club. **26 April:** The Chernobyl nuclear plant in the Ukraine explodes and releases a large radioactive cloud. **4 June:** Jonathan Pollard pleads guilty to espionage. **11 October:** Reagan meets Gorbachev in Reyk-javík, Iceland, for a summit. **3 November:** Lebanese paper *al-Shiraa* reports that the United States sold arms to Iran, marking the beginning of the Iran–Contra scandal. **13 November:** Reagan addresses the nation and denies selling arms to Iran for the release of hostages. **1 December:** Reagan appoints the Tower Commission to investigate Iran–Contra. **19 December:** Independent counsel Lawrence Walsh is appointed to investigate Iran–Contra.

**1987  5 January:** Reagan undergoes prostate surgery. **8 January:** Stock market closes at over 2,000 for the first time. **26 February:** The Tower Commission issues its report on Iran–Contra. While the commission finds no evidence that Reagan knew of the arms-for-hostages deal, he is criticized for failing to exercise adequate oversight of the National Security Council. **27 February:** Reagan fires chief of staff Donald Regan and replaces him with Howard Baker. **4 March:** Reagan addresses the nation and admits mistakes concerning Iran–Contra. **17 May:** An Iraqi plane fires a missile at the USS *Stark*. Thirty-seven sailors are killed. **12 June:** Reagan visits West Berlin. At the Brandenburg Gate he calls on Soviet leader Mikhail Gorbachev to "tear down this wall." **16 July:** British Prime Minister Margaret Thatcher visits Washington to demonstrate support for Reagan in the wake of Iran–Contra. **19 October:** "Black Monday"; the stock market drops 500 points. The federal budget deficit is cited as the reason. **23 October:** Senate rejects Robert Bork for the Supreme Court. **8 December:** Mikhail Gorbachev visits Washington. He and Reagan sign the Inter-mediate-Range Nuclear Forces (INF) Treaty.

**1988  11 February:** Anthony Kennedy appointed to the Supreme Court. **14 April:** Soviet Union begins withdrawal of troops from Afghanistan. **27 May:** Senate ratifies INF Treaty. **29 May:** Reagan travels to Moscow for a summit with Soviet leader Mikhail Gorbachev. Police charged with crowd control use unnecessary force to disperse the crowd, prompting Reagan to say the Soviet Union is "still a police state." **3 July:** Iran Air Flight 655 downed by USS *Vincennes*. **20 Au-**

**gust:** Iran–Iraq War ends. **8 November:** Vice President George H. W. Bush defeats Michael Dukakis for the presidency. **7 December:** Reagan and Soviet leader Gorbachev meet in New York. **21 December:** A bomb explodes aboard Pan Am Flight 103 over Lockerbie, Scotland. All 259 crew and passengers are killed, as well as 11 civilians on the ground. Libyan terrorists are suspected in the attack.

**1989** **20 January:** George H. W. Bush sworn in as the 41st president. **15 February:** Last of Soviet troops leave Afghanistan. **24 February:** Ayatollah Khomeini of Iran places a $3 million bounty on author Salman Rushdie for his book *The Satanic Verses.* **24 March:** *Exxon Valdez* runs aground in Alaska's Prince William Sound, spilling 11 million gallons of crude oil. **19 April:** Students begin demonstrations and occupy Tiananmen Square in Beijing, China. **4 June:** Chinese government cracks down on student protestors, killing hundreds. **7 November:** Douglas Wilder becomes first African American to be elected governor of Virginia. **9 November:** Berlin Wall falls. **30 November:** End of Communist rule in Czechoslovakia. **15 December:** Romanian revolution overthrows Communist rule. **20 December:** United States invades Panama to capture strongman Manuel Noriega. **25 December:** Romanian leader Nicolae Ceauşescu is executed.

**1990** **3 January:** Panamanian dictator Manuel Noriega surrenders to U.S. troops. **11 February:** South African anti-apartheid leader Nelson Mandela is released after 27 years in prison. **11 March:** The Baltic nation of Lithuania votes for independence. **19 March:** The Baltic nation of Latvia overturns Communist rule. **20 March:** Namibia gains independence after 75 years of South African rule. **29 May:** Boris Yeltsin is elected president of Russia. **2 August:** Iraqi dictator Saddam Hussein's army invades the nation of Kuwait. **7 August:** President George H. W. Bush orders U.S. troops to Saudi Arabia in Operation Desert Shield. **3 October:** East and West Germany are reunified. **5 November:** President Bush signs a budget bill that reduces spending and raises select taxes. **15 November:** President Bush signs Clean Air Act Amendments. **16 December:** Jean-Bertrand Aristide is elected president of Haiti, ending three decades of military rule.

**1991** **16 January:** Persian Gulf War begins with Operation Desert Storm. United States and coalition allies begin air raids on Iraqi military sites. **18 January:** Eastern Airlines fails and stops operating. **7 February:** Aristide is sworn in as Haiti's first democratically elected leader. **24 February:** Ground operations in Persian Gulf War begin; combat operations last only four days. **25 February:** Warsaw Pact dissolves military alliance. **6 April:** Official cease-fire is signed, ending the Persian Gulf War. **9 April:** Former Soviet Republic of Georgia affirms independence. **5 June:** South Africa repeals apartheid laws. **10 July:** Boris Yeltsin inaugurated as president of Russia. **31 July:** President Bush and Soviet leader Mikhail Gorbachev meet in a summit to negotiate the Strategic Arms Reduction Treaty (START). **18 August:** Failed coup against Gorbachev in Moscow. **25 August:** Baltic states of Latvia, Lithuania, and Estonia declare independence from the Soviet Union. **6 October:** Anita Hill accuses Supreme Court nominee Clarence Thomas of sexual harassment. **15 October:** Senate confirms Thomas by a 52–48 margin. **25 December:** Dissolution of the Soviet Union. Mikhail Gorbachev resigns, and Russia, Ukraine, and Byelorussia form the Commonwealth of Independent States (CIS).

**1992   15 January:** Yugoslav federation dissolves. **1 February:** President Bush and Russian President Boris Yeltsin declare a formal end to the Cold War. **27 April:** Panamanian dictator Manuel Noriega convicted on drug charges in the United States. **29 April:** The acquittal of four Los Angeles police officers in the beating of Rodney King precipitates a week of rioting in southern California. **1 July:** Bill Clinton nominated as the Democratic candidate for the presidency. **12 August:** North American Free Trade Agreement (NAFTA) between the United States, Canada, and Mexico is reached. **24 August:** Hurricane Andrew devastates south Florida. **31 August:** White supremacist Randy Weaver surrenders to federal authorities in Ruby Ridge, Idaho. **3 November:** The Democratic ticket of Bill Clinton and Al Gore defeats incumbent president Bush in a three-way race in which Reform Party candidate H. Ross Perot receives 19 percent of the popular vote. **25 November:** Czechoslovakia splits into the Czech Republic and Slovakia. **24 December:** President Bush pardons six Reagan Administration officials in the Iran–Contra scandal.

# Introduction

The 1980s and early 1990s were remarkable for the triumph of conservatism in the United States and its closest allies. The victories of presidents Ronald Reagan and George H. W. Bush in the United States were complemented by the electoral successes of Margaret Thatcher in the United Kingdom beginning in 1979 and Brian Mulroney in Canada in 1984. The relationship between Reagan and Bush and their conservative counterparts was particularly important in providing a united front on foreign policy, whether the target was the Soviet Union, communist insurgencies in Africa or Latin America, or Iraqi dictator Saddam Hussein.

Yet by the early 1990s the domestic climate began to change, in the United States as in the United Kingdom and Canada. Disaffected Tories ousted Thatcher in 1991 for her intransigence toward European integration, and voters jettisoned the conservatives altogether six years later. Against the backdrop of a struggling economy and high unemployment, estranged Republicans and independents shunned George H. W. Bush's reelection bid in 1992 and threw support to Ross Perot, aiding Bill Clinton's victory by a plurality of the national vote. And after two failed attempts to cement constitutional change for national unity, Brian Mulroney left Ottawa in 1993, just before his party was thoroughly decimated by the Liberals.

The image of leaders who championed market-oriented solutions for their domestic economies, sought to roll back the scope of the state, and dominated the international scene for over a decade in the struggle against communism faded rapidly into the annals of history, eclipsed as they were by their liberal successors and the end of the Cold War.

## AN ERA OF PARADOXES

On the campaign trail against incumbent Jimmy Carter in 1980, Ronald Reagan sought to revitalize the Oval Office and demonstrate to the country that the presidency was not "too much" for a single individual to manage. Ironically, his early legislative successes, Cold War leadership, and rhetorical acumen may have rekindled higher expectations for presidential leadership at a time when the constraints on officeholders began to grow dramatically, from the complexities of rapid globalization, trade politics, and intractable federal deficits to a seemingly chaotic international system that replaced the bipolar world of yesteryear. It was just such a context with which his successor, George H. W. Bush, had to contend. Yet Bush's leadership approach, predicated upon prudence and caution and putatively exacerbated by his antirhetorical and taciturn communication style, seemed strangely mismatched to his predecessor's eloquent oratory and interminable optimism.

The Reagan–Bush era must be appreciated for its many paradoxes—not only for the differences between the two individuals' practice of executive leadership but also for the contradictions within their respective terms. Stunning victories in the electoral realm, foreign policy, or in Congress were often overshadowed by scandals that resulted from internal mismanagement of the White House, protracted executive–legislative conflict, and economic conditions that produced a roller-coaster effect on public approval. Policy reversals were not uncommon, sometimes exasperating or alienating core supporters. Each president's relative success in using the "bully pulpit" to reach out to and inspire the electorate shaped public affect toward him. Mastery of public relations became a key factor in the ability—or inability—to weather the many storms that bore down on the White House, whether for reelection or congressional support or to brave public criticism. A brief survey of the two presidents' terms accentuates the policies, events, and choices that shaped politics and policies from 1981 to 1992.

## RONALD REAGAN'S IMPRINT

Reagan's rhetoric during the 1980 campaign and his imposing Electoral College victory created the impression of a policy mandate—even if he won only 50.7 percent of the popular vote. He adroitly exploited his electoral victory to push a bold agenda in Congress. The cornerstones of his first-year legislative successes, the Economic Recovery Tax Act and the Omnibus Budget Reconciliation Act, were earned through the deft use of public appeals and behind-the-scenes negotiation. His efforts to reach across the aisle to conservative Democrats caught that party's leadership in the House of Representatives off guard. A waning contingent of moderate southerners broke with the Democratic Party and joined almost all Republicans in the House to enable Reagan to surmount opposition-party control in the lower chamber. The result was a wholesale cut in taxes on individuals and corporations, reductions in domestic spending, and significant increases in military outlays.

But Reagan's legislative influence did not last indefinitely. While it may be argued that he had much of his agenda in place by the end of 1981, House Democrats did not stand idly by. They sought to thwart a minority of their conference from controlling floor outcomes to the president's benefit. Broad organizational reforms endowed the speaker with greater powers over agenda setting and referral of legislation to committees. The whip organization was reinvigorated. And restrictive rules on votes left conservatives without the tactical tools that had given Reagan substantial influence. For Reagan, the result was palpable. The Democratic-controlled House pronounced his budgets "dead on arrival." As early as 1982 Reagan turned to the veto as a primary instrument for negotiating the budget. On other matters he was less successful as his time in office progressed. The Senate rejected his nomination of Robert Bork to the Supreme Court. Bork's replacement, Douglas Ginsburg, withdrew his nomination after admitting to having smoked marijuana. And as Reagan's political capital ebbed toward the end of his second term, Congress overrode vetoes of South Africa sanctions and federal highway, water pollution, and civil rights legislation. The president's inability to keep his party behind his stances on these bills accentuates his changing fortunes vis-à-vis Congress over the course of his two terms.

Reagan's foreign policy victories were occasionally bittersweet. In 1983, just several days after a truck bomb killed 241 Marines and other U.S. service personnel in Beirut, Lebanon, the United States successfully invaded the island nation of Grenada. U.S. forces "rescued" 600 students and toppled the leftist government. The timing of the invasion was questioned by some in the media, as the brief "rally effect" for Reagan following "**Operation Urgent Fury**" eclipsed the worst terror attack on U.S. troops abroad to that point in time. Similarly, in 1986 Reagan sought to underscore to Libyan leader Muhammar Qaddafi the United States' resolve to take action against terrorism. In retaliation for alleged Libyan involvement in the bombing of a West Berlin night club frequented by U.S. service personnel, Reagan ordered air strikes on Tripoli, Benghazi, and Qaddafi's compound. But relations with France became strained when President François Mitterrand refused to allow U.S. jets to fly over French air space en route to the targets. Reagan instead turned to his friend and close ally, Margaret Thatcher, who enabled the United States to launch the attack from the United Kingdom.

Reagan's reversal vis-à-vis the Soviet Union was extraordinary. His advocacy of an arms buildup prompted the Bulletin of Atomic Scientists to move the clock forward toward midnight—a nuclear doomsday—only to turn the setting back sometime later. The president who had embarked on a massive increase of nuclear and conventional weapons to ensure "peace through strength" wound up negotiating away those very armaments with Soviet General Secretary Mikhail Gorbachev. To Reagan's supporters the expensive arms race, while responsible for massive domestic deficits, proved far more harmful to the Soviet economy. Reagan's championing of the Strategic Defense Initiative (SDI), or "Star Wars," putatively convinced the Soviets that they could not compete with the United States financially or technologically. Whether SDI was fantasy or a feasible enterprise may have made little difference. Gorbachev was visibly opposed to SDI and may well have thought it was possible for the United States to develop such a spaced-based anti-ballistic missile system. Reagan's supporters argue that the concept drove the final nail into the Soviet coffin and precipitated the collapse of the "evil empire." Skeptics suggest the demise of the Soviet Union was instead predicated on internal dynamics over which the United States had little influence or control. Whatever the case, Reagan's rhetoric certainly operated as one important contextual variable among the many factors involved in the Soviet Union's downfall.

Indeed, perhaps no president since Franklin Delano Roosevelt had mastered the levers of the rhetorical presidency better than Ronald Reagan. Even at what one could consider his worst moments, Reagan seemed able to bend the press and public opinion to his side. His rhetoric could have a hard edge, as when he traveled to Berlin and defied Mikhail Gorbachev to "tear down this wall." Yet what endeared many to Reagan was the personal sincerity that he conveyed. The nation was horrified in late March 1981 when the president was shot outside a Washington, D.C., hotel—just barely three months into his first term— by would-be assassin John Hinckley Jr. The bullet had narrowly missed the president's heart, but the incident scarcely detracted from Reagan's sense of optimism and humor. On a hospital gurney, he joked to reporters that he hoped the doctors were all Republicans. His return to Capitol Hill a month later to marshal support for his economic agenda was nothing short of triumphal, and the ordeal bolstered his public approval by eight to nine points.

Similarly, Reagan consoled the nation following the explosion of the space shuttle *Challenger* on 28 January 1986. His solemn speech to the nation, written by speechwriter Peggy Noonan, was among the most eloquent of any during his two terms as he spoke of the shuttle's crew: "We will never forget them, nor the last time we saw them, this morning, as they prepared for their journey and waved good-bye and slipped the surly bonds of Earth to touch the face of God." Even upon his announcement in 1994 that he had Alzheimer's disease, Reagan retained his optimistic spirit in a letter to the nation: "I now begin the journey that will lead me into the sunset of my life. I know that for America there will always be a bright dawn ahead."

Of course, Reagan also found the bully pulpit an important tool to stem the tide of political turmoil. By 1987 the "Great Communicator," who had mobilized the nation so successfully behind his tax and spending cuts in 1981, struggled to explain how he had failed to recognize that his White House national security staff had been selling arms to Iran in exchange for hostages and then diverting the funds to U.S.-backed insurgents in Central America. The former activity violated administration policy; the latter violated the Boland Amendment, a congressional statute. The end result was a potential constitutional crisis that could have rivaled Watergate. Reagan went on television once and denied the allegations. Later, he recanted and promised to correct the mistakes made by his administration. His forthrightness with Congress and the public after the Iran–Contra scandal broke, including his earnest implementation of the Tower Commission recommendations, arguably saved his presidency—and the office itself—from extensive damage.

The Iran–Contra fiasco underscored the profound impact of White House staffing choices on the fortunes of the president. Many historians, political scientists, and students of the policy process lauded Reagan's initial White House team. The "troika" composed of James A. Baker III (chief of staff), Michael Deaver (deputy chief of staff), and Edwin Meese (counselor) boasted competence and Washington experience that served the president extremely well in his first four years. But the fateful decision to alter the arrangement in 1985 foreshadowed the travails to come. The president ordered James Baker to exchange positions with Donald Regan, who had been secretary of treasury. Though Regan was never charged with a crime resulting from Iran–Contra, he employed his gatekeeper function as chief of staff to limit access to the president and insulate him from the illegal activities that contradicted the administration's stated policies. Reagan's choice of veteran senator Howard Baker as chief of staff in 1987 went a long way toward restoring confidence in the White House.

Finally, Reagan's public approval proved rather enigmatic over his two terms. His peaks came on the heels of his assassination attempt and rally effects from the Grenada invasion and Libya bombing. But the valleys were low, and none more so than from 1982 to 1983, when the country suffered from an economic downturn. Reagan's approval steadily tumbled more than 30 points from 1981 to 1983. In a like manner, the stock market crash of 1986 and revelations of the Iran–Contra scandal plunged the president's approval by almost 40 percent, erasing a steady recovery in public esteem and any lingering rally effect from the Libya bombing. Interestingly, Reagan's approval rebounded in the closing months of his second term. Up to that point in time, he joined only Dwight Eisenhower in leaving the presidency with popularity equal to or greater than when he came to the Oval Office. Reagan left the White House at 63 percent approval, six points higher than his first poll in January 1981. Nonetheless, surveys showed that the electorate made distinctions between Reagan's job approval and policy matters. Although many revered Reagan, he was frustrated that he could not win over the public on abortion, the environment, or Central America. Such are the limits of the bully pulpit.

## GEORGE H. W. BUSH:
## AN INGLORIOUS THIRD REAGAN TERM?

Ronald Reagan was precluded constitutionally from running for a third term. But for those who wished he could, Vice President George H. W. Bush seemed like an obvious choice to succeed Reagan. But Bush's persona and leadership style were dramatically different.

Bush won a sweeping victory over Democratic challenger Michael Dukakis in 1988. He ruffled Republicans' feathers when he called for a "kinder, gentler" America, which some interpreted as an indictment of Reagan. Regardless, the campaign between Bush and Dukakis was anything but kind and gentle. The Bush team's tactics were negative, unseemly, and at times vitriolic—but they worked. There was, however, little evidence of a presidential mandate. The electorate seemed only to confirm a preference for the status quo. Reagan left office squaring off against opposition majorities in both chambers of Congress. Bush would begin his term under the same circumstances and confront an increasingly programmatic and unified Democratic Party on Capitol Hill. And unlike Reagan, who from 1981 to 1986 had a Republican majority in the Senate he could use as leverage against the House, Bush had no such advantage.

Bush lacked an intrepid domestic agenda. Much of the 1988 election centered on character issues and emphasized Bush's foreign policy experience. Bush did make overtures about reducing the capital gains tax but never achieved the goal. Instead, much of what ended up on the legislative agenda was congressionally inspired or stemmed from the poor economic climate that he inherited. Bush was tasked with bailing out the failed savings and loan industry almost immediately upon entering the White House. And in 1989 he sparred with Congress over whether—or how much—to raise the minimum wage, vetoing one bill and reluctantly signing a compromise measure.

Indeed, much of Bush's relationship with Congress over his four years hinged on the veto power. His adroit use of the veto and veto threats as a negotiating tool to gain influence over Congress represented a different form of presidential leadership that defies the activist model championed by scholars and expected by the electorate. But the strategy was arguably successful in policy terms. Bush vetoed 44 measures in four years and was overridden only a single time. Keeping the Republicans in

Congress unified behind his vetoes, he stifled Democrats' attempts to liberalize abortion regulations 10 times and fought off two attempts to revoke China's most-favored-nation trade status after Tiananmen Square. The White House explicitly recognized the importance of "veto strength"—ensuring a minimum of a third of legislators would back the president's stand on any override attempt—as a key to winning policy concessions from Democrats.

Yet governance by veto sometimes proved a tough sell to the public and the media. Bush was roundly criticized when in 1990 he became the first president to veto a civil rights bill (though a compromise bill was enacted a year later). And he encountered other problems with Congress that proved embarrassing, including his failed nomination of John Tower as secretary of defense.

Economic management proved the most troublesome for Bush. The deficits that carried over from his predecessor had prompted lawmakers to enact legislation that provided for automatic cuts in entitlements and other domestic programs if Congress and the president could not agree on a budget. Pay-as-you-go (PAYGO) requirements mandated that any new spending had to be offset by reductions elsewhere in the budget. These requirements left neither congressional leaders nor the president much room to maneuver.

Bush became ensnarled in the budget in 1990. He engaged in "summitry" with congressional leaders to find a compromise on taxes and spending. Bush wanted to avoid automatic cuts; Democrats were unwilling to be scapegoated for raising taxes. Bush's ultimate acceptance of some new taxes in the budget agreement of 1990 infuriated conservatives, including Newt Gingrich, who contended the president had reneged on his "read-my-lips, no-new-taxes" pledge at the Republican National Convention in 1988. Bush took to the television to explain the budget and convince the nation of the necessity of compromise. Ironically, public support for the agreement *fell* after Bush's plea. The budget agreement subsequently collapsed in Congress under the weight of conservative Republicans angered by taxes and liberal Democrats upset by cuts to domestic programs. The budget fiasco marked what appeared to be the unraveling of his presidency by the midterm. Could the president turn to foreign affairs to save the day?

George Bush inherited a unipolar world that emerged with the fall of the Berlin Wall in 1989. With his Russian counterpart, Boris Yeltsin,

Bush proclaimed the end of the Cold War. Yet prudence—too much, in the eyes of his critics—marked his stance toward the breakup of the Soviet Union and how to aid Russia and the independent republics that emerged from the former communist behemoth. But prudence paid off in the Middle East. By late summer 1990, the budget debacle faded from memory as a new threat—Saddam Hussein—appeared on the horizon. In August 1990, Hussein invaded Kuwait, claiming the tiny emirate as a province of Iraq. Bush and his foreign-policy team worked indefatigably with the United Nations and bilaterally to assemble an impressive international coalition aimed at driving the Iraqi dictator's troops from Kuwait. When Hussein refused to comply with the 15 January 1991 deadline to withdraw from Kuwait, Bush launched Operation Desert Storm. That month the main hostilities of the Persian Gulf War began and ended in a military conflict that was broadcast live on television and featured reporters "embedded" in tanks and troop deployments.

The president's approval ratings peaked at 89 percent—an all-time high—and he seemed on top of his game once again. But to his detractors, Bush had not finished the job. It was not enough to simply restore Kuwait's independence. Rather, Saddam Hussein should have been removed from power. The problem is that the international coalition under the auspices of the United Nations had not adopted Hussein's ouster as an objective, and it is doubtful Bush could have won support for the endeavor. Of course, his son would rely largely on unilateral action and a "coalition of the willing" some 12 years later to topple Hussein's regime.

Bush's "rally effect" from the Gulf War victory proved ephemeral. As the media and the public refocused attention on the economic climate, Bush bore the brunt of anxiety over rising unemployment. Matters were made worse by the impression that the White House was in disarray. Bush's chief of staff, former New Hampshire Governor John Sununu, had already come under fire for using government aircraft for private and political travel. An abrasive figure who alienated both Democrats and Republicans, Sununu faced criticism for mismanaging the White House and was increasingly perceived as a liability by the end of 1991. As the president stood poised to address the economy, he replaced Sununu with Samuel Skinner, who as secretary of transportation earned the sobriquet "Master of Disaster" for his handling of the Pan Am 103 bombing and the San Francisco earthquake.

But the White House shake-up did little to improve Bush's fortunes, which were further damaged by media gaffes over barcode machines in grocery stores and his shock at the high prices of socks. By the New Hampshire primary of 1992, his approval rate had dropped below 50 percent, not a good omen for the fight he had to wage against fellow Republican Pat Buchanan for the GOP nomination. Bush, of course, won the nomination, but as he prepared to wage battle against Democratic standard-bearer Bill Clinton and Reform Party candidate Ross Perot, his approval tumbled to a nadir of 32 percent in July 1992. Unable to cull more than 35 percent of the popular vote in November, Bush's loss to Clinton was a stunning defeat—all the more so for the president, who could not understand how Americans would prefer, in his view, an untested candidate of questionable ethics and character in a complex and dangerous world.

In the final analysis, Clinton's succession to the presidency in 1992 and the opening of a new era in American politics owed much to Bush's topsy-turvy public approval. Through the spring and summer of 1991, when Bush's public approval soared, many potential Democratic candidates for the presidency, including such notables as New York Governor Mario Cuomo and West Virginia Senator John D. Rockefeller, decided not to run for the White House. Bush looked invincible and they were dissuaded from entering the primaries. As Clinton emerged as a viable candidate in 1992, Bush's approval sunk and the president appeared particularly vulnerable on the economy as unemployment reached 7 percent. The negative power of the veto that Bush had exercised so skillfully did little to provide him with a substantive record of achievement by 1992.

Americans were uninterested in Bush's leadership in foreign affairs. It may well be that Bush's ultimate demise in the election of 1992 was the economy, over which presidents have relatively little direct control. Some *macro*-level indicators were on the rise in 1992, yet voters always pay closest attention to *micro*-level, pocketbook issues. Right or wrong, the president is held accountable. On this score Bush was buffeted on either side by the critiques of Bill Clinton and Ross Perot.

But it may also be the case that Bush's inability to articulate a clear-cut vision for a second term was a major liability in his reelection effort. Perhaps the closest he came to Reaganesque inspiration was his passionate mention of a "thousand points of light" in 1988 to promote volunteerism. Bush later admitted, quite candidly, that he was not good at the "vision thing." Although personable and generally amiable in his relations with the media, Bush's terse one-liners and choppy syntax contrasted mightily with Reagan's flowing oratory. Uncomfortable in the fish-eye lens, he lacked the telegenic demeanor of his predecessor.

To his critics, Bush's term in office was a period of "drift" and "gridlock." Alternatively, it may be argued that Bush simply had a different conception of leadership—one focused on managing problems that arose in the present rather than defining future alternatives. Regardless, Bush's presidency and his defeat in 1992, like Reagan's two terms, provide important lessons and raise serious questions about the role of substance and style in our evaluation of modern chief executives.

# The Dictionary

## – A –

**ABBAS, ABU (1949–2004).** Abu Abbas was the name used by Muhammad Zaidan, the Palestinian **terrorist** and leader of the Palestinian Liberation Front who plotted the 1985 hijacking of the Italian ship *Achille Lauro*. He was held responsible for the murder of **Leon Klinghoffer**, an American Jew who was shot, killed, and thrown overboard during the hijacking. He later apologized for the hijacking and the murder of Klinghoffer. Abbas was captured in Iraq in 2003 following the United States' military invasion of that country. He was attempting to flee Baghdad for Syria. Italy demanded his extradition, but Abbas died on 8 March 2004 of natural causes while detained by U.S. forces.

**ABORTION.** Defined as the medically induced termination of a pregnancy, abortion was legalized by the U.S. **Supreme Court** in the landmark *Roe v. Wade* decision of 1973. The justices who wrote the majority opinion contended that a **woman**'s right to choose whether to terminate a pregnancy was protected in an inherent "right to privacy" in the Constitution. Prior to *Roe*, states had legislated varying degrees of access to abortion services, and some banned abortion procedures altogether.

Presidents **Ronald Reagan** and **George H. W. Bush** were steadfastly opposed to abortion in their rhetoric and policy preferences, which heightened a growing national debate on the issue in the 1980s and 1990s. Reagan was outspoken in his opposition to abortion. In 1983 he penned an article entitled "Abortion and the Conscience of the Nation," which was published in the *Human Life Review* and coincided with the 10th anniversary of the *Roe* decision.

1

Reagan's influential article eschewed the debate about when life begins and instead focused on abortion as a serious moral crisis facing the United States. He also allegedly had the controversial film *The Silent Scream* screened at the White House. The film depicts the alleged pain that a fetus undergoes during an abortion. Finally, Reagan used part of his 1986 State of the Union address to underscore his view that abortion was "a wound in our national consciousness."

In policy terms Reagan was unable to significantly challenge the basic underpinnings of *Roe*. But he did sign the so-called Hyde amendment, which restricted public funding of abortions. He also supported the 1984 "Mexico City" policy, which prohibited federal funding for any organization that performed or promoted abortions abroad.

By Reagan's second term, abortion foes engaged in greater public activism. In 1986 Randall Terry founded Operation Rescue. The group's objective was to organize mass protests at abortion clinics around the nation. Operation Rescue filed suit against a number of clinics, as well as against the National Organization for Women (NOW), which is staunchly pro-choice. In 1988 the Supreme Court dismissed the racketeering charges brought by Operation Rescue.

George H. W. Bush used his veto power extensively to ward off the Democratic congressional majority's attempt to liberalize abortion policies. Between 1989 and 1992 Bush vetoed a total of 10 bills that included provisions to loosen restrictions on abortion access or public funding for abortions. Not a single vetoed bill was successfully challenged in Congress. Moreover, Bush used the threat of the veto to substantively alter other bills that contained such language or policy "riders."

Bush's actions coincided with two key Supreme Court decisions during his term. The 1989 case **Webster v. Reproductive Health Services** confirmed states' ability to restrict public funds for abortion as long as such policies did not constitute an "undue burden" on women's ability to secure an abortion. The 1992 decision in *Planned Parenthood v. Casey* modified the constitutional basis for the right to an abortion by emphasizing the Fourteenth Amendment's due process clause instead of *Roe*'s "right to privacy" rationale. Most importantly, *Planned Parenthood v. Casey* emphasized the right to an abortion contingent upon the viability of a fetus outside the womb rather than *Roe*'s "trimester" formula.

**ABRAMS, ELLIOTT (1948– ).** A graduate of Harvard Law School, Abrams got his start in politics by working for Democratic senator Daniel Patrick Moynihan of New York in the 1970s. He held several positions in the administration of **Ronald Reagan**, including assistant secretary of state for human rights and later for inter-American affairs. He came under intense congressional scrutiny in 1982 following allegations made by investigative reporters of civilian massacres by right-wing death squads in **El Salvador**. Abrams was later implicated in the **Iran–Contra** scandal. Indicted for lying to special prosecutor **Lawrence Walsh** about his knowledge of the cover-up, he ultimately reached a plea agreement to avoid jail. Abrams, along with five others, was pardoned by President **George H. W. Bush** in 1992. Widely regarded as a staunch neoconservative, Abrams worked for several think tanks in the 1990s, including the Project for the New American Century (PNAC), co-founded by **Richard (Dick) Cheney**. President **George W. Bush** tapped Abrams for the **National Security Council** and promoted him to deputy **national security advisor** during his second term. Abrams is author of *Faith or Fear* (1997).

*ACHILLE LAURO.* This Italian passenger sea liner was hijacked in Egypt on 7 October 1985 by four members of the Palestinian Liberation Front. The hijacking was in apparent retaliation for **Israel**'s bombing of the headquarters of the **Palestinian Liberation Organization (PLO)** in Tunis, Tunisia, six days earlier. The hijackers forced the crew to sail the ship to Syria, where it was refused permission to dock. They then killed passenger **Leon Klinghoffer**, an American Jew who was confined to a wheelchair. The hijackers provoked further international outrage when they threw his body over the side of the ship because he was Jewish. The ship returned to Egypt, where the hijackers negotiated the release of the passengers in exchange for safe passage to Tunisia via an Egyptian aircraft. The U.S. Navy intercepted the plane on 10 October and forced it to land at a NATO air base in Sigonella, Italy (Sicily). The hijackers were subsequently arrested and two were convicted. **Abu Abbas**, PLO leader and mastermind of the hijacking, left Italy and was convicted in absentia. The PLO was sued over Klinghoffer's death, but the suit was eventually dropped when the organization paid an undisclosed sum to Klinghoffer's family.

**ACQUIRED IMMUNE DEFICIENCY SYNDROME (AIDS).** The Federal Centers for Disease Control published a report on 5 June 1981 that identified AIDS as a disease that destroys the human immune system. The term *AIDS* was adopted by the scientific and medical communities in 1983. AIDS is a result of infection from the Human Immunodeficiency Virus (HIV). The infection devastates the immune system's T cells, preventing the body from warding off infection. The disease is believed to have originated in Africa and jumped species from primates to humans. In the 1980s, AIDS infections in the United States became widespread among gay men and intravenous drug users, who are at higher risk for transmission of the disease. Gay rights activists and others reproached President **Ronald Reagan**'s handling of the AIDS crisis. **Larry Speakes**, Reagan's press secretary, joked about the matter. When asked about the "gay plague" by a reporter, Speakes replied, "I don't have it; do you?" Reagan was criticized for a slow federal response to AIDS and for failing to enable Surgeon General **C. Everett Koop** to confront the disease more aggressively through sex education. However, Reagan did appoint a commission to investigate workplace protections for AIDS victims as scientists and doctors learned more about the disease and its transmission. Between 1982 and 1988 federal funding for AIDS virtually doubled, reaching nearly $2 billion by the end of Reagan's presidency. AIDS touched Reagan personally and raised his awareness of the issue when his friend, actor **Rock Hudson**, died of the disease in 1985.

**AFGHANISTAN.** The **Soviet Union** invaded the central Asian country on 24 December 1979 to prevent an Islamist government from displacing the Communist leadership. The invasion was consistent with the **Brezhnev Doctrine**—that countries under the Soviets' sphere of influence had no right to challenge the Communist Party's monopoly on power. In protest of the invasion, President **Jimmy Carter** announced a boycott of the 1980 Summer Olympics in Moscow. In 1983 the **United Nations** passed Resolution 37/37, which called for withdrawal of Soviet troops. Soviet troops nonetheless remained in Afghanistan for a decade, sinking into a quagmire of guerilla warfare with **mujahadeen** insurgents backed by the United States. President **Ronald Reagan** referred to the mujahadeen as "freedom fighters." The **Central Intelligence Agency (CIA)** spent over $2 billion in weapons and logistical support for the anti-Soviet opposition. The war caused 1.5 million casualties and displaced 6 million people. Soviet troops began pulling out in May 1988 and completed their withdrawal in February 1989, after which time Afghanistan descended into civil war as various mujahadeen factions took up arms against one another. In 1996 the Taliban clerics seized power and imposed Islamic Sharia law in Afghanistan. The Taliban also gave succor to **Osama bin Laden** and his **terrorist** organization, al-Qaeda. The United States invaded Afghanistan in 2001 and toppled the Taliban when links between bin Laden and al-Qaeda and the terrorist attacks on New York and Washington, D.C., on 11 September 2001 were discovered.

**AĞCA, MEHMET ALI.** *See* POPE JOHN PAUL II.

**AGRICULTURAL CREDIT ACT (1987).** This legislation stemmed from the farming crisis of the 1980s (*see* BLOCK, JOHN RUSLING). The bill allowed farmers to reacquire or lease agricultural property foreclosed or transferred by deed. The bill also mandated that the Farmer's Home Administration could not foreclose on a family farmer unless the organization would make more money through foreclosure than it would by investing in the farm to make it profitable. President **Ronald Reagan** signed the bill in early January 1988. The group **Farm Aid**, which had worked to call public attention to the plight of farmers, applauded the bill.

**AIRBORNE WARNING AND CONTROL SYSTEM.** *See* AWACS.

**AIR TRAFFIC CONTROLLER'S STRIKE.** *See* PROFESSIONAL AIR TRAFFIC CONTROLLERS ORGANIZATION (PATCO).

***AL-SHIRAA.*** This Lebanese magazine broke the story on 3 November 1986 that the United States had sold arms to Iran to procure the release of seven American hostages. The story was confirmed by the Iranian government. The publication of the article touched off the **Iran–Contra** scandal.

**ALEXANDER, LAMAR (1940– ).** Alexander was born in Maryville, Tennessee, and is a graduate of Vanderbilt University and New York

University Law School. Following law school he served as a clerk for John Minor Wisdom of the U.S. Court of Appeals in New Orleans and a legislative assistant to U.S. Senator **Howard Baker**, and he worked for Bryce Harlow, counsel to President Richard Nixon. After an unsuccessful campaign for Tennessee governor in 1974, he rebounded in his second bid for the office in 1978. Walking 1,000 miles across the state in his trademark plaid shirt, Alexander won election in 1979 and reelection four years later. Following his governorship, he held the presidency of the University of Tennessee (1988–91). President **George H. W. Bush** appointed him as secretary of education in 1991, and he served out the rest of the president's term. Following two failed attempts to gain the Republican presidential nomination (1996, 2000), Alexander won election to the U.S. Senate from his home state in 2002.

**AMERICANS WITH DISABILITIES ACT (ADA).** President **George H. W. Bush** signed the Americans with Disabilities Act into law on 26 July 1990. The **civil rights** bill was aimed at providing protections from discrimination for individuals with handicaps. Further, the bill required public and private entities to provide "reasonable accommodation" to individuals with disabilities. Despite the law's intentions, which were hailed by civil rights activists, critics charge that because the onus for reporting violations of the act is on the disabled, the law has not lived up to its potential. The Equal Employment Opportunity Commission (EEOC), which is tasked with investigating claims, quickly became overwhelmed by complaints. As of 2006, a huge backlog of cases remains, and the EEOC continues to lack the human resources adequate to investigate allegations in a timely manner.

**ANDEAN INITIATIVE.** President **George H. W. Bush** met with the leaders of Bolivia, **Colombia**, and Peru to launch a systematic effort to address **drug trafficking**. The agreement was reached in February 1990 in Cartagena, Colombia, and provided for U.S. economic and military aid to battle the drug trade in South America, including the replacement of cocaine production with alternative crops.

**ANDROPOV, YURI (1914–1984).** Born in Stavropol, Imperial Russia, in 1914, Andropov succeeded **Leonid Brezhnev** as general secretary of the **Soviet Union** from November 1982 until his death in February 1984. Andropov was stationed at the Soviet embassy in Budapest during the Soviet invasion of Hungary in 1956. He headed the Soviet **KGB** from 1967 to 1982. U.S.–Soviet arms control negotiations stalled during Andropov's secretariat. The United States deployed **Pershing II missiles** in Western Europe to counter Soviet **SS-20** intermediate-range missiles. Relations with the United States became strained when Soviet fighter jets shot down **Korean Airlines Flight 007** (KAL 007). The plane mistakenly strayed into Soviet airspace in September 1983. All on board were killed, including 61 Americans. Andropov is best remembered in the United States for extending a personal invitation to a fifth-grade schoolgirl to visit the Soviet Union. **Samantha Smith** had written Andropov a letter in which she expressed concern about the possibility of nuclear war. Smith later visited the Soviet Union, partaking in a number of highly publicized peacemaking events across the country.

**ANGOLA.** A former Portuguese colony, this southwest African country gained independence in 1975. However, civil war immediately followed and ravaged the country for nearly a quarter century as Marxist and anti-Communist, nationalist factions battled for power. The internal conflict in Angola was a metaphor for the **Cold War** as the United States and **Soviet Union** vied for influence in the developing world. The United States financially and militarily supported **Jonas Malheiro Savimbi**, leader of UNITA (*União Nacional para a Independência Total de Angola*, or National Union for the Total Independence of Angola), in his struggle against the Cuban- and Soviet-backed Marxist government. Savimbi was killed in February 2002. A cease-fire between the government and opposition groups was reached the same year.

**ANTI–BALLISTIC MISSILE (ABM) TREATY.** The ABM Treaty between the United States and **Soviet Union** was signed by President Richard Nixon and Soviet General Secretary **Leonid Brezhnev** in May 1972. The purpose of the treaty was to prevent either country from developing or deploying systems capable of destroying incoming nuclear weapons. Both the United States and Soviet Union viewed ABM systems as destabilizing to the doctrine of **Mutually**

**Assured Destruction (MAD)**. If, for example, the United States developed a system capable of defending against an attack, the Soviets might have reason to launch a preemptive first strike—thinking that the presence of ABM systems might ultimately prompt the United States to do so first. Paradoxically, precluding deployment of ABM systems left both countries vulnerable but restored confidence in **deterrence**; neither had a strategic advantage in launching a first strike. Soviet consternation was palpable when President **Ronald Reagan** proposed the **Strategic Defense Initiative (SDI)**, a space-based ABM system. SDI would have violated the ABM Treaty and potentially threatened the foundation of MAD. Although SDI was never developed, the United States withdrew from the ABM Treaty in June 2002. President **George W. Bush** proposed a program analogous to SDI—not to protect against Russian missiles but to guard against **terrorism**.

**APARTHEID.** In the Dutch-based language of Afrikaans spoken in South Africa, *apartheid* means "separation." In practice, the word connotes the de jure segregation of the black majority in South Africa from the white minority, which maintained political control until the early 1990s. Black South African **Desmond Tutu**, an Anglican bishop, appealed to the West to impose economic sanctions on South Africa as a means to expedite political change. Congress passed the Anti-Apartheid Act of 1986 in a move to prohibit imports from South Africa or investments in the country. President **Ronald Reagan** vetoed the package. The bill was ultimately passed when both chambers overrode the veto. *See also* MANDELA, NELSON ROLIHLAHLA; SOUTH AFRICA SANCTIONS.

**ARAFAT, YASSER.** *See* PALESTINIAN LIBERATION ORGANIZATION (PLO).

**ARISTIDE, JEAN-BERTRAND (1953– ).** Born in Port-Salut, Haiti, on 15 July 1953, Aristide is a former Catholic priest who became president of the island nation in 1991. He was overthrown in a military coup just seven months later. Aristide's ouster precipitated a wave of refugees, who took to makeshift boats en route to Florida to escape the military regime during 1991–92. These "boat people"—

numbering more than 40,000—were repatriated or taken to the U.S. base at Guantanamo Bay, Cuba, by the U.S. Coast Guard. President **George H. W.** Bush was criticized by some African Americans for failing to offer asylum to the refugees or allow them to reach the United States. U.S. troops occupied Haiti in 1994 after the military regime stepped down under international pressure, and Aristide resumed his presidency until 1996, when new elections took place (Aristide was precluded by law from serving two consecutive terms). He was elected again in 2000 under a cloud of allegations of electoral fraud. In 2004 rebels opposed to Aristide seized several cities in Haiti, prompting him to flee the country. He was flown by U.S. aircraft to the Central African Republic and then relocated to South Africa. Aristide maintains he was kidnapped by U.S. troops and forced into exile, though the circumstances surrounding his ouster are a matter of contention.

**ARMS CONTROL.** Controlling the proliferation of nuclear arms by the United States and **Soviet Union** was an issue of paramount importance in the 1980s—the closing decade of the **Cold War. Deter-rence** theory, based on the notion of **Mutually Assured Destruction**, posited that the risk of nuclear war could be diminished if neither superpower had a strategic advantage in launching a first strike against the other. To this end, advocates of **détente** such as President Richard Nixon negotiated the **Anti–Ballistic Missile (ABM) Treaty** with the Soviets and sought a reduction in nuclear weapons through the Strategic Arms Limitation Treaty (SALT I).

President **Ronald Reagan** took a different approach to the Soviet Union, which he called an "**evil empire.**" He campaigned for an increase in nuclear weapons stockpiles to counter a perceived Soviet advantage, particularly with respect to short-range weapons stationed against Western European countries in **Warsaw Pact** nations. In 1984 Reagan won German chancellor **Helmut Kohl's** approval to place short-range **Pershing II missiles** in West Germany to counter Soviet **SS-20 missiles** in Eastern Europe. Reagan also marshaled congressional approval for the development and deployment of **MX missiles**—long-range **intercontinental ballistic missiles (ICBMs)**—that could carry multiple nuclear weapons and increased submarine-based **Trident II missiles** and **cruise missiles**.

Reagan's "reversal" of positions on the arms buildup began with Mikhail Gorbachev's accession to the post of general secretary of the Communist Party of the Soviet Union in 1985 following the death of Konstantin Chernenko. Reagan's advocacy of the Strategic Defense Initiative (SDI), a space-based anti–ballistic missile system, troubled Gorbachev and threatened to undermine the ABM Treaty. Reagan and Gorbachev met for a summit in Reykjavík, Iceland, which paved the way for the Intermediate-Range Nuclear Forces (INF) Treaty of 1987. The INF Treaty eliminated Soviet SS-20 missiles in Eastern Europe, Pershing II missiles in North Atlantic Treaty Organization (NATO) countries, and short-range cruise missiles. Reagan later negotiated the first Strategic Arms Reduction Treaty (START) with the Soviets in 1988, and President George H. W. Bush finalized a second round of START in 1991. Both agreements limited the number of nuclear weapons the United States and Soviet Union could possess.

Arms control remained an issue for the administration of George H. W. Bush, but with the dissolution of the Soviet Union in 1991 and a proclaimed end of the Cold War, concern was focused on control of the Russian warheads that might be sold on the international black market. *See also* GROMYKO, ANDREI ANDREYEVICH; WEINBERGER, CASPAR WILLIARD; YELTSIN, BORIS NIKOLAYEVICH.

**AWACS.** The acronym for Airborne Warning and Control System, AWACS is a radar system mounted on aircraft and designed for in-flight surveillance. In a controversial move, President Ronald Reagan won congressional approval to sell AWACS to Saudi Arabia in 1981. Reagan linked the sale to Saudi engagement in Middle East peace processes and sought to shore up Saudi Arabia's alliance with the United States. *See also* ISRAEL.

**– B –**

**B1-B BOMBER.** The B1-B is a long-range, supersonic bomber that was a precursor to the Stealth Bomber. Built by Rockwell, its design made it difficult to detect by radar devices. President Ronald Reagan restarted the program in 1981 after it had been stopped by the administration of **Jimmy Carter** in 1977.

**BAKER, HOWARD HENRY, JR. (1925– ).** A Tennessee native, graduate of the University of Tennessee School of Law (1949), and **World War II** veteran of the navy, Baker served three terms in the United States Senate between 1967 and 1985. He made a brief, unsuccessful bid for the Republican presidential nomination in 1980. He was best known for his legislative leadership as Senate minority leader from 1977 to 1981 and as majority leader in 1981 after Republicans gained a majority in the Senate on President **Ronald Reagan**'s election coattails. He was instrumental in marshaling much of Reagan's legislative agenda through the upper chamber and providing leverage over the Democratic-controlled House of Representatives during Reagan's first term. Baker remained majority leader through 1984, at which time he decided to retire from the Senate. He was awarded the Presidential Medal of Freedom in 1984 for his public service. President Reagan asked him to serve as **chief of staff** in 1987 to replace **Donald T. Regan**, and during his tenure he was credited with rehabilitating the image of White House internal management in the wake of the **Iran–Contra** scandal. In 1996 Baker married his former Senate colleague from Kansas, Nancy Landon Kassebaum. President **George W. Bush** named Baker ambassador to **Japan** in 2001. Baker remained in that post until 2004, returning to the private sector as an advisor to the Citigroup financial firm.

**BAKER, JAMES ADDISON, III (1930– ).** A native Texan, Baker has been a prominent figure in Republican presidential administrations and elections since the mid-1970s. Baker graduated from Princeton University in 1952, and after two years in the Marine Corps, went to the University of Texas, where he received a law degree in 1957. President Gerald Ford appointed him undersecretary of commerce in 1975, and later chairman of his national election committee in 1976. Baker was chairman of **George H. W. Bush**'s 1980 campaign for the presidency. When **Ronald Reagan** clinched the Republican nomination and chose Bush as his running mate, Baker subsequently joined Ronald Reagan's campaign as senior advisor for the general election. He served as President Ronald Reagan's White House **chief of staff**

from 1981 to 1985, after which he was appointed secretary of the treasury (1985–89). He was also a member of the **National Security Council** and the Economic Policy Council during Reagan's second term. President Bush appointed him secretary of state in 1989, and Baker held that position until August 1992, when he became the White House chief of staff. In 1991 he was awarded the Presidential Medal of Freedom for his leadership in the Communist transitions of 1989 following the demise of the **Soviet Union** and fall of the **Berlin Wall.** He was also commended for his service with respect to the reunification of Germany and the allied invasion of Iraq in the **Persian Gulf War** in 1991.

Baker published *The Politics of Diplomacy* in 1995 and in 1997 served as the personal envoy for the **United Nations** secretary general for the Western Sahara. After returning to the private sector as a senior partner to his law practice of Baker Botts and as senior counsel to the Carlyle Group, he became President **George W. Bush**'s principal legal advisor during the Florida recount controversy following the 2000 election (*see* BUSH, JOHN ELLIS). President George W. Bush appointed him as a special envoy in 2003 to work with foreign countries to relieve Iraq's debt after dictator **Saddam Hussein**'s regime was toppled by American and coalition forces earlier that spring.

**BAKKER, JIM (1939– ).** Television evangelist and co-host with his wife, Tammy Faye Bakker, of the *PTL Club* ("Praise the Lord"), Bakker was convicted in August 1989 for fraud and **tax** evasion. His staff had paid over $200,000 to purchase the silence of Jessica Hahn, a **woman** who had sexual relations with Bakker. Bakker had also committed fraud regarding his theme park, Heritage USA, when he sold more shares in the hotel than the number of persons the facility could accommodate. Bakker spent five years in prison and was released on parole in 1993. His conviction, not to mention his excessively lavish lifestyle, cast a pall over television evangelists in the late 1980s.

**BALDRIGE, MALCOLM (1922–1987).** Born in Nebraska and educated at Yale, Baldrige entered the manufacturing industry in 1947 after serving in the Pacific theater during **World War II**. As head of

Scovill, Inc., beginning in 1962 Baldrige turned a financially insolvent mill operation into a profitable and diversified company. President **Ronald Reagan** appointed Baldrige secretary of commerce in 1981, and he remained in the post until 1987. Baldrige was heavily involved in trade policy and is credited for brokering technology transfers to India and **China**. He also negotiated access for American firms to markets in the **Soviet Union** and championed the Export Trading Company Act of 1982, which was aimed at facilitating and expanding exports from the United States. Baldrige won acclaim for his streamlined management of budget and personnel practices in the Department of Commerce. Congress named the Malcolm Baldrige National Quality Award in his honor. He died in July 1987 in a rodeo accident in California.

**BALTIC STATES.** Comprising Latvia, Lithuania, and Estonia, the Baltic States were among the first of the former Soviet republics to establish autonomous governments following the dissolution of the **Soviet Union**. The three countries were recognized as independent in September 1991 by the Soviet ruling counsel.

**BARR, WILLIAM PELHAM (1950– ).** A graduate of law from George Washington University, Barr was employed at the **Central Intelligence Agency** from 1973 to 1977. He served as a law clerk to Judge Malcolm Wilkey of the U.S. Court of Appeals for the District of Columbia Circuit from 1977 to 1978. He was employed by the Washington law firm of Shaw, Pitman, Potts & Trowbridge before serving as assistant U.S. attorney general for the Office of Legal Counsel from 1989 to 1990, deputy attorney general from May 1990 to August 1991, and acting attorney general in 1991. He was appointed attorney general by President **George H. W. Bush** in 1991 and served until the end of Bush's term. Barr resumed private practice and served on the board of directors of the College of William and Mary and several corporations following his public service.

**BEIRUT, LEBANON.** U.S. Marines arrived in Beirut in August 1982 as part of an international peacekeeping force after **Israel**'s invasion of Lebanon. On 23 October 1983, a suicide bomber driving a truck with 12,000 pounds of TNT crashed into the Marines' barracks at the

Beirut International Airport. The force of the explosion leveled the four-story building, killing 241 people, of whom 220 were Marines, 18 navy, and 3 army personnel. The **terrorist** attack was the most deadly ever recorded overseas. President **Ronald Reagan** contemplated military action against **Hezbollah**, the organization believed to be responsible for the incident. Reagan and Defense Secretary **Caspar Weinberger** originally targeted Baalbek, Lebanon, thought to be a Hezbollah training outpost run by the Iranian Revolutionary Guard. Reagan and his cabinet scrapped those plans for fear of jeopardizing relations with other Arab nations in the region. The Marines in Beirut were subsequently moved offshore, and in February 1984 the international peacekeeping force withdrew from Lebanon. The country fell into deepening chaos and civil war. Reagan was accused by some of trying to draw attention away from the Marine barracks bombing when U.S. forces invaded the island nation of **Grenada** on 23 October 1983—just two days after the tragedy. However, Reagan had been readying an invasion of Grenada well in advance of the Beirut debacle, following a coup on the island and the execution of Marxist Prime Minister Maurice Bishop by leftist radicals. A week prior, the president had ordered a navy flotilla to change direction from Lebanon to the tiny Caribbean island.

**BELL, TERREL HOWARD (1921–1996).** Bell was born in Lava Hot Springs, Idaho. He was secretary of education under President **Ronald Reagan** from 1981 to 1984. He served in the Marine Corps during **World War II** (1942–46). He graduated from Southern Idaho College of Education (1946) and earned a doctorate in education from the University of Utah in 1961 while teaching in public schools. He was named the Utah state superintendent of public instruction (1962–70), worked in the U.S. Office of Education (1970–71), and was U.S. commissioner of education under presidents Richard Nixon and Gerald Ford. In the administration of Ronald Reagan, Bell was acclaimed for his work on the commission that wrote *A Nation at Risk*, which prompted reforms of public schools. The author of eight books, including *Mothers, Leadership and Success* (1990), *Excellence* (1990), and *How to Shape Up Our Schools* (1991), Bell died from pulmonary fibrosis in 1996.

**BENGHAZI, LIBYA.** *See* OPERATION EL DORADO CANYON.

**BENNETT, WILLIAM JOHN (BILL) (1943– ).** An outspoken and prominent conservative, Bennett was born in New York and holds a doctorate in philosophy from the University of Texas and a law degree from Harvard. He served as an assistant to the president of Boston University (1972–76) before becoming executive director (1976–79) and later president and director (1979–81) of the National Humanities Center in North Carolina. President **Ronald Reagan** appointed Bennett to chair the National Endowment for the Humanities (1981–85). In that position, Bennett was a vocal critic of government support for programs and events he viewed as harmful to traditional values and culture, earning him much praise from conservatives. President Reagan later appointed Bennett secretary of education (1985–88). Bennett devoted much time to publicly debating his attempts to implement educational reforms centered on "content, character, and choice." He remained in public service under President **George H. W. Bush**, serving as director of the newly created **Office of National Drug Control Policy**, a position dubbed the "drug czar" (1989–90). *See also* DRUG TRAFFICKING.

Leaving the White House in 1990, Bennett became codirector of the nonprofit Empower America, a conservative policy organization, and co-founded and chairs K12, Inc., an Internet-based home school program. He also chairs Americans for Victory over Terrorism, an organization dedicated to strengthening public resolve in support of the war on **terrorism** following the attacks of 11 September 2001. A profuse writer on contemporary social issues, Bennett's books include *Our Children and Our Country: Improving America's Schools and Affirming the Common Culture* (1988), *The De-valuing of America: The Fight for Our Children and Our Culture* (1992), *The Death of Outrage: Bill Clinton and the Assault on American Ideals* (1998), *The Broken Hearth: Reversing the Moral Collapse of the American Family* (2003), and *Why We Fight: Moral Clarity and the War on Terrorism* (2003).

**BENTSEN, LLOYD MILLARD, JR. (1921– ).** A native of Mission, Texas, a graduate of the University of Texas Law School (1942), and a **World War II** European theater veteran, Democrat Lloyd Bentsen served three terms in the House of Representatives from 1948 to 1954. He then left public service until 1970, when he successfully unseated incumbent Texas senator Ralph Yarborough in the Democratic primary and later won the general election. Bentsen was reelected in 1976, 1982, and 1988. In 1988, Democratic presidential nominee **Michael Dukakis** chose Bentsen—12 years his elder—as his vice-presidential running mate, primarily for Bentsen's **foreign policy** experience in the Senate and his moderate political stances. Bentsen issued a memorable quip during the vice-presidential debates that earned him some distinction. When Indiana senator and Republican vice-presidential candidate **J. Danforth Quayle** tried to liken himself to slain president John F. Kennedy, Bentsen retorted, "Jack Kennedy was a friend of mine. Senator, you're no Jack Kennedy." After he and Dukakis lost the 1988 election, Bentsen returned to the Senate and finished out his fourth term. President **William Clinton** chose him as secretary of the treasury in 1993. Bentsen retired from that post in 1994 and returned to private life.

**BERGEN–BELSEN CONCENTRATION CAMP, GERMANY.** Originally established as a prisoner of war camp in 1940, Bergen–Belsen was transformed into a concentration camp in 1942. Between 1942 and the liberation of the camp in 1945 by British soldiers, approximately 50,000 Jews, Eastern Europeans, anti-Nazis, homosexuals, and others captured by the German Nazi regime died in Bergen–Belsen, including Dutch-born Anne Frank (author of *The Diary of Anne Frank*). Though the presence of gas chambers at Bergen–Belsen is disputed, the camp was known for its horribly overcrowded conditions, malnutrition of prisoners, and rampant disease, including typhoid. President **Ronald Reagan** visited Bergen–Belsen with German chancellor **Helmut Kohl** on 5 May 1985 during the 40th anniversary of the defeat of Adolph Hitler. Reagan was criticized by many, including Holocaust survivor Elie Wiesel, for having first visited nearby Bitburg Cemetery in West Berlin, which contains the graves of members of Hitler's SS (*Schutzstaffel*, or paramilitary branch of the Nazi Party that notoriously persecuted Jews).

**BERLIN WALL.** Built in 1961 by the East German government, the Wall (*der Mauer* in German) completely encompassed West Berlin.

It was constructed to prevent East Germans from defecting to the West during the **Cold War**. President **Ronald Reagan** visited the Brandenburg Gate at the Berlin Wall on 12 June 1987. There he made an impassioned appeal to the Soviet general secretary **Mikhail Gorbachev** that sounded the death knell of Soviet domination of Eastern Europe: "Mr. Gorbachev, open this gate! Mr. Gorbachev, tear down this wall!" In December 1988, Gorbachev formally abandoned the **Brezhnev Doctrine** in favor of the "**Sinatra Doctrine**,"so named for singer Frank Sinatra's song "My Way." The Soviet Union would no longer intervene in the affairs of **Warsaw Pact** nations, and they alone could determine their own futures. In November 1989, East German protests against the Communist regime in that country followed the resignation of leader **Erich Honecker**. The successor government, headed by **Egon Krenz**, mistakenly announced that all travel restrictions to the West had been lifted. No longer under the threat of Soviet intervention, East Germans rushed to the Wall on 9 November and overwhelmed security forces. They were joined by festive West Germans on the other side who were armed with shovels and sledge hammers and began dismantling the fortification. The fall of the Berlin Wall marked the road to reunification of Germany, which took place on 3 October 1990.

**BHOPAL, INDIA.** Bhopal is the site of a fatal gas leak at a Union Carbide pesticide plant on 3 December 1984. Approximately 40 tons of poisonous gas escaped into the atmosphere near the town in central India. The Indian government claimed nearly 15,000 people died and over a half million became ill with maladies such as cancer, kidney failure, and liver disease, or had babies with birth defects. Union Carbide, an American company, paid $470 million in compensation as part of a settlement with the Indian government in 1989. The company has certified that the site of the leak has been cleaned up adequately, but skeptics argue that the groundwater still suffers from contamination.

**BILINGUAL EDUCATION.** See *CASTAÑEDA V. PICKARD* (1981).

**BIN LADEN, OSAMA.** Born in Riyadh, Saudi Arabia, bin Laden inherited a fortune from his father's construction business. In the 1980s he established Maktab al-Khadamat (Office of Order), which supported and supplied the **mujahadeen** fighters with money, arms, and human resources following the **Soviet Union**'s invasion of **Afghanistan**. The extent of U.S. support for, or covert involvement in, support of bin Laden's organization and its jihad (holy war) against the Soviets in Afghanistan is a matter of speculation. From the extremist elements of Maktab al-Khadamat, bin Laden formed a new group of militant Islamists called al-Qaeda in 1988. Following the **Persian Gulf War** he called for the ouster of U.S. troops from Saudi Arabia, which houses the holy cities of Mecca and Medina. The Saudi royal family expelled bin Laden from the country in 1991, and he fled to Sudan. Bin Laden's family disowned him in 1994, the same year Saudi Arabia formally revoked his citizenship. After Sudan expelled him under international pressure, bin Laden took up refuge in Afghanistan, where he received succor from the Taliban government. Bin Laden is suspected of causing a string of **terrorist** attacks, including hotel bombings in Egypt and Yemen; U.S. embassy bombings in Dar es Salaam, Tanzania, and Nairobi, Kenya; and the hijackings of four aircraft used in the 11 September 2001 attacks on New York and Washington, D.C. *See also* TERRORISM.

**BITBURG, GERMANY.** *See* BERGEN–BELSEN CONCENTRATION CAMP, GERMANY.

**BLOCK, JOHN RUSLING (1935– ).** Born in Galesburg, Illinois, Block transformed a family farm into a thriving agribusiness in the 1960s. He became Illinois secretary of agriculture in 1977. President **Ronald Reagan** appointed him secretary of agriculture in 1981, and he remained in that position until 1986. In the 1980s farmers blamed Block for the worst recession to hit rural America since the Great Depression. In 1985 the devastating effect of the economic downturn prompted singers **Willie Nelson**, **Neil Young**, and **John Mellencamp** to organize **Farm Aid**, a series of fundraising concerts. The concerts were aimed at calling public attention to farmers who were losing their livelihood to bank foreclosures. Congress later passed the **Agricultural Credit Act** of 1987 to halt the rate of failed farms. Upon leaving the Department of Agriculture, Block became president of the National-American Wholesale Grocers' Association (later named

Food Distributors International), a trade association. In 2000 he joined the board of directors of MetaMorphix, an agricultural biotechnology firm.

**BOLAND AMENDMENT.** Named for Representative Edward Boland of Massachusetts, this amendment to the House appropriations bill of 1982 (HR 2698, for Fiscal Year 1983) prohibited the administration of **Ronald Reagan** from utilizing congressionally appropriated funds for covert activities in **Nicaragua**. It also revoked funding for the **Contra** rebels battling the Marxist **Sandinista** government in that country. Congress adopted the amendment following **Central Intelligence Agency (CIA)** actions in Nicaragua against that government that never received congressional assent. The courts never settled the question of whether Congress overstepped its authority in the realm of the presidential conduct of foreign relations. The Boland Amendment forbade the U.S. intelligence agencies from providing material or support "for the purpose of overthrowing the Government of Nicaragua," a goal that the Reagan administration supported. The Reagan administration violated the Boland Amendment when Admiral **John M. Poindexter** and Colonel **Oliver North**, members of the **National Security Council**, secretly channeled funds to **Contra** rebels after selling weapons to Iran for the release of U.S. hostages. The Lebanese newspaper ***al-Shiraa*** broke the story on 3 November 1986, touching off the **Iran–Contra** scandal.

**BORK, ROBERT HERON (1927– ).** A Pennsylvania native and graduate of the University of Chicago Law School, Bork taught law at Yale University in the 1960s and 1970s. An "originalist" in his judicial philosophy, Bork advocates interpreting the Constitution based on the intentions of the Founders. From 1972 to 1977 he served under presidents Richard Nixon and Gerald Ford as solicitor general in the Justice Department. Bork earned fame—or infamy—for his role in President Nixon's "Saturday Night Massacre" of October 1973. Nixon ordered the Justice Department to fire special prosecutor Archibald Cox, who was investigating Watergate, and demanded that the president turn over tapes of White House conversations. Attorney General Elliott Richardson and Deputy Attorney General William Ruckelshaus both resigned rather than carry out Nixon's order. As the number three in rank at Justice, Bork became acting attorney general and fired Cox.

In 1982 President **Ronald Reagan** appointed Bork to the U.S. Circuit Court of Appeals for the District of Columbia. Five years later, Reagan nominated Bork to the **Supreme Court** to replace retiring justice Lewis Powell. The Senate confirmation battle over his nomination was one of the most spectacularly vitriolic up to that point in time. In his testimony, Bork affirmed that the Constitution did not contain an inherent "right to privacy"—a notion used to justify **abortion** rights in the 1973 case *Roe v. Wade*. His candidacy galvanized the opposition of **women**'s groups, and the Democratic-controlled Senate rejected his nomination by a vote of 42–58. He returned to the bench for a final year on the Appeals Court and left in 1988. He joined the conservative think tank American Enterprise Institute and has written numerous books, including *Slouching Towards Gomorrah: Modern Liberalism and American Decline* (1996), and (ed.) *A Country I Do Not Recognize: The Legal Assault on American Values* (2005). *See also* GINSBURG, DOUGLAS HOWARD; KENNEDY, ANTHONY MCLEOD.

**BOSNIA–HERZEGOVINA.** Part of Tito's Yugoslavia following **World War II**, the region of Bosnia–Herzegovina declared independence in October 1991. Bosnian Serbs boycotted the subsequent referendum in February 1992. They took up arms alongside Serbians against Croats (largely Catholic) and Bosnians (largely Muslim) in order to force the division of the republic along ethnic and religious lines. Under President **George H. W. Bush**, the United States sent troops to the former Yugoslavia under the **United Nations** Protection Force (UNPROFOR) for peacekeeping, for the delivery of humanitarian aid, and for ensuring the safety of demilitarized "safe zones" for refugees.

**BOWEN, OTIS RAY (1918– ).** A graduate of Indiana University medical school (1942), Bowen served with a medical unit in Okinawa during **World War II**. Following his military service, he returned to his native Indiana, where he set up a medical practice. He entered state politics in 1957 and spent nearly two decades in the Indiana statehouse, where he served as speaker from 1967 to 1973. He was elected to two successive terms as governor of Indiana in 1972 and 1976, and served as chair of the National Governors' Association. He left public life briefly between 1981 and 1985 to become a professor of family medicine at Indiana University. Bowen headed the Advisory Commission on **Social Security** from 1982 to 1984, and served as President **Ronald Reagan**'s secretary of Health and Human Services from 1985 to 1989.

**BRADY, JAMES SCOTT (1940– ).** Born in Centralia, Illinois, Brady was press secretary for President **Ronald Reagan** from 1981 to 1989. Brady began his career in public service as a staff member in the office of Illinois Republican senator Everett Dirksen. He later worked on the faculty of Southern Illinois University and held positions in public relations. He became special assistant to the secretary of housing and urban development from 1973 to 1975 under presidents Richard Nixon and Gerald Ford, special assistant to the director of the Office of Management and Budget from 1975 to 1976, and assistant to the secretary of defense from 1976 to 1977. He joined the staff of Delaware Republican senator William J. Roth from 1976 to 1977 before serving as press secretary to former Texas governor and presidential candidate John Connally of Texas. Brady is remembered for **John Hinckley Jr.**'s attempt on President Reagan's life on 30 March 1981. Brady suffered a serious head injury from a bullet, which left him partially paralyzed and in a wheelchair. Brady retained the title of press secretary for the duration of Reagan's two terms in office, though he did not return to the White House after the assassination attempt. Deputy Press Secretary **Larry Speakes** assumed day-to-day **media** operations. Brady and his wife, Sarah, were indefatigable advocates for stricter handgun control laws. The Brady Handgun Violence Prevention Act, dubbed the "Brady Bill," was signed into law under President **William Clinton** in 1993. The bill requires federally licensed gun dealers to perform background checks on customers.

**BRADY, NICHOLAS FREDERICK (1930– ).** Born in New York City and educated at Yale and Harvard in business, Brady's long career in the banking industry dates to 1954, when he was first employed at Dillon, Read and Company, Inc., where he eventually became chairman of the board. He later directed several large corporations, included the H. J. Heinz Company. Prior to joining the administration of **Ronald Reagan** as treasury secretary in 1988, he served on numerous presidential commissions, including Strategic Forces (1983), the National Bipartisan Commission on Central America (1983), the Commission on Security and Economic Assistance (1983), the Blue Ribbon Commission on Defense Management (1985), and the Presidential Task Force on Market Mechanisms (1987). President **George H. W. Bush** retained Brady as treasury secretary for the duration of his term (1989–93).

**BREZHNEV DOCTRINE.** In 1968 **Leonid Brezhnev** elaborated the official position that the **Soviet Union** was entitled to intervene in Communist states in Eastern Europe in order to "safeguard socialism" and protect the integrity of governments in the **Warsaw Pact**. This doctrine, used by Brezhnev to justify interventions in **Czechoslovakia** in 1968 and **Afghanistan** in 1979, represented a longer-standing policy dating to Nikita Khrushchev. Khrushchev utilized a similar rationale to put down the Hungarian Revolution led by Imre Nagy in 1956. Nagy had announced intentions to withdraw Hungary from the Warsaw Pact. The policy differs from the so-called **Sinatra Doctrine** of Soviet General Secretary **Mikhail Gorbachev**, who allowed Warsaw Pact nations to decide their own futures in the late 1980s without fear of Soviet intervention.

**BREZHNEV, LEONID ILYCH (1906–1982).** Born in Dniprodzerzhyns'k, Ukraine, in 1906, Leonid Ilych Brezhnev was general secretary of the Communist Party of the **Soviet Union** from 1964 until his death on 10 November 1982. A **Cold War** icon, Brezhnev ordered **Warsaw Pact** troops to invade **Czechoslovakia** and remove **Alexander Dubček** from power in 1968, presided over a deepening rift with **China** (the Sino-Soviet split), and supported North Vietnam during the Vietnam War. Yet he was also secretary during a period of growing **détente** with the United States. He signed the Strategic Arms Limitation Treaty (SALT I) with Richard Nixon and later the Helsinki Accords on human rights with President Gerald Ford in the 1970s. However, Brezhnev's decision to invade **Afghanistan** in December 1979 soured relations with the United States. President **Ronald Reagan** adopted a rhetorically confrontational stance against the Soviet Union and sought to counter a perceived Soviet military advantage. Reagan never met Brezhnev. Brezhnev had a stroke in March 1982, and suffered a fatal heart attack later that year. He was succeeded by **Yuri Andropov**. *See also* ARMS CONTROL; CHERNENKO, KONSTANTIN; GORBACHEV, MIKHAIL SERGEYEVICH.

**BROCK, WILLIAM EMERSON (1930– ).** Congressman and senator from his native Tennessee, William Brock served as President **Ronald Reagan**'s labor secretary from 1985 to 1987. A graduate of Washington and Lee University (1953), Brock served in the navy from 1953 to 1956 and then worked for his family's business, Brock Candy Company, rising through the ranks to become director of the corporation in 1961. He won election to the U.S. House of Representatives from the third district of Tennessee in 1963, and was re-elected thrice before successfully running for the Senate in 1970. Brock chaired the Republican National Committee from 1977 to 1981, and was President Ronald Reagan's trade representative from 1981 to 1985. Brock resigned his position as secretary of labor in 1987 to chair **Robert Dole**'s presidential committee. He resides in Annapolis, Maryland, and in 1994 failed to win a Senate seat in that state.

**BUCHANAN, PATRICK JOSEPH (1938– ).** Buchanan, a native of Washington, D.C., served in the administrations of Richard Nixon, Gerald Ford, and **Ronald Reagan,** and unsuccessfully ran for the presidency three times—twice as a Republican (1992, 1996) and in 2000 under the **Reform Party** banner after a bitter court battle over that party's internal nomination politics. A conservative Catholic and graduate of Georgetown University in English and philosophy (1961) and Columbia University in journalism (1962), Buchanan entered politics during Richard Nixon's first presidential campaign. He joined the Nixon administration as a speechwriter in 1969. When Nixon resigned in August 1974, Buchanan stayed on briefly in the same capacity under President Ford before leaving to take up a career in broadcast and print **media**. He became a regular contributor and host on television programs such as the *McLaughlin Group* (Public Broadcasting Corporation) and the Cable News Network's *Crossfire*, where he elaborated his traditionalist conservative views on social and **foreign policy**. Buchanan was also a widely read syndicated columnist before joining the White House in Ronald Reagan's second term. From 1985 to 1987 he served as director of White House communications.

In 1992 Buchanan challenged **George H. W. Bush** for the Republican presidential nomination. Though he lost the New Hampshire primary and later dropped out of the race, Buchanan's brief campaign fostered resentment among many Republicans for President Bush's decision to accept **tax** increases in the **1990 Budget Agreement** with Democrats, which Buchanan argued violated the president's 1988 convention pledge "**read my lips, no new taxes**." Buchanan's campaign is often regarded as a key factor in some Republicans' support of **Reform Party** candidate **Ross Perot** in 1992, which many scholars and pundits argue robbed Bush of reelection. Buchanan also gave a fiery discourse at the 1992 Republican convention, often dubbed the "culture war" speech, in which he excoriated Democratic presidential candidate **William J. Clinton** on social issues such as **abortion**.

Buchanan entered the 1996 Republican presidential primaries on a platform against the **North American Free Trade Agreement (NAFTA)**, immigration, and social issues such as abortion. Although he prevailed narrowly in the New Hampshire primary, Buchanan dropped out of the race several months later when rival and eventual nominee, **Robert Dole**, swept subsequent contests. Buchanan left the Republican Party in 1999, arguing that it had abandoned its historical stances on anti-New Deal policies and limited American engagement in **foreign policy**. He ran as the Reform Party candidate for president in 2000, but won less than a percent of the national popular vote. Buchanan continues his criticism of Republican policies under President **George W. Bush**. He advocates tougher policies on immigration, restrictions on abortion, and tax reductions. Critics contend his rhetoric contains elements of anti-Semitism. Buchanan is also highly critical of the Bush administration's engagement in the Middle East, which he argues verges on imperialism. He is author of *Where the Right Went Wrong: How Neoconservatives Subverted the Reagan Revolution and Hijacked the Bush Presidency* (2004), *The Death of the West: How Dying Populations and Immigrant Invasions Imperil*

*Our Country and Civilization* (2002), *A Republic, Not an Empire: Reclaiming America's Destiny* (2002), and *The Great Betrayal: How American Sovereignty and Social Justice Are Being Sacrificed to the Gods of the Global Economy* (1998).

**BUCKLEY, WILLIAM F. (1928–1985).** Buckley was an American **Central Intelligence Agency (CIA)** operative in **Beirut, Lebanon**. He was captured in March 1984 and held hostage for 444 days by a group called Islamic Holy War with ties to the **terrorist** organization **Hezbollah**. He was tortured and died during his captivity. Buckley's body lies in rest at Arlington National Cemetery.

**BUDGET AGREEMENT (1990).** Critics contend that the 1990 budget agreement reached by **George H. W. Bush** and congressional Democrats and Republicans was a betrayal of the president's **"read my lips, no new taxes"** pledge made at the 1988 Republican convention. The agreement was the result of a confluence of complex forces. Rising federal deficits spilling over from the 1980s had prompted Congress to pass deficit reduction measures such as **Gramm–Rudman–Hollings** (1985, 1987), which mandated automatic spending cuts if Congress and the president could not agree on how to offset new spending with reductions in the budget. As entitlements such as **Social Security** and **Medicare** took a greater proportion of federal outlays and narrowed discretionary spending, the Democratic majority in Congress was unwilling to shoulder the blame for any new **tax** increases. With the 1992 election looming, Bush was fearful of a government shutdown and wary of the potential effects of deficits on interest rates and economic growth. The president entered into negotiations with top Democrats and Republicans and reached a budget deal through a process of "summitry." The agreement angered rank-and-file Democrats because of proposed cuts to Medicare and infuriated conservative Republicans, such as **Newt Gingrich**, because of income and luxury tax increases. Despite a televised plea to the American public, Bush could not generate majority support for the budget in Congress. The budget was defeated in the House of Representatives by a margin of 75 votes—and by a majority of both Democrats and Republicans. Following Bush's veto of a continuing resolution to keep the government in operation, Congress passed the

Omnibus Budget Reconciliation Act of 1990, which Bush called a compromise. However, the bill was even less commensurate with his stated goals of removing the capital gains tax and avoiding new taxes. Bush's reversal on the tax increase issue became a major point of criticism by **Patrick Buchanan**, who challenged Bush during the 1992 Republican primaries. *See also* BUDGET ENFORCEMENT ACT (1990); PEROT, H. (HENRY) ROSS; "REAGANOMICS".

**BUDGET ENFORCEMENT ACT (1990).** Adopted by Congress in 1990, the Budget Enforcement Act replaced **Gramm–Rudman–Hollings**, which failed to reduce the federal deficit to statutory targets. The legislation required pay-as-you-go (PAYGO) provisions for all direct government spending and receipts. PAYGO mandated that new spending must be offset by reductions in spending elsewhere in the budget. The goal was to cap domestic spending and reduce the deficit over five years. The legislation enabled the president to authorize the **Office of Management and Budget (OMB)** to "sequester," or block funds, for bills that violated the PAYGO requirement.

**BURNLEY, JAMES HORACE (1948– ).** A native of North Carolina, Burnley earned a B.A. degree at Yale (1970) and a law degree from Harvard (1973). Following graduation, he entered private law practice at Brooks, Pierce, McLendon, Humphrey and Leonard (1973–1975), and then became a partner at Turner, Enochs, Foster, Sparrow and Burnley (1975–1981). He entered government service in 1981, and served as director of Volunteers in Service to America (VISTA), a program started in 1965. He was associate deputy attorney general at the Department of Justice from 1982 to 1983. Burnley then moved to the Department of Transportation, taking a position as general counsel (1983), before becoming deputy secretary (1983–1987) and serving as President **Ronald Reagan**'s third transportation secretary from 1987 to 1989.

**BUSH, BARBARA PIERCE (1925– ).** First Lady Barbara Bush was born in Rye, New York. She married her husband, President **George H. W. Bush**, in early 1945, shortly before he shipped off to the South Pacific as a navy pilot in **World War II**. She is mother to six children, including President **George W. Bush**, Florida Governor **John Ellis (Jeb) Bush**, Pauline Robinson (1949–53), Neil, Marvin, and Dorothy Walker. As first lady, Barbara Bush's role in the White House was more understated than her immediate predecessors. Yet her strong support of the causes of literacy and homelessness exemplified her husband's call to voluntarism. She worked with the Project Literacy U.S. (PLUS) and became a board member of Reading Is Fundamental. From the White House in 1989, she established the Barbara Bush Foundation for Family Literacy. She engaged in fundraising activities for such organizations as the United Negro College Fund and Morehouse College School of Medicine. She also actively volunteered in various hospitals and clinics. She is the author of three books, including *C. Fred's Story* (1984), *Millie's Book* (1990), and *Barbara Bush: A Memoir* (1994). She used the proceeds from her first book, a story about one of the Bush family's dogs, to support Laubach Literacy Action and Literacy Volunteers of America. She donated earnings from *Millie's Book*, a recounting of the "First Dog's" White House life, to the Barbara Bush Foundation for Family Literacy. Barbara resides with her husband in Houston, Texas, and at their home in Kennebunkport, Maine.

**BUSH, GEORGE HERBERT WALKER (1924– ).** The 41st president of the United States was born on 12 June 1924 in Milton, Massachusetts, to Dorothy Walker and Prescott Bush. His father was a U.S. senator from Connecticut from 1952 to 1963. He attended the prestigious Phillips Academy in Andover, Massachusetts, and joined the U.S. Navy in 1942 on his 18th birthday. During Bush's service as a naval aviator, his plane was shot down by the Japanese during an otherwise successful raid on Chi Chi Jima in the South Pacific. Bush survived a crash landing in the sea and was rescued, but the other three members of his crew perished. He received the Distinguished Flying Cross for his mission. He subsequently flew 58 combat missions in the **Philippines** and also received medals of valor for his service aboard the USS *San Jacinto*.

After World War II he enrolled in Yale University, where he became president of the Delta Kappa Epsilon fraternity and was inducted into the secret Skull and Bones society. Bush married **Barbara Pierce (Bush)** on 6 January 1945. His children include George

Walker (Texas governor and 43rd president of the United States), Pauline Robinson (died 1953), **John Ellis (Jeb)** (Florida governor), Neil, Marvin, and Dorothy Walker.

Following his degree at Yale, Bush moved to Texas and joined Dresser Industries to pursue oil exploration. He entered Republican politics in Texas in 1964, unsuccessfully challenging incumbent senator Ralph Yarborough. He turned his attention to the seventh district of Texas in 1966, and won election to the House of Representatives twice. Yet his second run at the Senate ended in defeat by Democrat **Lloyd Bentsen** in 1970. Bush caught the attention of President Richard Nixon for his support of Nixon's agenda in Congress. Nixon appointed him ambassador to the **United Nations** (1971–72). Bush returned to the United States to chair the Republican National Committee in 1972. His assignment was a difficult one, as he sought to minimize the damage to Republican electoral politics as the Watergate scandal unfolded. In 1974 President Gerald Ford appointed him to the U.S. liaison office in Beijing, **China**, where he remained until he assumed the directorship of the **Central Intelligence Agency (CIA)** in 1976. Bush returned to the private sector in Texas following the 1976 election of President **Jimmy Carter**.

In 1980 Bush entered the Republican presidential primaries, only to lose to **Ronald Reagan**. The primary contests became bitter when the more moderate Bush called Reagan's **tax**-cut program "**voodoo economics**"—a phrase that would surface time and again following the massive deficits of the 1980s. Nevertheless Reagan chose Bush as his vice-presidential candidate, largely because of his **foreign policy** experience. After eight years as vice president, Bush ran for the Oval Office in 1988 and beat back early primary challenges from prominent Republican senator **Robert (Bob) Dole** and television evangelist **Pat Robertson**. The dynamics of the 1988 Republican convention were especially important for Bush. In a surprise move, he chose a relatively unknown conservative senator—**J. Danforth (Dan) Quayle**—of Indiana as his running mate. He also made a commanding speech in which he outlined his vision of America as a "**thousand points of light**" and pledged not to raise taxes in a phrase that would later haunt him: "**read my lips, no new taxes**." The general campaign pitted the Bush–Quayle ticket against Democratic presidential nominee **Michael Dukakis** of Massachusetts and vice-presidential candidate Lloyd Bentsen of Texas. The campaign was notable as one of the most bitter and negative in recent history. The Bush–Quayle team used scathing television ads that lambasted Dukakis's record on crime as Massachusetts governor. Particularly controversial was the **Willy Horton** ad, which portrayed an African American man serving a life sentence who was released on a weekend furlough and committed rape. Another ad depicted the furlough program as a "revolving door" of criminals coming and going to and from prison. Despite a slow pre-convention start in the polls, Bush ultimately prevailed in the election with 54 percent of the popular vote and 426 Electoral College votes. Yet Democrats retained both chambers of Congress, and Republicans actually lost seats in the House of Representatives in 1988.

Bush did not have a far-reaching domestic agenda. Nevertheless, Congress passed a minimum wage increase, the **Americans with Disabilities Act**, and a federal bailout of the failed **savings and loan** industry in his first two years in office. Relations with the Democratic Congress became more strained as time passed, and Bush turned increasingly to the veto to halt objectionable legislation. He became the first president to veto a **civil rights** bill in 1990, which he argued placed quotas for the hiring of minorities. A compromise version of the bill passed a year later. Bush's apparent reneging on his pledge not to raise taxes in the **Budget Agreement of 1990** cost him much political capital among conservative Republicans in Congress and in the electorate.

Foreign policy drove the more successful side of Bush's term. The president cautiously approached the disintegration of the **Soviet Union**, lending his support to an aid bill for the **Commonwealth of Independent States** (CIS). He declared an end to the **Cold War** alongside Russian President **Boris Yeltsin** in 1992.

When Iraqi dictator **Saddam Hussein** invaded **Kuwait** in August 1990, Bush built an impressive international coalition through the United Nations and drove Iraqi forces out of the country. The **Persian Gulf War** of 1990–91 boosted his public approval to unprecedented heights following successful resolution of the conflict. Some critics suggest that Bush squandered his high approval—over 90 percent—by failing to translate the "rally effect" of the war into tangible domestic programs, though there is little evidence the Democratic Congress would have necessarily followed his lead. As the electorate turned to domestic issues following the **Persian Gulf War**, Bush came under increased scrutiny for rising unemployment and an economic slowdown.

The entry of **Reform Party** candidate and millionaire **H. Ross Perot** confounded Bush's reelection bid in 1992, as Perot and Democratic candidate **William J. Clinton** indefatigably criticized him on the economy. Perot also criticized Bush's negotiation of the **North American Free Trade Agreement (NAFTA)** with Canada and Mexico, arguing that the trade bill would export American jobs to Mexico where labor is cheaper. Perot's candidacy cost Bush a sizable number of votes among disaffected Republicans. With 19 percent of the popular vote, Perot arguably enabled Clinton to prevail in the election with a plurality—43.3 percent to Bush's 37.7 percent.

Upon leaving office, Bush made the controversial decision to pardon six key figures in the **Iran–Contra** scandal. He granted pardons to **Caspar Weinberger**, **Elliott Abrams**, and **Robert McFarlane** along with three employees of the **Central Intelligence Agency**. Bush's autobiography, *All the Best, George Bush*, was published in 1994. The George Bush Presidential Library opened in 1997 and is situated on the campus of Texas A&M University in College Station, Texas. The former president and his wife, Barbara, reside in Houston and at the family compound in Kennebunkport, Maine.

**BUSH, GEORGE WALKER (1946– ).** The 43rd president of the United States, George W. Bush is the oldest son of **George H. W. Bush** and **Barbara Bush**. He was born in New Haven, Connecticut, on 6 July 1946, but was raised in Texas. He attended the Philips Academy in Andover, Massachusetts, just as his father had. He earned a bachelor's degree in history from Yale (1968). He served in the Texas Air National Guard during the Vietnam War. He later completed a master's of business administration degree at Harvard (1975).

Bush got his start in politics in 1978 via an unsuccessful bid for a seat in the U.S. House of Representatives. In between oil ventures, he worked on his father's campaigns—including his successful race against **Michael Dukakis** in 1988. Bush bought a large holding in the Texas Rangers baseball club and became general manager in 1989. In 1994 he defeated incumbent Democrat Ann Richards for the Texas governorship. Bush improved significantly on his margin in 1998 to win reelection handily with nearly two-thirds of the state vote. He forged a working relationship with the Democratic legislature and lieutenant governor and was a promoter of education reform.

Bush won the Republican nomination for the presidency in 2000 and chose **Richard (Dick) Cheney**, who had served as secretary of defense under his father, as running mate. The Bush–Cheney ticket faced Democrats **Albert Gore** and Joseph Lieberman in the general election. The outcome ultimately hinged on Florida's 25 Electoral College votes. Ballot disputes in Palm Beach County and a court-ordered recount of ballots in select counties culminated in a **Supreme Court** case, *Bush v. Gore*, which effectively ended the controversy. **James Baker III** represented the Bush campaign in the electoral dispute. Florida secretary of state Katherine Harris, an appointee of Bush's brother **John Ellis (Jeb) Bush**, who was governor of Florida, certified that Bush had received 537 more votes than Gore. Despite losing the popular vote by over 500,000 nationally, Bush won a majority of the Electoral College and thus the presidency. The administration of George W. Bush has included many figures from his father's presidency, including **Elliott Abrams**, **Howard Baker**, **Andrew Card**, and **Colin Powell**.

Bush won reelection in 2004 on the theme of national security and was the first candidate to win a majority of the popular vote since his father in 1988. His presidency was profoundly transformed by the 11 September 2001 **terrorist** attacks on New York and Washington, D.C. He responded to the attacks with military force against **Afghanistan**, whose Taliban government had given succor to terrorist **Osama bin Laden** and his followers. Bush later turned his attention to **Saddam Hussein**, contending that the Iraqi leader had developed weapons of mass destruction that he planned to use on the United States and its allies. Unlike his father in the lead-up to the **Persian Gulf War,** Bush was unable to garner an international consensus on military action in Iraq in the **United Nations**. In March 2003 the United States and a "coalition of the willing" preemptively invaded Iraq and toppled the Hussein regime. No weapons of mass destruction were located. At the time of writing more than 130,000 American troops remain in Iraq.

**BUSH, JOHN ELLIS (JEB) (1953– ).** Born on 11 February 1953, Jeb is the second son of President **George H. W. Bush** and **Barbara**

**Bush**, and the younger brother to President **George W. Bush**. A graduate of the University of Texas at Austin (1973), he married Columbo Garnica Gallo, a Mexican national, in 1974 and has three children.

Bush gained business experience in Texas, south Florida, and Latin America in banking and real estate ventures. Although he aided his father's failed bid for the Republican presidential nomination in 1980, he did not enter politics until a few years later when he became chair of the Dade County, Florida, Republican Party. In 1986 he used his position to help elect **Robert (Bob) Martinez** to the governorship. In 1988 he again supported his father's electoral bid for the presidency, and a year later worked on south Florida congresswoman Ileana Ros-Lehtinen's successful campaign.

Bush lost the 1994 governor's race in Florida by a narrow margin to popular incumbent Lawton Chiles. He returned to the campaign trail in 1998 to defeat Lieutenant Governor Buddy MacKay handily and was reelected in 2002. Bush bills himself as an environmentalist and has played an important role in the restoration of the Everglades. He has also taken a strong interest in education and advocates statewide testing of students to evaluate school performance. Nevertheless, he found himself at the center of controversy in the 2000 presidential election when the secretary of state he had appointed, Katherine Harris, certified that his brother George had defeated Democratic candidate **Al Gore** by just 537 votes. The certification guaranteed that all of Florida's 25 electoral votes would go to George W. Bush and that he would carry the Electoral College, even though he lost the popular vote nationally. Harris's certification came in the midst of allegations that the flawed "butterfly" ballot in Palm Beach County had confused elderly voters, and that black voters around the state had been erroneously placed on a felons list that annulled their right to vote.

Bush has been rumored as a possible Republican candidate for the presidency in 2008, but as of 2006 he has repeatedly denied that he intends to run.

## – C –

**CARD, ANDREW H., JR. (1947– ).** A graduate in engineering from the University of South Carolina, Card's career has spanned the public and private sectors, and he has had a close relationship with the family of **George H. W. Bush**. He got his start in politics by serving in the Massachusetts statehouse from 1975 to 1983, where he was active in ethics issues. In 1980 he was campaign chair for Bush's presidential bid. He served in President **Ronald Reagan**'s White House as special assistant to the president for intergovernmental affairs and later as director of intergovernmental affairs, charged with developing relations with governors and state officials. Card served President Bush as his deputy chief of staff (1988–92) before he was appointed secretary of transportation (1992–93). Card won praise for his oversight of federal disaster relief efforts following **Hurricane Andrew**, which devastated south Florida in 1992. He returned to the private sector from 1993 to 1998, becoming president and chief executive officer of the American Automobile Manufacturers Association (AAMA), which disbanded in 1998. President **George W. Bush** appointed Card his **chief of staff** following the 2000 presidential election and he remained in that post until April 2006.

**CARLUCCI, FRANK CHARLES, III (1930– ).** Born in Pennsylvania and a graduate of Princeton (1952), Carlucci was an officer in the navy from 1952 to 1954. He began a 13-year career with the State Department in 1956, during which he was an operative in the **Central Intelligence Agency**'s (CIA) Congo mission and allegedly took part in the assassination of Congolese prime minister Patrice Lumumba. He developed a close relationship with **Caspar Weinberger** as undersecretary of Health, Education and Welfare (HEW) in the early 1970s. Carlucci was appointed ambassador to Portugal in 1974 and served in that position until 1977, after which time he became deputy director of the Central Intelligence Agency (1978–1981). He was reunited once again with Weinberger in 1981, serving as deputy defense secretary until 1986, and as **national security advisor** from 1986 to 1987. He became secretary of defense in 1987 when Weinberger resigned. Carlucci was considered less confrontational in his approach with the **Soviet Union**. He is chairman emeritus of the Carlyle Group, an international investment firm, and is affiliated with the Project for the New American Century and the RAND Corporation.

**CARTER, JAMES EARL (JIMMY) (1924– ).** The 39th president was born in Plains, Georgia. He earned a B.S. degree from the U.S.

Naval Academy in 1946. That same year he married his wife, Rosalynn. For seven years he served on submarines in both the Atlantic and the Pacific as a nuclear engineer. He left the navy and returned to Plains in 1953 to assume leadership of his father's peanut business. Carter got his political start in the Georgia state senate, where he served two terms in the 1960s. He was elected governor of Georgia in 1970 on a campaign theme of reform, and took a strong stance against racial discrimination.

His entry into the Democratic primaries of 1976 marked the first presidential nomination to take place following the McGovern–Fraser reforms. Those reforms changed the party's nominating rules and stripped party leaders of the power they once had over the choice of the eventual nominee. Although he was little known outside Georgia or the South, Carter built an impressive grassroots campaign. His "outsider" campaign struck a chord with the electorate following the Watergate scandal and Richard Nixon's resignation in 1974. After winning his party's nomination, Carter prevailed over incumbent Republican Gerald Ford with 50.1 percent of the popular vote. On the domestic front, Carter's presidency was plagued by inflation and high unemployment—"stagflation"—which was aggravated by soaring oil prices and an energy crisis. In the realm of **foreign policy**, Carter helped Egypt and **Israel** achieve peace with the signing of the Camp David Accords, turned over control of the Panama Canal to Panama, and negotiated the second round of the Strategic Arms Limitation Treaty (SALT II) with the **Soviet Union**. However, the **Iranian hostage crisis** overwhelmed Carter's final years in office. When Carter allowed the deposed **shah of Iran** asylum in the United States, Iranian militants captured and occupied the U.S. embassy in Teheran in 1979. The militants took 100 Americans hostage, often blindfolding them, mistreating them, and forcing them to march around for cameras. As the hostage crisis lingered into 1980, a failed rescue attempt further diminished public confidence in Carter's leadership.

Republican nominee **Ronald Reagan** made Carter's foreign policy a major issue in the 1980 campaign, calling it "weak" and "indecisive." Losing his bid for reelection in 1980, Carter has arguably had a successful post-presidency. He is a devout Christian and has focused many of his efforts on human rights and international conflict resolution through the Carter Center in Atlanta, Georgia, the site of the Carter Presidential Library. Carter and his wife have also been particularly active in Habitat for Humanity, which promotes housing for the poor. And Carter is only the third president to have won the Nobel Peace Prize. His many books include *Keeping Faith: Memoirs of a President* (1995), *A Government as Good as Its People* (1996), and *Sources of Strength: Meditations on Scripture for a Living Faith* (1997).

**CASEY, WILLIAM JOSEPH (1913–1987).** A New York City native, Casey graduated from St. John's University Law School in 1937. He worked for the Office of Strategic Services during **World War II**, which was involved in intelligence-gathering activities. He headed the Securities and Exchange Commission in the administration of Richard Nixon from 1971 to 1973. He gained prominence in 1980 as chair of **Ronald Reagan**'s presidential campaign. Reagan, impressed with his acumen, appointed him to head the **Central Intelligence Agency (CIA)** in 1981, a post Casey held until 1987. Casey expanded the CIA's activities significantly and oversaw major covert operations in **Afghanistan** and, most notably, Central America. He was implicated in the **Iran–Contra** scandal for having coordinated military aid to the Nicaraguan **Contras**. However, a brain tumor precluded him from testifying before Congress about his role in the arms-for-hostages deal. Casey died on 6 May 1987 and is buried in Westbury, New York. *See also* NICARAGUA.

*CASTAÑEDA V. PICKARD* **(1981).** This case, decided by the Fifth Circuit Court of Appeals, is often heralded as the most significant decision in bilingual education after *Lau v. Nichols* (1974). The appellate court set forth a three-pronged test by which bilingual programs are measured for compliance with the Equal Educational Opportunities Act of 1974. Under the court's interpretation, school districts must have a pedagogically sound plan for students with limited proficiency in the English language, sufficient and qualified staff to implement the plan, and a system to evaluate the program. The decision did not require bilingual education programs to meet certain standards. Rather, it required only that "appropriate action to overcome language barriers" be implemented.

**CAVAZOS, LAURO FRED, JR. (1927– ).** A Texas native and graduate of Texas Tech University and Iowa State University (Ph.D. in physiology), Cavazos was on the faculty of Tufts University School of Medicine from 1964 to 1980, and became president of Texas Tech University in 1980. He was appointed by President **Ronald Reagan** as secretary of education in 1988, and was the first Hispanic to hold a cabinet-level position. He continued his tenure under President **George H. W. Bush** through the end of 1990.

**CEAUŞESCU, NICHOLAE (1918–1989).** Leader of Communist Romania from 1965 until 1989, Ceauşescu and his wife, Elena, were executed by a firing squad on 25 December 1989. Their executions followed the fall of his regime and a mass rebellion that culminated in the Romanian Revolution. *See also* BERLIN WALL; BREZHNEV DOCTRINE; SINATRA DOCTRINE; WARSAW PACT.

**CENTRAL INTELLIGENCE AGENCY (CIA).** The Central Intelligence Agency was created by the National Security Act of 1947 under President Harry Truman. The director of the CIA heads the agency, coordinates foreign intelligence-gathering activities, and advises the president on intelligence matters. The CIA is precluded from domestic intelligence gathering.

President **Ronald Reagan** appointed two directors to the CIA, both of whom were instrumental in his **Cold War foreign policy**. His first director, **William Casey**, served from 1981 to 1987. Casey sought to expand the agency's foreign intelligence-gathering capacity and covert operations against pro-Soviet factions in the developing world. He resigned in 1987 due to complications with a brain tumor. Casey was alleged to have been involved in the **Iran–Contra** affair, but **Lawrence Walsh**, the **independent counsel** investigating the matter, did not investigate Casey due to his illness.

Reagan's second CIA director, **William Webster**, began his service in 1987 and continued his service into the administration of **George H. W. Bush**. Webster played an important role in efforts to halt **drug trafficking** into the United States as well as in the **Persian Gulf War**. Webster was succeeded by **Robert Gates**, who served as CIA director from 1991 to 1993. As deputy director of intelligence at the CIA under President Reagan, Gates was implicated in the Iran–Contra affair but was not indicted due to lack of evidence.

**CHALLENGER (SPACE SHUTTLE).** The successor shuttle to *Columbia*, *Challenger* made its first flight and orbit on 4 April 1983. The shuttle completed another eight successful missions from 1983 to 1985. On 28 January 1986, Challenger exploded 73 seconds after takeoff when an O-ring seal failed and ignited the hydrogen-filled booster tank. All six astronauts, as well as the first civilian in space, schoolteacher **Christa McAuliffe**, were killed. Several hours after the tragic accident, President **Ronald Reagan** made a televised speech to the nation. His final comments were among the most memorable of his presidency when he said: "The crew of the space shuttle Challenger honored us by the manner in which they lived their lives. We will never forget them, nor the last time we saw them, this morning, as they prepared for their journey and waved good-bye and slipped the surly bonds of Earth to touch the face of God." *See also* NOONAN, PEGGY.

**CHENEY, RICHARD BRUCE (DICK) (1941– ).** Born in Lincoln, Nebraska, Cheney was raised in Casper, Wyoming. After beginning and halting his studies at Yale, he eventually completed undergraduate and graduate work at the University of Wyoming in political science. His early political experience included service in the Nixon White House on the Cost of Living Council and the Office of Economic Opportunity. Cheney was named President Gerald Ford's **chief of staff** in 1975 and managed Ford's election campaign in 1976. He later sought and won a seat to Congress from his home state of Wyoming in 1978, and was reelected five times, serving as chair of the House Republican Policy Committee (1981–87), chair of the House Republican Conference (1987), and minority whip (1988). In 1989 President **George H. W. Bush** selected Cheney as secretary of defense. Cheney was instrumental in directing **Operation Just Cause** in Panama, which ousted dictator **Manuel Noriega**, as well as **Operation Desert Storm** during the **Persian Gulf War**. He earned the Presidential Medal of Freedom in 1991.

Exiting public service in 1993, Cheney joined the conservative think tank, the American Enterprise Institute, in 1993 before becoming chair and chief executive officer of Halliburton (an energy corporation). In 1997 he co-founded the Project for the New American Century, a **foreign policy** think tank. He resigned from the Halliburton chairmanship in 2000 when **George W. Bush** asked him to run on the Republican ticket as the vice-presidential candidate. Cheney has been an energetic and visible vice president during President George W. Bush's two terms in campaigning and fundraising, developing foreign and defense policy, and making the public case for the invasion of Iraq in spring 2003. But he has also been criticized for Halliburton Corporation's alleged gains from defense contracting and its prominent role in the rebuilding of Iraq. Cheney, who suffers from a bad heart, made it known in early 2005 that he would not seek the Republican presidential nomination in 2008.

**CHERNENKO, KONSTANTIN (1911–1985).** Siberian-born Chernenko succeeded **Yuri Andropov** as general secretary of the Soviet Communist Party in February 1984. He died 13 months later. His brief secretariat marked a return to the hard-line policies of the **Leonid Brezhnev** era, particularly with regard to the repression of internal dissent in the **Soviet Union. Mikhail Gorbachev** replaced Chernenko in 1985 and broke with the Brezhnev exemplar by promoting internal political and economic reforms. *See also* BREZHNEV DOCTRINE; *GLASNOST*; *PERESTROIKA*; SINATRA DOCTRINE.

**CHERNOBYL, UKRAINE.** This city near the border of Belarus was the site of the explosion and meltdown of a nuclear reactor on 26 April 1986. The incident is regarded as the worst accident in the history of nuclear power. Scientists who studied the reasons for the disaster first attributed it to human error. The International Atomic Energy Agency later blamed the meltdown on fundamental defects in the reactor's design. The immediate death toll was 31, including 28 workers who died from radiation exposure while trying to control the fires. Due to the heat and intensity of the fire, much of the radioactive material released during the accident reached the upper atmosphere and formed a cloud that contained radioactive Cesium-137. That cloud contaminated parts of the Ukraine, Belarus, and what is today the Russian Federation, exposing hundreds of thousands of people to the dangers of radiation. Soviet officials kept the incident secret until Swedish workers at a nuclear power plant found unexpectedly high levels of radiation on workers at a plant in Forsmark and determined that the material came from elsewhere. The Soviets evacuated a 30-kilometer radius around the disaster site and launched a massive cleanup effort. Cases of thyroid cancer in the contaminated areas have increased dramatically, and the longer-term effects of radiation exposure on humans, as well as the ecosystems of contaminated areas, remain unknown.

**CHIEF OF STAFF.** The White House chief of staff serves at the president's pleasure and does not require confirmation by the Senate. The chief of staff manages personnel in the White House, oversees the president's calendar, and supervises access and paper flow to the president. For this reason the function of the chief of staff is frequently referred to as "gatekeeper." Chiefs of staff also variably take on other roles, including personal and political advice to the president. *See also* EXECUTIVE OFFICE OF THE PRESIDENT (EOP).

**CHINA, PEOPLE'S REPUBLIC OF.** China occupied an important place in the **foreign policy** of presidents **Ronald Reagan** and **George H. W. Bush**. The United States' close ties and sales of arms to Taiwan, which China views as a breakaway province of the mainland, had been a sore point in bilateral relations. In 1982 Reagan proposed ending the arms sales gradually, contingent upon China's acceptance of a peaceful settlement of Taiwan's precarious status. In 1984 Reagan made a six-day state visit to China and became the only president since Richard Nixon to visit the nation since Mao Zedong declared the republic Communist in 1949. China was, in fact, the first Communist nation Reagan had visited. During his stay, Reagan explored greater trade opportunities between the United States and China and emphasized common concerns about the **Soviet Union**, especially the 1980 invasion of **Afghanistan**. Reagan also signed a nuclear cooperation agreement with China in 1984, which was not implemented until 1998. He came under criticism from many in Congress when he stated that the Chinese "weren't really Communists." Reagan did not substantively alter U.S.–Chinese relations, but he sought to maintain a cordial relationship with Communist leaders while simultaneously supporting Taiwan.

China's brutal crackdown on pro-democracy student protestors in **Tiananmen Square** in June 1989 drew George H. W. Bush's immediate attention. Bush sought to implement a policy of "constructive engagement" with China, rebuffing with his veto power two attempts by Congress to tie most-favored-nation trade status to improvements to human rights. Bush posited that moderating Chinese attitudes on democracy would be made easier by continued trade and contact between the two countries. *See also* COLD WAR; ZEMIN, JIANG.

**CHRISTIAN COALITION.** The Christian Coalition was established by former presidential candidate **Pat Robertson** in 1988. A grassroots political organization comprising members of various faiths (protestant evangelicals, Christian fundamentalists, and Catholics), the Christian Coalition is associated with political conservatives. The organization was active in voter mobilization in the early 1990s, when it reached the acme of its membership strength. Robertson relinquished leadership of the organization in 1989. Ralph Reed led the organization until 1997, but left after failing to oust **William Clinton** from the White House and elect a conservative Christian to the presidency. The organization has arguably atomized since, with prominent members such as Reed working for members of the Republican Party.

**CISNEROS, HENRY GABRIEL (1947– ).** A San Antonio, Texas, native, Cisneros holds a doctorate from George Washington University in public administration. He got his start in politics on the San Antonio City Council in 1975, becoming the youngest member ever elected. In 1981 he successfully ran in the city's mayoral race to win the distinction of becoming the first Hispanic mayor elected in a major U.S. city. He later served as Secretary of Housing and Urban Development under President **William Clinton** from 1993 to 1997.

**CIVIL RIGHT(S).** A civil right is a privilege, constitutional protection, or statutory right that is enforceable through government action. Civil rights are different from civil liberties, such as the Bill of Rights, which outline actions that government is prohibited from taking *against* individuals. During the presidencies of **Ronald Reagan** and **George H. W. Bush,** civil rights concerning **women** and minorities took center stage. Both presidents were opposed to affirmative action programs for minorities, including quotas for race and ethnicity in the workplace, school bussing to achieve integration, and contract "set-asides" by state and federal governments for minority-owned businesses.

Critics of Reagan's civil rights stances charged him with racism or, at a minimum, with failing to address or understand the concerns of African Americans. Reagan's supporters suggest that his stances were simply a reflection of his desire for minimal government interference in individuals' lives and emphasis on self-reliance. Nevertheless, Reagan's characterization of poor black women as "welfare queens" who lived in luxury infuriated black leaders, and his support of Bob Jones University, which tried to regain tax-exempt status despite its historically segregated campus, further alienated many African Americans. In 1988 Reagan vetoed the Civil Rights Restoration Act. Congress passed the act following a 1984 **Supreme Court** decision, *Grove City v. Bell*, in which the Court contended that only specific programs or departments in colleges and universities that received federal aid had to comply with federal nondiscrimination policies. The Civil Rights Restoration Act forced the entire institution to comply with nondiscrimination guidelines concerning women, minorities, the elderly, and the handicapped. In a stunning defeat for the president, Congress overrode Reagan's veto by large margins. Reagan proposed a less-comprehensive bill that he argued would have minimized federal intrusion into the private sector.

Bush was also criticized for his confrontations with Congress over civil rights. In 1990 he vetoed a civil rights bill for putatively mandating racial quotas in the hiring of minorities. The Democratic Congress had attempted to overturn several Supreme Court decisions, namely the *Wards Cove v. Atonio* and *Price Waterhouse v. Hopkins* cases, in which the high court shifted the burden of proof on discrimination cases to employees and made it more difficult to sue employers. The allegations of sexual harassment that surfaced against **Clarence Thomas** during his confirmation hearings in 1991 also spurred Congress to action. A reconstituted civil rights bill passed in 1991, which Bush signed, contending it did not mandate quotas. The signing ceremony turned into a contentious event, however, after a draft memo written by Bush's counsel **C. Boyden Gray** was leaked. In that memo Gray suggested Bush use the occasion to terminate federal affirmative action programs. Bush did not take that action, but his insistence that the 1991 bill be narrowly interpreted proked anger among many congressional Democrats. *See also* KING, RODNEY GLEN; RACE RIOTS (LOS ANGELES).

**CLARK, WILLIAM PATRICK (1931– ).** A graduate of Loyola Law School, Clark served in the army in the Counter Intelligence Corps before presiding as a judge in the Superior Court of California from 1969 to 1971. He was an associate justice on the California Supreme Court from 1973 to 1981. Before serving as President **Ronald Reagan**'s secretary of the interior (1983–85), Clark had served as deputy secretary of state (1981–82) and as assistant to the president for national security affairs (1982–83). After Clark left the administration in 1985, President Reagan tapped him to chair the Task Group on Nuclear Weapons Program Management. He is also a trustee of the Ronald Reagan Presidential Foundation. Clark returned to the private sector as chief executive officer of the Clark Company and as senior counsel to his law firm, Clark, Cali and Negranti.

**CLEAN AIR ACT AMENDMENTS (1990).** The amendments adopted in 1990 updated and expanded the scope of the Clean Air Act of 1970. The bill mandated more stringent emissions standards for motor vehicles, including buses and trucks. The bill also called for the use of cleaner fuels in the nation's most polluted urban areas to reduce carbon monoxide emissions and hydrocarbons that affect the ozone layer.

**CLINTON, WILLIAM JEFFERSON (BILL) (1946– ).** Born William Jefferson Blythe III and adopted by Roger Clinton, his mother's second husband, the 42nd president of the United States graduated from Georgetown University, was a Rhodes Scholar at Oxford University in the United Kingdom, and later earned a law degree from Yale University. After serving as an assistant to Arkansas senator J. William Fulbright, Clinton ran unsuccessfully for the House of Representatives in 1974. Two years later he was elected attorney general of Arkansas, which he used as a springboard to the governor's mansion. Clinton was elected to five terms as governor of the state of Arkansas (1978–80, 1982–92). He headed the National Governors' Association and then the centrist Democratic Leadership Council, 1990–91.

Clinton's presidential aspirations were aided by President **George H. W. Bush**'s extremely high popularity following victory in the **Persian Gulf War**, which convinced many senior Democrats to eschew a run for the White House in the 1992 election. Clinton emerged as a Democratic challenger following Bush's slide in public approval as the electorate and the **media** focused intensely on domestic politics and a sluggish economy. Clinton lost the Iowa caucuses to rival and Iowa native Tom Harkin, and finished second behind favorite son Massachusetts senator Paul Tsongas in the first-in-the-nation New Hampshire primary. Clinton's early primary campaign was marred by scandals surrounding Vietnam and his draft deferral as well as allegations of extramarital affairs that he and his wife, Hillary Clinton, would address candidly on national television. His strong showing in New Hampshire despite these obstacles gave him a label he would carry through his two terms—the "comeback kid." Clinton swept subsequent primaries and won the Democratic nomination. He chose Tennessee senator **Albert Gore Jr.** as his running mate.

The general campaign pitted Clinton and **Reform Party** candidate **H. Ross Perot** against George H. W. Bush. Like Perot, Clinton's campaign focused on domestic politics. His campaign strategist James Carville hung a sign in the "war room" of the Clinton campaign headquarters that read, "It's the economy, stupid—and don't forget health care" to keep the message on track. Clinton focused on the need for change and promised to address rising health care costs, while Perot criticized Bush for his economic policies and the risks of further job losses with the **North American Free Trade Agreement (NAFTA)**. Bush emphasized his steady leadership in **foreign policy** and his broad experience from **World War II** to his days in the **United Nations**, calling into question Clinton's fitness to be commander in chief. Clinton ultimately won the 1992 election with 43 percent of the popular vote to Bush's 37 percent. Perot's 19 percent was the best showing for a third-party candidate for president since Teddy Roosevelt's "Bull Moose" Party in 1912, and is believed to have cost Bush more votes than Clinton.

Despite a Democratic majority in both chambers of Congress, Clinton's first two years in the Oval Office were scarred by battles over gays in the military, gun control, the federal budget, and his health care proposal, which gave a far-reaching regulatory role to the national government—but never came to a vote in Congress. By 1994 Clinton's popularity reached a nadir, and in the 1994 midterm elections Republicans won a stunning victory by gaining control of the House of Representatives for the first time in 40 years and winning a majority in the Senate, which they had lost in 1986. House Speaker **Newt Gingrich** supplanted Clinton's legislative agenda with the GOP's conservative program entitled the "Contract with America," much of which Clinton eventually vetoed. Clinton won reelection in 1996 against Republican candidate **Robert Dole,** largely on a defensive campaign that emphasized the need to keep the GOP majority in Congress in check. He achieved victory again with only a plurality of the national vote—49 percent—to Dole's 41 percent and Perot's 8 percent. Clinton faced a Republican majority in Congress for the duration of his second term.

He became only the second president in U.S. history to be impeached. Following his denial of an affair with a White House intern, Monica Lewinsky, the House of Representatives approved two articles of impeachment against Clinton: perjury and obstruction of justice. He was acquitted by the Senate on both counts in February 1999. Despite the scandal and impeachment, in his second term Clinton did negotiate a compromise budget that reduced the deficit and a bill that fundamentally altered federal welfare programs. He also turned his attention to foreign policy, attempting to broker peace negotiations in Northern Ireland and between **Israel** and the Palestinians. Clinton maintains a high profile in the Democratic Party alongside his wife, Hillary, whom he helped successfully campaign for the junior Senate seat from the state of New York in 2001. He published his memoirs, *My Life*, in 2004.

**COLD WAR.** Coined by Bernard Baruch, an advisor to presidents Woodrow Wilson, Franklin Roosevelt, Harry Truman, and John Kennedy, the term *Cold War* connotes the ideological, technological, and military rivalry between the United States and the **Soviet Union** following **World War II**, and by extension, between the countries of the **North Atlantic Treaty Organization (NATO)** and **Warsaw Pact** nations. The Cold War arguably began when President Truman called upon Congress to support efforts to rebuild Europe following the war and preclude Communist victories in Greece and Turkey. The fall of the **Berlin Wall** in 1989 signaled the closing stages of the Cold War, which ended with the dissolution of the Soviet Union in 1991.

The doctrine of **deterrence** and the certainty of mutual annihilation (*see* MUTUALLY ASSURED DESTRUCTION [MAD]) through the use of nuclear weapons precluded open conflict between the United States and the Soviet Union. Instead, the period was notable for each country's overt and covert support of opposing factions in the developing world (Angola, Mozambique, Central America) and direct military intervention (Korea, Vietnam, **Grenada** for the United States, and **Afghanistan** for the Soviet Union). The Cuban Missile Crisis of 1962 was the sharpest direct confrontation between the two superpowers. The Cold War pushed both countries to invest heavily in nuclear weaponry and sparked costly arms races with intermittent periods of **détente** notable for bilateral agreements to reduce those weapons.

The Cold War continued to rage during the presidency of **Ronald Reagan**. As part of Reagan's **foreign policy** agenda, the United States invested heavily in nuclear weapons in the 1980s to offset a perceived Soviet advantage. The deployment of **MX missiles** in the continental United States was aimed at countering Soviet **intercontinental ballistic missiles (ICBMs)**. Reagan persuaded German chancellor **Helmut Kohl** to station **Pershing II** short-range missiles in Germany to counterbalance short-range Soviet **SS-20 missiles** deployed in Warsaw Pact nations. The United States also deployed **Trident II** nuclear warheads and **cruise missiles** aboard submarines. Reagan's plan for a space-based missile defense system—the **Strategic Defense Initiative (SDI)**—drew sharp Soviet criticism. SDI would have abrogated the **Anti–Ballistic Missile (ABM) Treaty** between the Soviet Union and the United States. Anti–ballistic missile systems could destabilize the doctrine of deterrence by providing one side with a strategic advantage to launch a first strike. When Reagan met with Soviet General Secretary **Mikhail Gorbachev** in **Reykjavík**, Iceland, to discuss **arms control**, the two leaders nearly reached an accord to scrap their entire strategic nuclear arsenals, but the agreement fell apart over the issue of SDI. Nevertheless, the meeting paved the way for the **Intermediate-Range Nuclear Forces (INF) Treaty** a year later, which eliminated short-range weapons in Europe.

The Cold War dissipated by the late 1980s as Gorbachev made it clear that the Soviet Union was not interested in expansionism. He repealed the **Brezhnev Doctrine** that the Soviet Union had the right to intervene in the internal affairs of its Warsaw Pact neighbors to counter any challenge to Communist governments. Gorbachev enunciated the so-called **Sinatra Doctrine**, which allowed Eastern European countries to determine their own futures without the threat of Soviet interference. With the fall of the Berlin Wall in 1989, Warsaw Pact nations began transitions to democracy and free market economies, and Germany was reunified by 1991. Gorbachev's internal reforms, *glasnost* and *perestroika*—transparency and economic rebuilding—placed the Soviet Union on a course toward imminent dissolution. With the accession of **Boris Yeltsin** to the presidency of Russia and the establishment of the **Commonwealth of Independent States** in 1991, the Soviet Union ceased to exist and Gorbachev resigned as general secretary in late December of that year. President **George H. W. Bush** and Yeltsin declared an end to the Cold War in 1992.

**COLOMBIA.** The South American country is the largest supplier of cocaine to the United States. In 1989 Colombian "drug lords" declared total war on the government and the **Medellín cartel** embarked on a campaign of extensive violence. President **George H. W. Bush**'s **Andean Initiative** was aimed at shoring up and expanding counternarcotic operations not only in Colombia but also in Bolivia and Peru through foreign and military aid as well as equipment and advisors. The effort marked the first systematic effort to stem the flow of illegal narcotics into the United States and evolved into the **"war on drugs."** *See also* DRUG TRAFFICKING.

*COLUMBIA* **(SPACE SHUTTLE).** *Columbia* was the first space shuttle built for manned flight by the National Aeronautics and Space Administration (NASA). *Columbia* made its maiden flight on 12 April 1981. The shuttle completed another 26 successful flights between 1981 and 2002, deploying deep-space telescopes such as the Hubble, and enabling two decades worth of research experiments. *Columbia*'s final mission ended in disaster. On 1 February 2003, the shuttle exploded and broke off into several pieces upon re-entering the Earth's atmosphere, killing all seven members of the crew and scattering debris over eastern Texas. The explosion was caused by a tile that had been damaged by a piece of insulation foam that fell from the shuttle's external fuel tank just after its launch. The disaster marked the second loss of a shuttle. The first was *Challenger*, which was lost in 1986.

**COMMONWEALTH OF INDEPENDENT STATES.** The Commonwealth of Independent States (CIS) was originally formed by 11 former Soviet republics, including Armenia, Azerbaijan, Belarus, Kazakhstan, Kyrgyzstan, Moldova, Russia, Tajikistan, Turkmenistan, Ukraine, and Uzbekistan. Georgia joined the CIS in 1993, following Russian military intervention to bolster the government of **Eduard Shevardnadze** during a bloody civil war. The CIS treaty followed official Soviet recognition of the independence of the **Baltic States** Estonia, Latvia, and Lithuania several months earlier. The ratification of the treaty on 21 December 1991 marked the formal dissolution of the Soviet Union. It also represented the end of a yearlong power struggle between Soviet General Secretary **Mikhail Gorbachev** and president of the Russian Republic **Boris Yeltsin**. Gorbachev resigned three days after the treaty was ratified. Yeltsin originally brokered the voluntary treaty with Ukrainian leader Leonid Kravchuk and Belarusian leader Stanislau Shushkevich following the Ukraine's declaration of independence. The treaty was aimed at providing a framework for political, economic, and military cooperation among the former Soviet republics.

**CONTRAS.** Opponents of the leftist **Sandinista** government in **Nicaragua** in the 1980s, the Contras derived their name from the word *counterrevolutionary* (*contrarevolucionarios*) in Spanish. The term was widely used by the U.S. **media** to describe the panoply of groups that sought to overturn the Cuban-backed Sandinista government. During the administration of **Ronald Reagan**, the Contras received military and financial support from the U.S. government. Congress outlawed direct military assistance to the Contras in 1982 with the **Boland Amendment**. Reagan's national security staff, notably Admiral **John Poindexter** and Colonel **Oliver North**, was accused of violating the statute when the Lebanese newspaper *al-Shiraa* reported that the administration had traded arms to Iran for the return of hostages and then covertly diverted proceeds from the arms sales to fund the Contras. In 1984 the Sandinista government sued the United States in the **United Nations** International Court of Justice over U.S. involvement in the mining of Nicaragua's harbors. The Sandinista government won a judgment against the United States, which Reagan refused to acknowledge. *See also* IRAN–CONTRA; TOWER COMMISSION.

**COUNCIL ON COMPETITIVENESS.** Chaired by Vice President **J. Danforth (Dan) Quayle**, the Council on Competitiveness (also known as the Quayle Council) was established in 1991. The purpose of the council was to oversee congressional regulatory efforts, apply cost-benefit analyses to agency rulemaking, and push for deregulation that would benefit the private sector. Congressional Democrats charged that the council was a backdoor mechanism for business to do an end-run around regulatory agencies and attempted to de-fund the council in 1992, but the effort failed narrowly in the Senate. Consumer advocate organizations such as Public Citizen were skeptical of the council. Of particular concern was the council's ability to over-rule decisions of agencies such as the **Environmental Protection Agency** and Food and Drug Administration. The secretiveness of the council also drew criticism, since it was not required to disclose contacts with lobbyists or make public its proceedings.

**CRUISE MISSILES.** Cruise missiles are "drones," or unmanned rockets. They may carry nuclear warheads or conventional explosives, and they may be launched from naval vessels, from aircraft, or from ground operations. Their flight path is low, which enables them to escape radar detection. They are typically short-range weapons that travel 200–700 miles and fly below the speed of sound. Many of the ground-based devices deployed by the United States in Europe during the **Cold War** were eliminated under the **Intermediate-Range Nuclear Forces (INF) Treaty** negotiated by President **Ronald Reagan** and Soviet General Secretary **Mikhail Gorbachev**. *See also* ARMS CONTROL; DETERRENCE; INTERCONTINENTAL BALLISTIC MISSILES (ICBMs); MUTUALLY ASSURED DESTRUCTION (MAD); NORTH ATLANTIC TREATY ORGANIZATION (NATO); REYKJAVÍK (SUMMIT); WARSAW PACT.

**CZECHOSLOVAKIA.** This central European country was founded in 1918 following World War I. In 1938 German dictator Adolph Hitler annexed the Sudetenland, an area of primarily German-speaking residents, and occupied the entire country by 1939. Following **World War II**, Czechoslovakia became a satellite state of the **Soviet Union** and a member of the **Warsaw Pact.** In 1968 Czech leader **Alexander Dubček** embarked on a series of political and economic reforms he qualified as "socialism with a human face." Those reforms were met by Warsaw Pact troops that promptly put down the reform effort and removed Dubček from power. With the fall of the **Berlin Wall** in 1989, Czechoslovakia broke free from Soviet domination. Soviet General Secretary **Mikhail Gorbachev's Sinatra Doctrine** of allowing former Eastern bloc countries to decide their own futures enabled playwright **Václav Havel** to lead the country toward democratic governance and a market economy in the **Velvet Revolution** of 1989. On 1 January 1993, Czechoslovakia split into two independent countries, the Czech Republic and Slovakia. The peaceful partition is often referred to as the "Velvet Divorce." *See also* BREZHNEV DOCTRINE; COLD WAR.

## – D –

**DARMAN, RICHARD GORDON (1943– ).** Born in North Carolina and a graduate of Harvard Business School (1967), Darman shifted employment between the private and public spheres over the course of his career. He was director of ICF, Inc. (1974–75) before becoming assistant secretary of commerce under President Gerald Ford (1976–77). President **Ronald Reagan** selected him as deputy **chief of staff** (1981–85), and later he was appointed as deputy secretary of the treasury (1985–87). He left the White House for two years in 1987 to become managing director of Shearson Lehman Brothers, Inc., a Wall Street brokerage firm. President **George H. W. Bush** appointed him as director of the Office of Management and Budget, where he served from 1989 to 1993. An economic pragmatist, Darman was criticized harshly by more ideological Republicans, including Republican House Minority Whip **Newt Gingrich,** for his willingness to accept tax increases to address the federal deficit—and for allegedly convincing President Bush to recant his **"read my lips, no new taxes"** pledge during negotiations with Congress over the 1990 budget. Darman is author of *Who's in Control? Polar Politics and the Sensible Center* (1996). He became managing director at the Carlyle Group, an investment firm, in 1993.

***THE DAY AFTER.*** This Emmy Award–winning film aired on the American Broadcasting Corporation (ABC) network on 20 November 1983. Viewed by 100 million Americans, the film portrayed the effects of a nuclear war between the United States and the **Soviet Union** on the residents of Kansas City, Missouri, and the nearby university town of Lawrence, Kansas. The cast starred actors Jason Robards, John Lithgow, and JoBeth Williams. The plot develops from a Soviet military buildup around West Berlin, an eventual invasion of West Germany, and a gradual escalation in nuclear warfare that reaches a full strike by both sides—though the film never clarifies which country launched its arsenal first. The rest of the film follows the lives of survivors of the nuclear bombs in the greater Kansas City area. It paints a grim portrait of the survivors, who develop radiation sickness and find themselves without shelter or medical assistance—and ultimately lose hope. The gripping film is a **Cold War** classic that challenged the doctrine of **Mutually Assured Destruction**, or MAD, the notion that neither the United States nor the Soviet Union would launch a first strike on the other because it would end in the reciprocal destruction of the two societies. In a follow-up to the film, ABC hosted a debate between conservative writer William F. Buckley Jr. and scientist Carl Sagan. During the debate, Sagan introduced the controversial theory of a "nuclear winter," arguing that the long-term effects of fires, smoke, and radiation from a global nuclear war would far outshadow the immediate effects on survivors by blotting out the sun and destroying the food chain. Gerald Degroot, author of *The Bomb: A Life* (2005), reports that President **Ronald Reagan** wept after seeing the film, though the account is not verifiable. *See also* ARMS CONTROL; DÉTENTE; DETERRENCE; INTERCONTINENTAL BALLISTIC MISSILES (ICBMs).

**DEATH PENALTY.** *See* SUPREME COURT.

**DEAVER, MICHAEL KEITH (1938– ).** Born in Bakersfield, California, Deaver spent three decades as one of President **Ronald Reagan**'s most trusted aides. The relationship began in the 1960s when Reagan was elected governor of California. Deaver was a savvy image-maker during Reagan's 1980 and 1984 presidential campaigns, and served as assistant to the president and deputy **chief of staff** from 1981 to 1985. He left the Reagan White House under a cloud. He was investigated for unethical lobbying activities and was convicted on three counts of perjury, for which he received a stiff fine. He currently serves as international vice chairman for Edelman Worldwide. He is the author of several books detailing his close relationship with President and Mrs. Reagan in *A Different Drummer: My Thirty Years with Ronald Reagan* (2001) and *Nancy: A Portrait of My Years with Nancy Reagan* (2004).

**DERWINSKI, EDWARD JOSEPH (1926– ).** A native of Illinois, Derwinski became the first secretary of the **Department of Veterans Affairs** in 1989 and remained in that post through the end of President **George H. W. Bush**'s term. A veteran of **World War II**, Derwinski served in the army infantry in the South Pacific and in occupied **Japan**. He graduated from Loyola University in Chicago in 1951, and was president of West Pullman Savings and Loan Association from 1950 to 1975. During this time he served a single term in the Illinois statehouse (1957–58) and was a delegate to the **United Nations** General Assembly (1971–72). A 12-term member of the U.S. House of Representatives, Derwinski first won election to Congress from Illinois in 1958.

**DÉTENTE.** A French word that translates literally as "relaxation," the term refers to efforts by the United States and **Soviet Union** to ease tensions between the superpowers during the **Cold War**. Increased diplomatic, commercial, and cultural contacts and exchanges were aimed at improving bilateral relations. When he took office in 1981, President **Ronald Reagan** was less favorable to détente than his predecessors. The loss of international prestige from the **Iranian hostage crisis** and the **Soviet Union**'s invasion of **Afghanistan** in 1979 convinced Reagan that the Soviet threat required increased military expenditures and weaponry. By his second term, however, Reagan forged a working relationship with Soviet General Secretary **Mikhail Gorbachev** that marked a return to détente. The **Reykjavík Summit** paved the way for the **Intermediate-Range Nuclear Forces (INF) Treaty**, signed by the United States and Soviet Union in December 1987. Over a three-year period, the treaty eliminated vast quantities of short-range ballistic and **cruise missiles**, including U.S. **Pershing II missiles** and Soviet **SS-20 missiles**. *See also* ANTI–BALLISTIC MISSILE (ABM) TREATY; ARMS CONTROL; DETERRENCE; MUTUALLY ASSURED DESTRUCTION (MAD); NORTH ATLANTIC TREATY ORGANIZATION (NATO); STRATEGIC ARMS REDUCTION TREATY (START); STRATEGIC DEFENSE INITIATIVE (SDI); WARSAW PACT.

**DETERRENCE.** The theory of deterrence is closely linked to the **Cold War** doctrine of **Mutually Assured Destruction** that drove the nuclear arms race between the United States and **Soviet Union**. The theory prescribes the deployment by the superpowers of weapons capable of massive retaliation. The guaranteed reciprocal damage the adversary would sustain would deter leaders on either side from preemptive attacks. With any advantage for a first strike erased, equilibrium is (theoretically) the result. *See also* ANTI–BALLISTIC MISSILE (ABM) TREATY; ARMS CONTROL; DÉTENTE; MUTUALLY ASSURED DESTRUCTION (MAD); NORTH ATLANTIC TREATY ORGANIZATION (NATO); WARSAW PACT.

**DOBRYNIN, ANATOLY FYODOROVICH (1919– ).** Born in Krasnaya Gorka, Russia, and an aviation engineer by training, Dobrynin studied at the Soviet Higher Diplomatic School of the Ministry of Foreign Affairs in the 1940s. He was appointed Soviet ambassador to the United States in 1962 by Nikita Khrushchev six months before the Cuban Missile Crisis. He served as ambassador to six presidents, including President **Ronald Reagan**. He was recalled to Moscow in 1986 to direct the Communist Party secretariat's international department. He retired in 1988. He is author of *In Confidence: Moscow's Ambassador to America's Six Cold War Presidents* (1995). *See also* COLD WAR; SOVIET UNION.

**DOLE, ELIZABETH HANFORD (1936– ).** A North Carolina native and wife of former senator and Republican presidential candidate **Robert J. Dole**, Elizabeth Hanford Dole earned an undergraduate degree at Duke University (1958) before pursuing a graduate and law degree at Harvard (1965). She worked as a public defender in Washington, D.C., was deputy assistant for consumer affairs for President Richard Nixon (1971–73), and was a member of the Federal Trade Commission (1973–79). Before President **Ronald Reagan** appointed her secretary of transportation in 1983 (a post she held until 1987), she was his assistant for public liaison from 1981 to 1983. President **George H. W. Bush** appointed her secretary of labor in 1989, a position from which she resigned in 1991 to become president of the American Red Cross. After unsuccessfully seeking the Republican presidential nomination in 2000, Dole won a seat to the Senate in 2002 from North Carolina. She is the author, with her husband, of *Unlimited Partners: Our American Story* (1996).

**DOLE, ROBERT JOSEPH (BOB) (1923– ).** A native of Russell, Kansas, Dole served in the U.S. Army during World War II. He received two Purple Hearts for injuries he sustained while fighting the German army in northern Italy, and which left his right arm paralyzed. Dole entered politics in 1950 when he won a seat to the Kansas legislature. He completed a law degree at Washburn University (1952), and returned to Russell to open a law practice. From 1960 to 1968 he served in the U.S. House of Representatives. He successfully ran for the Senate in 1968, and was reelected four times before resigning in 1996 to run for the presidency. He served as Senate majority leader from 1985 to 1987, during which time Republicans had control of the upper chamber. He served as minority leader from 1987 to 1995 and was a prominent spokesman for Republican policy stands during the presidency of **George H. W. Bush**.

Dole's presidential aspirations date to 1976, when incumbent president Gerald Ford chose him as his vice-presidential candidate. He made a brief run for the Republican nomination in 1980. In 1988 Dole entered the primaries against George H. W. Bush. The campaign, which Bush eventually won, was bitter. Dole accused Bush of lying about his Senate record. In 1996, after resigning his Senate seat,

Dole set his sights on the Republican nomination in the bid to oust Democratic incumbent president **William Clinton**. He faced a crowded Republican primary field that included **Pat Buchanan**, **Lamar Alexander**, and millionaire Steve Forbes. Dole lost the first-in-the-nation New Hampshire primary to Buchanan, but eventually gathered enough delegates in other states to secure the Republican nomination.

Nonetheless, Dole was forced to spend much more money than expected in the primary contests. Because he had accepted federal funds, he faced spending limits in the general campaign against Clinton—who did not have any opposition in the Democratic Party in 1996. Dole's campaign was lackluster. He chose former representative **Jack Kemp** as his running mate, but was criticized by some Republicans for distancing himself from House Speaker **Newt Gingrich**, whose policy platform entitled the "Contract with America" had stalled in the Senate under Dole's leadership. Dole emphasized a sweeping **tax** cut of 15 percent, but the idea did not catch hold. Moreover, his campaign was hampered by the entry of millionaire **H. Ross Perot**. On election day, Clinton earned 49 percent of the popular vote to Dole's 40 percent. Dole exited politics thereafter and has since become a prominent spokesperson for pharmaceuticals for erectile dysfunction and for the soft drink Pepsi. In 2003 he established the Robert J. Dole Institute of Politics, located on the University of Kansas campus in Lawrence. He has been married to **Elizabeth Hanford Dole** since 1975. He is author of *One Soldier's Story: A Memoir* (2005).

**DONOVAN, RAYMOND JAMES (1930– ).** Born in Bayonne, New Jersey, and a graduate of Notre Dame Seminary in New Orleans in 1942, Donovan served as President **Ronald Reagan**'s secretary of labor from 1981 to 1985, during which time he was investigated and charged with having ties to organized crime. He resigned his post in the administration when two **independent counsel**s and a New York state investigation examined charges that he had given false testimony to a grand jury and engaged in larceny and fraud concerning his employment at Schiavone Construction Company, where he had become executive vice president in 1971. The federal investigations were suspended and Donovan was acquitted of any wrongdoing by a

New York State court in 1987. As labor secretary, Donovan headed the president's efforts to decrease labor regulations, cut federal jobs, and ease rule enforcement.

**DREXEL, BURNHAM, LAMBERT.** Drexel, Burnham, Lambert was a highly successful Wall Street investment firm in the 1970s and 1980s. However, the firm was caught in the "**junk bond**" scandals of the late 1980s. Drexel agreed to pay penalties of $650 million in late 1988 for insider trading and other securities violations—the largest settlement to that date. The firm dissolved and reorganized into several smaller components in 1990 after filing bankruptcy.

**"DRUG CZAR."** *See* BENNETT, WILLIAM JOHN (BILL); MARTINEZ, ROBERT (BOB); OFFICE OF NATIONAL DRUG CONTROL POLICY.

**DRUG PROBLEM.** *See* DRUG TRAFFICKING; MEDELLÍN CARTEL; NANCY REAGAN; OFFICE OF NATIONAL DRUG CONTROL POLICY; "WAR ON DRUGS."

**DRUG TRAFFICKING.** The import and sale of illegal drugs such as marijuana, cocaine, and heroin in the United States became a central concern during the administrations of **Ronald Reagan** and **George H. W. Bush**. In the **war on drugs** that began under Reagan, Congress imposed stiffer federal criminal penalties for drug smuggling and selling and poured more resources into the coast guard and federal agencies for drug interdiction. First Lady **Nancy Reagan** embarked on a "just say no" campaign to encourage young Americans to avoid drugs. President Reagan supported a 1986 crime bill that mandated that convicted drug offenders serve at least 85 percent of their sentences.

In 1988 Congress passed the Anti-Drug Abuse Act, which Reagan supported. The act established an **Office of National Drug Control Policy** (ONDCP) in the **Executive Office of the President**, whose director was often referred to as the "drug czar." The first director of ONDCP, **William Bennett**, took up his position under President George H. W. Bush in 1989, and was charged with coordinating federal drug-interdiction efforts. In 1990 Bush launched the **Andean**

**Initiative** and met with the leaders of Bolivia, **Colombia,** and Peru to discuss ways to halt cocaine trafficking to the United States. Bush also provided military and intelligence support to the Colombian government in its battle with the **Medellín cartel**, one of the largest exporters of cocaine to the United States. *See also* MARTINEZ, ROBERT (BOB); NORIEGA MORENO, MANUEL ANTONIO; "WAR ON DRUGS."

**DUBČEK, ALEXANDER (1921–1992).** Born in Uhrovec, **Czechoslovakia** (now part of the Republic of Slovakia), Dubček was a Nazi resistor during the German occupation of Czechoslovakia during **World War II**. He became secretary of the Czech Communist Party in 1968, and attempted to undertake reforms to promote "socialism with a human face." In what became known as the "Prague Spring," Soviet forces entered Czechoslovakia that year to quash a perceived insurrection. The Soviet invasion was consistent with the **Brezhnev Doctrine** that challenges to Communist governments in the **Soviet Union**'s sphere of influence would not be tolerated. Dubček was ultimately expelled from the Communist Party in 1970. He was a central figure in Czechoslovakia's **Velvet Revolution** in 1989 and a supporter of President **Václav Havel**. Dubček became speaker of the Czech federal assembly in 1989. He died in 1992 from complications subsequent to a car crash. *See also* BERLIN WALL; GORBACHEV, MIKHAIL SERGEYEVICH; SINATRA DOCTRINE; WARSAW PACT.

**DUBERSTEIN, KENNETH M. (1944– ).** Duberstein is a graduate of Franklin and Marshall College (1965) and received a master's degree from American University (1966). He began his government service as an assistant to New York Republican senator Jacob Javits, and later became deputy undersecretary of labor for President Gerald Ford. He served in the administration of **Ronald Reagan** as assistant to the president for legislative affairs (1981–83), and was then deputy chief of staff (1987) before taking over the **chief of staff** job from **Howard Baker** in 1988. Duberstein was awarded the President's Citizens Medal in January 1989. He held several positions in the private sector, including the vice presidency of Timmons and Company, Inc., a government-relations firm, prior to his service to President Reagan.

His lobbying skills prompted President **George H. W. Bush** to hire him as a key spokesman for **Supreme Court** nominee **Clarence Thomas**. Duberstein is chairman of the Ethics Committee for the U.S. Olympics Committee and served as vice chairman of the independent Special Bid Oversight Reform Commission for the U.S. Olympics Committee. He also serves on the board of directors of numerous corporations, including the Federal National Mortgage Association.

**DUKAKIS, MICHAEL STANLEY (1933– ).** The son of Greek immigrants, the Massachusetts native attended Swarthmore College and earned a law degree at Harvard University (1960). He began his political career in the Massachusetts state legislature, winning four terms starting in 1962. He won the 1974 governor's race in Massachusetts but was defeated in the Democratic primary four years later when the state's high property and sales **taxes** were the focal point of the campaign. In 1974 Dukakis had promised not to raise taxes, but balancing the budget forced him to renege on his pledge. He made a comeback in 1983 and served as governor again until 1990, riding Massachusetts's economic boom, which stemmed largely from high-tech firms around Boston. Dukakis took credit for his state's economic turnaround and defeated a crowd of Democratic challengers in the 1988 presidential primaries. Winning the Democratic nomination, he chose Texas Senator **Lloyd Bentsen** as his running mate.

The general campaign between Dukakis and incumbent vice president **George H. W. Bush** was especially bitter and personal. The Bush campaign went on the offensive, casting a highly negative light on Dukakis's record as governor and portraying him as a liberal, particularly on crime. The **Willie Horton** television ad showed how an inmate on a weekend prison furlough program supported by Dukakis had assaulted a man and raped his girlfriend. In a public relations disaster during a presidential debate, Dukakis admitted that he would be against the death penalty even if his wife had been raped and murdered. The Bush campaign also ran ads challenging Dukakis's ability to act as commander in chief. The most infamous ad showed an uncomfortable-looking Dukakis on a tank with an oversized helmet. And Bush challenged his environmental record. Citing the cleanup of the highly polluted Boston Harbor as the most expensive on record, a Bush campaign ad stated, "And now Michael Dukakis wants to do for America what he's done for Massachusetts." Dukakis lost the election by over seven million votes. Following his defeat, he returned to finish his term as governor, and presently teaches political science at Northeastern University in Boston.

## – E –

**EAGLEBURGER, LAWRENCE SIDNEY (1930– ).** A native of Milwaukee, Wisconsin, Eagleburger is a career foreign service officer who was a deputy to Henry Kissinger and spent several decades in the former Yugoslavia. A moderate Republican, Eagleburger was appointed ambassador to the former Yugoslavia by President **Jimmy Carter** in 1977, and served in that post until 1981. President **Ronald Reagan** named him assistant secretary for European affairs in 1981. He served as Secretary of State **James Baker III**'s deputy from 1989 to 1992, and finished out President **George H. W. Bush**'s term as his secretary of state when Baker moved to the position of White House **chief of staff**. In 2002 Eagleburger chaired the international commission on compensation for Holocaust victims of **World War II**.

**EASTERN AIRLINES STRIKE.** Machinists for Eastern Airlines went on strike on 4 March 1989 after refusing to accept a pay cut demanded by owner Frank Lorenzo. As the dispute between labor unions and management continued into fall 1989, Congress passed a bill calling for federal mediation. President **George H. W. Bush** vetoed the bill, and Congress was unable to override it. The machinists remained on strike a total of 686 days—until Eastern Airlines went out of business on 18 January 1991. The strike compounded the troubled airline's financial difficulties and declining sales and market share.

**ECONOMIC RECOVERY TAX ACT (1981).** Along with the Omnibus Budget Reconciliation Act of 1981, the Economic Recovery Tax Act of 1981 was a cornerstone of President **Ronald Reagan**'s first-year legislative agenda. The legislation cut income **tax** rates by 25 percent over three years, amounting to a $749 billion loss of revenue to the federal government. The plan was originally developed by congressional Republicans **Jack Kemp** and William Roth in 1977, and Reagan latched on to the idea. In spring 1981, following an assassination attempt by **John W. Hinckley Jr.**, Reagan made a televised plea for the bill that yielded a significant grassroots response. Reagan also worked behind the scenes and negotiated with an important group of moderate, mostly southern Democrats to win support for the bill. *See also* GRAMM–RUDMAN–HOLLINGS ACT; "REAGANOMICS"; "VOODOO ECONOMICS."

**EDWARDS, JAMES BURROWS (1927– ).** Born in Hawthorne, Florida, Edwards was educated in South Carolina and began his career in public service and medicine there. He received a bachelor of science degree from Charleston College (1950) and a doctor of medical dentistry degree from the University of Louisville (1955). Having served in the U.S. Maritime Service as a deck officer from 1944 to 1947, Edwards later worked as a dental officer in the navy (1955–57) and was lieutenant commander in the naval reserve from 1957 to 1967. He entered politics in 1972 as a state senator from Charleston County. He made history in 1974 as the first Republican to be elected governor of South Carolina since Reconstruction. President **Ronald Reagan** selected him as secretary of energy in 1981. Edwards left the administration in 1982 to accept the presidency of the Medical University of South Carolina, and is now retired.

**EL SALVADOR.** The Central American country endured a civil war that began in 1980 and spanned the 12 years of presidents **Ronald Reagan** and **George H. W. Bush.** The conflict pitted Marxist rebels known as the Farabundo Martí National Liberation Front (FMLN) against the government of President Alfredo Cristiani, who was supported by the United States. Right-wing death squads killed thousands during the civil war, including the Catholic archbishop of San Salvador, Oscar Romero, who had spoken out against violations of human rights. President **Ronald Reagan** dispatched Marines to train the Salvadoran army against the Marxist rebels as part of his struggle against Communist insurgencies in Central America. Although officials in the Reagan administration denied that U.S. armed forces took part in combat operations, some journalists and members of Congress suspected otherwise. The United States spent $4 billion in economic and military aid during the civil war, which ended in January 1992 following an accord between rebels and the government. *See also* COLD WAR; CONTRAS; NATIONAL SECURITY DECISION DIRECTIVE (NSDD) 32; NICARAGUA.

**ENDARA GALIMANY, GUILLERMO DAVID (1936– ).** Endara won the Panamanian election of May 1989 by nearly a 3–1 margin over **Manuel Noriega**, but Noriega refused to step down from power. Noriega's hold on Panama was broken when the United States invaded the country in December 1989 in **Operation Just Cause**. Noriega was captured and taken to the United States for trial, and Endara became president in December 1989. He left office in September 1994.

**ENVIRONMENT.** The environmental policies of presidents **Ronald Reagan** and **George H. W. Bush** sparked intense criticism from environmental groups. Both presidents attempted to roll back federal environmental regulations that businesses considered costly, even though each considered himself pro-environment. Two of Reagan's appointments—**James G. Watt** as secretary of the interior and Anne Gorsuch as administrator of the **Environmental Protection Agency (EPA)**—stirred considerable controversy. Watt's staunch support for the development of natural gas and other energy resources on federal lands and his off-color comments forced his resignation in 1983. EPA Administrator Gorsuch undertook efforts to cut the agency's budget for environmental protection by more than 25 percent in 1981. Moreover, she reduced enforcement of environmental regulations under statutes such as the **Clean Air Act** by trimming the number of cases filed against alleged violators by over 75 percent. Reagan's pro-business stance on environmental issues was met with congressional discord in 1987 when he vetoed the Clean Water Act, charging that the bill imposed costly regulations on the private sector. The Democratic-controlled House and Senate promptly overrode his veto with considerable support from congressional Republicans.

Bush did not so much reverse Reagan's environmental policies as moderate them. Billing himself as an environmentally friendly presidential candidate in 1988, Bush had traveled to Massachusetts and lambasted Democratic candidate **Michael Dukakis** for his failure to clean up Boston Harbor. In the Oval Office, however, Bush continued to push for federal deregulation. He appointed Vice President **J. Danforth Quayle** to head up the **Council on Competitiveness**, which applied cost-benefit analyses to agency regulations, including the EPA. Nonetheless, Bush did sign the 1990 **Clean Air Act amendments**, which updated environmental standards for air pollution, as well as a water bill in 1992 that protected the Grand Canyon. In June 1992, Bush also participated in the **United Nations** Conference on Environment and Development, better known as the "Earth Summit," which took place in Rio de Janeiro, Brazil. Although he signed a treaty on climate change and global warming, Bush refused to sign an accord on biodiversity and was roundly criticized in the domestic and international **media**. In his bid for reelection, one of Bush's principal concerns was how such a treaty might negatively affect the U.S. economy. *See also* ENVIRONMENTAL PROTECTION AGENCY (EPA); OFFICE OF INFORMATION AND REGULATORY AFFAIRS (OIRA); OFFICE OF MANAGEMENT AND BUDGET (OMB).

**ENVIRONMENTAL PROTECTION AGENCY (EPA).** Established by Congress in 1970, during the presidency of Richard Nixon, the EPA is an independent federal agency that oversees the regulation of air and water quality, treatment and disposal of land-based pollutants and hazardous waste, and the protection of natural species that have become endangered. President **Ronald Reagan** sought to scale back environmental regulation as part of his 1980 campaign. He appointed Anne Gorsuch to head the agency in 1981. Gorsuch reduced the EPA's budget dramatically and cut staff by nearly one quarter. She was particularly skeptical of Superfund enforcement, the congressionally mandated reserve of funds dedicated to hazardous-waste cleanup. Gorsuch resigned in 1983 amidst congressional investigation and left her successors to restore the agency's credibility with Congress. President **George H. W. Bush** appointed William K. Reilly to head the agency from 1989 to 1992. Reilly was instrumental in passing the **Clean Air Act amendments** in 1990 and also provided input into the negotiation of the **North American Free Trade Agreement (NAFTA)** with respect to environmental issues. However, the EPA came under criticism in 1990 when the agency declared that homes along Love Canal in Niagara Falls, New York, were again safe for habitation. Love Canal was the site of one of the nation's worst toxic waste dumps in the late 1970s. *See also* ENVIRONMENT.

**"EVIL EMPIRE."** President **Ronald Reagan** used the term *evil* numerous times to describe the totalitarian nature of the **Soviet Union** in a speech to the House of Commons in the United Kingdom on 8 June 1982. He used the phrase *evil empire* in reference to proponents of a **nuclear freeze** while addressing the National Association of Evangelicals on 8 March 1983: "I urge you to beware the temptation of pride—the temptation of blithely declaring yourselves above it all and label both sides equally at fault, to ignore the facts of history and the aggressive impulses of an evil empire, to simply call the arms race a giant misunderstanding and thereby remove yourself from the struggle between right and wrong and good and evil." Reagan's portrayal of the Soviet Union as evil was aimed at giving a moral dimension to the ideological struggle between totalitarianism and democracy. Conservatives applauded the description, while liberals tended to view the rhetoric as unnecessarily exacerbating tensions between the United States and Soviet Union. Reagan withdrew his description following reformist **Mikhail Gorbachev**'s accession to power in 1985. *See also* ANDROPOV, YURI; ARMS CONTROL; BREZHNEV, LEONID; CHERNENKO, KONSTANTIN; COLD WAR; DÉTENTE.

**EXECUTIVE OFFICE OF THE PRESIDENT (EOP).** The Executive Office of the President comprises White House offices and agencies, including the **Office of Management and Budget (OMB)**. These offices are staffed largely by career civil servants and select appointees. The various EOP offices help develop and implement the policy and programs of the president. *See also* OFFICE OF INFORMATION AND REGULATORY AFFAIRS (OIRA).

***EXXON VALDEZ.*** This oil tanker ran aground on Bligh Reef in Prince William Sound, Alaska, on 24 March 1989. The accident caused a massive oil spill that spanned over 1,000 miles of Alaskan coastline and killed substantial numbers of fish and bird life. It was the worst oil spill in U.S. history. The captain of the vessel, Joseph Hazelwood, allegedly an alcoholic, was acquitted of charges. The ExxonMobil Corporation, however, paid over $3 billion in cleanup costs. Exxon-Mobil was indicted by the federal government and contended with a myriad of lawsuits by fishermen and other residents of the devastated area. The corporation paid $1 billion to settle the criminal penalties and civilian damages but continues to appeal other lawsuits. The oil spill prompted Congress to pass the Oil Pollution Act of 1990, which enhanced the federal government's ability to manage tanker accidents and toughened industry enforcement provisions by the **Environmental Protection Agency**.

## – F –

**FALKLAND ISLANDS WAR.** Situated off the coast of Argentina, the Falkland Islands (*Islas Malvinas* in Spanish) have been disputed between the United Kingdom and Argentina for several centuries. War broke out between the two countries on 2 April 1982, when the Argentine Army, under orders from President Leopoldo Galtieri, invaded the islands. Galtieri, who led a military junta in Argentina, hoped to divert public attention away from the country's economic problems and spark a wave of patriotism. He miscalculated that the British would not respond to the invasion. Diplomatic efforts by the United States and other nations failed to resolve the conflict peacefully. Early in the conflict, President **Ronald Reagan** attempted to maintain neutrality but eventually sided with Britain. The government of British Prime Minister **Margaret Thatcher** responded swiftly to the invasion, sending the Royal Air Force and a naval armada to take back the islands by force. Fighting began three weeks after the Argentine invasion and lasted six weeks. On 14 June, Argentine forces surrendered, though Argentina has not relinquished its claim to the islands. Britain lost 255 soldiers, the Argentines 652. Galtieri was chased from power and tried in court, and spent five years in prison. Britain's victory in the short war bolstered Thatcher's position in advance of her second successful electoral bid in 1983.

**FARM AID.** In 1985, musicians **Willie Nelson**, **John Mellencamp**, and **Neil Young** organized a concert to call public and government attention to the plight of American farmers in the midst of the worst economic conditions since the Great Depression. Farm Aid developed into an annual event, with organizers and participants urging governmental action. As a result, Congress passed the **Agricultural Credit Act (1987)**, which President **Ronald Reagan** signed in early 1988. *See also* BLOCK, JOHN RUSLING.

**FEDERAL BUREAU OF INVESTIGATION (FBI).** The FBI was formed as a force of special federal agents in 1908 called the Bureau of Investigation. Its name was changed in 1935, and it is housed as an agency within the Department of Justice, headed by the attorney general of the United States. The bureau's primary responsibility includes investigating federal crimes and cases of espionage and providing assistance to state and local law enforcement authorities. Following the **terrorist** attacks of 11 September 2001, more than 3,000 of the bureau's approximately 11,000 employees have been redirected to counterterrorism and counterespionage activities.

**FEDERAL EMERGENCY MANAGEMENT AGENCY (FEMA).** FEMA is the federal agency that coordinates disaster relief efforts between federal, state, and local governments. FEMA came under criticism in 1992 when **Hurricane Andrew** devastated south Florida. The agency's slow response to victims prompted President **George H. W. Bush** to appoint Transportation Secretary **Andrew Card** to oversee the federal effort. FEMA was transformed from an independent agency to a part of the Department of Homeland Security in March 2003.

**FEDERAL RESERVE SYSTEM.** The Federal Reserve, often referred to by the **media** simply as the "Fed," is the central bank of the United States. The system was created in 1913 by the Federal Reserve Act. The Fed's primary directive is to control national monetary policy, or the supply of money available to banks for consumer and corporate lending. The Fed manages the federal funds rate, which is the rate banks charge one another for overnight loans of federal funds, which are the reserves held by banks at the Fed. The Fed also sets the discount rate, which is the amount that banks pay for direct borrowing from the federal government. Lower federal-funds and discount rates typically provide larger sums of money for banks to lend. When the Fed is concerned with inflation, raising these key indices is aimed at slowing consumer and corporate borrowing and spending.

There are 12 districts in which the Federal Reserve has branches. Seven members of the Federal Reserve's board of governors direct the bank's operations and are appointed by the president for 14-year terms. The president is legally mandated to make those appointments with an eye to ensuring "fair representation of the financial, agricultural, industrial, and commercial interests and geographical divisions of the country." The president also appoints the chair of the Fed, who serves a four-year term. All appointments require Senate confirmation.

President **Ronald Reagan** reappointed **Paul Volcker** as chairman of the Fed in 1983. Volcker was widely hailed for limiting the money supply in the early 1980s as a way of bringing inflation under control. When Volcker stepped down from the Fed in 1987, Reagan appointed **Alan Greenspan** as chair. Greenspan was subsequently reappointed by presidents **George H. W. Bush**, **William Clinton**, and **George W. Bush**. Greenspan maintained the Fed's low interest rate policy through his unprecedented five terms as chair and is credited with the long-term economic growth in the United States that spanned the 1980s to the early years of the new millennium. *See also* "REAGANOMICS"; "VOODOO ECONOMICS."

**FERRARO, GERALDINE (1935– ).** Born in Newburgh, New York, Ferraro was the first female candidate for vice president. She joined the Democratic ticket headed by **Walter Mondale** in 1984, but was defeated in President **Ronald Reagan**'s landslide reelection. While pursuing a law degree at Fordham University, Ferraro worked as a schoolteacher. She later joined the Queens County, New York, district attorney's office. She got her start in politics by winning election to Congress in 1978, and serving two subsequent terms. While on the Mondale ticket, Ferraro, who is Catholic, was criticized for her pro-choice stance on **abortion**. Questions were also raised by the **media** about husband John Zaccaro's alleged ties to organized crime. After an unsuccessful bid for the U.S. Senate in 1992, Ferraro frequented political news programs and joined a consulting firm. She is author of *Ferraro: My Story* (1985).

**FITZWATER, MARLIN (MAX) (1942– ).** Fitzwater served in the administrations of **Ronald Reagan** and **George H. W. Bush** as press secretary from 1983 to 1993. He is the longest-serving press secretary to date. Born in Kansas, Fitzwater is a graduate in journalism from Kansas State University. He worked for various newspapers in Kansas before taking positions in the federal government, including the Appalachian Regional Commission, Department of Transportation, **Environmental Protection Agency**, and Department of the Treasury. He was named Outstanding Civil Servant in government in 1980, and received the nation's second-highest civilian award, the Presidential Citizens Medal, in 1992. He is author of a memoir of his White House years entitled *Call the Briefing* (1997) and published his first novel, *Esther's Pillow*, in 2001.

**FLAG BURNING.** See *TEXAS V. JOHNSON*.

**FOLEY, THOMAS STEPHEN (1929– ).** A native of Spokane, Foley earned a law degree from the University of Washington in Seattle (1957) and entered private practice. Three years later he went to work for the state attorney general's office. He moved to Washington, D.C., in 1961 and served as special counsel for a Senate committee. In 1964 he won election to the House of Representatives from Washington's fifth district. He was reelected 14 times. Foley ascended through the ranks of the Democratic leadership, working as majority whip from 1981 to 1987 and as majority leader from 1987 to 1989. He was elected Speaker of the House in 1989 when **James Wright** resigned following an ethics probe. As Speaker, Foley's support of President **George H. W. Bush** was vital in winning congressional authorization for the use of force in the **Persian Gulf War**. Foley narrowly lost his seat in Congress in 1994 when Republicans gained a majority in the House of Representatives for the first time in four decades. He was the first sitting Speaker in 130 years to be defeated. In 1997 President **William Clinton** appointed Foley ambassador to **Japan**. Foley remained in the post until 2001.

**FOREIGN POLICY.** The **Cold War** between the United States and the **Soviet Union** guided foreign policy during the administration of **Ronald Reagan**. Following the disintegration of the Soviet Union in late 1991, President **George H. W. Bush** and Russian President **Boris Yeltsin** declared an end to the Cold War a year later. The **Persian Gulf War** against Iraqi dictator **Saddam Hussein** dominated foreign affairs during Bush's term.

Both Reagan and Bush suffered significant foreign policy setbacks during their terms. Reagan's foreign policy leadership was jeopardized by the **Iran–Contra** affair. Bush and Congress struggled to find an appropriate response to Communist **China**'s massacre of pro-democracy demonstrators in **Tiananmen Square**. At the same time, Reagan is often credited with hastening the breakup of the Soviet Union by successfully challenging its technological capacity with the **Strategic Defense Initiative (SDI)** while simultaneously seeking a reduction in nuclear weapons with Soviet General Secretary **Mikhail Gorbachev**. Bush's assembly of an unprecedented international coalition against Saddam Hussein following the Iraqi dictator's invasion of **Kuwait** stands as the high point of his term.

Reagan, like each of his post–**World War II** predecessors, subscribed to the policy of containment vis-à-vis the Soviet Union—the notion that all efforts should be made to ensure resistance to the spread of Communism around the world. During Reagan's two terms the United States militarily and financially supported the **Contras** in their struggle against the Marxist government in **Nicaragua**, as well as rebel leader **Jonas Savimbi** in his fight against the Cuban- and Soviet-backed Marxist government in **Angola**. Reagan also ordered a military invasion of the Caribbean island of **Grenada** to rescue American students on the island, oust a hard-line Communist from power, and restore order in the tiny country, despite British Prime Minister **Margaret Thatcher**'s opposition to the intervention.

Reagan also took military action to counter **terrorist** attacks on U.S. interests abroad. He ordered the bombing of Libyan dictator **Muhammar Qaddafi**'s compound on 14 April 1986 (*see* OPERATION EL DORADO CANYON). The raid, which killed Qaddafi's adopted daughter, injured two of his sons, and left 30 civilians dead, was in retaliation for suspected Libyan involvement in the bombing of a West Berlin nightclub frequented by U.S. service personnel. Relations with France were strained when Reagan could not win approval from French President **François Mitterrand** to allow U.S. planes to fly over France en route to Libya. Reagan convinced British

Prime Minister Margaret Thatcher to launch the assault from U.S. bases in England.

Reagan's stature was greatly damaged by the Iran–Contra scandal that broke in November 1986. When the Lebanese newspaper *al-Shiraa* reported that the president and his national security staff had traded arms to Iran in exchange for the return of U.S. hostages—and then diverted the proceeds of the arms sales to support the Contras in Nicaragua, in clear defiance of the **Boland Amendment**—Congress launched multiple investigations. Reagan denied knowing about the policy and appointed Senator **John Tower** to head an independent commission to investigate the allegations. Although Reagan was ultimately cleared of any wrongdoing, the **Tower Commission** report was highly critical of Reagan for failing to properly supervise his national security staff, including Colonel **Oliver North** and Admiral **John Poindexter**, both of whom were later indicted and cleared on criminal charges for their involvement in the Iran–Contra affair. Reagan addressed the nation in a televised speech on 4 March 1987 in which he admitted that he had made mistakes and summarized plans to revamp the national security structure along the lines recommended by the Tower Commission. The success of his speech in convincing the American public of his sincerity arguably saved his presidency from further congressional investigation or impeachment.

Reagan was also dealt a severe blow to his prestige on the international stage when Congress overrode his veto of a bill mandating sanctions on the **apartheid** regime in South Africa. Despite the call of many black South Africans, including Bishop **Desmond Tutu,** for western countries to halt international commerce with South Africa, Reagan took the position that economic sanctions would only harm the black population. The Democratic-led Congress disagreed and passed the 1986 Anti-Apartheid Act over Reagan's objections (*see* SOUTH AFRICA SANCTIONS). The act restricted U.S. investment in South Africa and represented one of the worst defeats for a president in foreign policy matters since Congress's override of Richard Nixon's veto of the War Powers Resolution in 1973.

Reagan was also skeptical of the **United Nations**. He appointed **Jeane Kirkpatrick**, a staunch critic of the UN's alleged anti-American stances, as ambassador to the international organization. Under her leadership and with Reagan's support, the United States withdrew from the United Nations Educational, Scientific and Cultural Organization (UNESCO), refused to contribute to the UN's population fund because of disagreements about **abortion** and family planning, and supported reducing U.S. funding to the UN by a quarter unless the UN amended its fundamental charter. Finally, the Reagan administration refused to recognize the jurisdiction of the UN's International Court of Justice when the United States was found to have violated international law by mining **Nicaragua**'s harbors in the bid to weaken the Marxist regime in that country.

Reagan's anti-Communist posture was irrefutable. He often directed his rhetorical skills against the Soviet Union, which he described as an "**evil empire**." While at Berlin's Brandenburg Gate in 1987, he defiantly called upon **Mikhail Gorbachev** to tear down the wall separating West and East Berlin (*see* BERLIN WALL). In policy terms, Reagan's stance was similarly unambiguous. In 1982 he issued **National Security Decision Directive (NSDD) 32**, which set forth the goal of undermining the Soviet Union by economic means and limiting its influence in the developing world through covert operations and military assistance to anti-Communist movements.

Some observers contend that Reagan's stance on **arms control** was contradictory. During his first term, Reagan won congressional support for considerable new funding for a military buildup—in particular, nuclear weapons such as **intercontinental ballistic missiles (ICBMs)**, **Trident II missiles** aboard submarines, **cruise missiles**, **MX missiles**, and short-range **Pershing II missiles** deployed in Western Europe. Yet in 1987, following the **Reykjavík Summit** with Soviet leader Gorbachev, Reagan signed the **Intermediate-Range Nuclear Forces (INF) Treaty**, which dismantled U.S. Pershing II missiles in West Germany and Soviet **SS-20** warheads stationed in **Warsaw Pact** countries of Eastern Europe. Reagan's "great reversal"—engaging in a costly and potentially dangerous arms race with the Soviet Union only to oversee the destruction of those very weapons in his second term—remains a controversial legacy.

President George H. W. Bush took a cautious approach to the disintegration of the Soviet Union in late 1991. In 1992 he ultimately urged Congress to pass legislation to aid in Russia's transition to democracy and a free market economy and in the securitization of the former Soviet Union's nuclear arsenal. He also jointly declared the end of the Cold War with Russian President **Boris Yeltsin**.

Bush employed the phrase "**new world order**" to suggest that the end of the Cold War would bring about not only better U.S.–Russian cooperation but also a larger positive impact on international cooperation. Critics suggested, instead, that Bush was advocating a "world government" run by the United Nations. Regardless, Bush had made it clear throughout his term that he was willing to take unilateral action or seek international cooperation to protect U.S. interests abroad, depending upon the circumstances.

Bush struggled throughout his presidency to find a compromise policy vis-à-vis **China** following the brutal crackdown on pro-democracy student protestors in Beijing's **Tiananmen Square** in spring 1989. Bush sought "constructive engagement" with the Chinese leadership, of which he had an intimate knowledge from his days as envoy to the country. He argued that economic sanctions against China would curtail, rather than bolster, the ability of the United States to influence China's human rights policies. Many of Bush's detractors in Congress, particularly Democratic senator George Mitchell of Maine, challenged Bush's stance and attempted to rescind China's "most-favored-nation" (MFN) status as a trading partner of the United States with preferential treatment. Twice Bush vetoed congressional legislation that would have revoked China's MFN status. Critics charged that Bush's stance failed to have substantive effects on moderating China's hard-line policy on internal dissent.

In late December 1989, Bush ordered U.S. forces to invade the Central American nation of Panama to oust strongman and alleged drug trafficker **Manuel Noriega** from power. Noriega was eventually captured, returned to the United States for trial, and convicted on **drug trafficking** charges. **Guillermo Endara**, the presumptive victor in the Panamanian presidential race had Noriega not canceled the elections, was sworn in as president. Bush justified the invasion on the grounds that Noriega posed an imminent threat to the security of the Panama Canal, which links the Gulf of Mexico with the Pacific Ocean.

Bush supported sanctions against the apartheid regime in South Africa and sought to hasten political change in that country. In 1990 he met with both F. W. de Klerk, a progressive white leader on the apartheid issue, and black leader **Nelson Mandela**, who had recently been freed from prison. Ronald Reagan had previously charged that Mandela was a **terrorist** for his attempts to overthrow the South African government. In 1991 Bush lifted the economic sanctions that had been in place against South Africa since 1986, as the system of apartheid was dismantled (*see* SOUTH AFRICA SANCTIONS).

Bush won acclaim for his handling of the Persian Gulf War in 1991. Following Iraqi dictator Saddam Hussein's invasion of the emirate of Kuwait in August 1990, Bush skillfully used his personal relations with international leaders, as well as the United Nations Security Council, to assemble an unprecedented international coalition of forces—first to protect Saudi Arabia from any Iraqi aggression (*see* OPERATION DESERT SHIELD), and then to restore the status quo when Hussein refused to withdraw his troops by January 1991 (*see* OPERATION DESERT STORM). Bush's efforts were aided by his foreign policy team, including Joint Chiefs Chairman **Colin Powell** and Secretary of Defense **Richard Cheney**, and the decisive command of General **Norman Schwarzkopf** amidst the ground fighting. The initial air campaign lasted less than 96 hours, destroying Iraqi air forces and setting up the successful ground campaign (*see* OPERATION DESERT SABRE), which brought about a cease-fire between Hussein and the coalition forces just a little more than five weeks after the military conflict began. Although Bush's public approval reached record levels for a president in the post–World War II era, some criticized his refusal to chase Hussein from power—though as Bush pointed out, correctly, Hussein's ouster was not part of the UN mandate. *See also* ARMS CONTROL; CENTRAL INTELLIGENCE AGENCY (CIA).

**FRANKLIN, BARBARA HACKMAN (1940– ).** Born in Pennsylvania and a graduate of Harvard, Franklin served as a staff assistant to President Richard Nixon (1971–73). She was appointed to head the U.S. Consumer Product Safety Commission in 1973, and held that position until 1979. Only the second **woman** to serve as secretary of commerce, Franklin was appointed to that post by President **George H. W. Bush** in February 1992. She has since served on numerous corporate boards.

**FSX FIGHTER JET.** During **George H. W. Bush**'s presidency, the United States and **Japan** agreed to co-develop a new fighter aircraft known as the FSX. The joint venture became embroiled in Congress over issues pertaining to ongoing trade disputes between the two countries. The Democratic-controlled Senate placed restrictions on technology transfer to Japan as part of the agreement, with critics arguing the deal would otherwise give Japanese firms an unfair future advantage. On 31 July 1989, President Bush vetoed the bill, and a Senate override failed several months later. President Bush reasoned that provisions in the bill were unconstitutional intrusions into his ability to conduct **foreign policy**. In February 1990, Mitsubishi Industries and U.S.-based General Dynamics agreed to develop the aircraft, with the American company taking responsibility for 40 percent of the project's development.

## – G –

**GATES, ROBERT MICHAEL (1943– ).** A Kansas native, Gates earned a doctoral degree in Russian and Soviet history from Georgetown University (1974). He joined the **Central Intelligence Agency (CIA)** in 1966. He served on the **National Security Council** from 1974 to1979 under presidents Gerald Ford and **Jimmy Carter** before returning to the CIA. He became deputy director of the CIA under President **Ronald Reagan** in 1986. President **George H. W. Bush** named Gates deputy **national security advisor** in 1989, and he remained in that post during the **Persian Gulf War**. Bush nominated him to direct the CIA in 1991 after **William Webster** announced his retirement. Gates remained at the CIA until President **William Clinton** took office in January 1993, and he was appointed Secretary of Defense in 2006 by President **George W. Bush**. He is the recipient of numerous medals, including the Presidential Citizens Medal and the National Security Medal. In 2002 he became president of Texas A&M University. He is author of *From the Shadows: The Ultimate Insider's Story of Five Presidents and How They Won the Cold War* (1996).

**GENERAL AGREEMENT ON TARIFFS AND TRADE (GATT).** The precursor to the World Trade Organization, GATT is an international agreement among nations that seeks to liberalize trade. Member nations grant each other "most-favored-nation" trading status for the exchange of goods. GATT organized global trade negotiations called "rounds," including the **Uruguay Round** from 1986 to 1998.

**GINGRICH, NEWTON LEROY (NEWT) (1943– ).** A native of Pennsylvania, Gingrich attended Emory University in Atlanta and graduated with a master's and doctorate in history from Tulane University. He taught at West Georgia College (now the University of West Georgia) from 1970 to 1978. He first won election to the House of Representatives from the sixth district of Georgia in 1978, and was reelected 10 consecutive times. In 1983 he founded the "Conservative Opportunity Society," a caucus for congressional Republicans. The objective was to strategize and reverse decades of Democratic control of Congress. Gingrich became known as a "bomb-thrower" in Congress, coordinating two-minute speeches by Republicans that criticized the Democrats' agenda on the cable television network C-SPAN. In 1987 he leveled ethics charges against House Speaker **Jim Wright** of Texas, and a subsequent congressional investigation prompted Wright to resign. Gingrich became minority whip in 1989 when President **George H. W. Bush** tapped **Richard (Dick) Cheney** as his secretary of defense. Gingrich was among disgruntled Republicans angry at Bush for his acceptance of the **Budget Agreement of 1990** that included **tax** increases. Gingrich spearheaded a resolution by the House Republican Conference calling the taxes unacceptable.

Gingrich ultimately realized the dream of a Republican congressional majority by creating an electoral platform—the "Contract with America"—on which GOP candidates successfully campaigned in the 1994 midterm elections. Gingrich was elected Speaker of the House of Representatives from 1995 to 1999. He resigned from office in 1999 after Republicans lost seats in the 1998 midterm elections, which took place as the House stood ready to impeach President **William Clinton**. He joined the American Enterprise Institute, a conservative think tank, and is a frequent commentator on the cable television FOX News Channel. He is author of several books, including *Winning the Future: A 21st Century Contract with America* (2005).

**GINSBURG, DOUGLAS HOWARD (1946– ).** A graduate of the University of Chicago Law School (1973), Ginsburg was a law clerk to

Supreme Court Justice Thurgood Marshall before teaching law at Harvard University from 1975 to 1983. President **Ronald Reagan** appointed him to the U.S. Circuit Court of Appeals for the District of Columbia in 1986, where he became chief justice. A year later Reagan nominated him to fill a vacancy on the **Supreme Court**. Reagan had previously nominated **Robert Bork** to replace retiring justice Lewis Powell, but the Senate rejected him definitively. Under pressure from conservatives in the Reagan White House, including Education Secretary **William Bennett**, Ginsburg ultimately withdrew his name from consideration. Senate hearings revealed that he had not only smoked marijuana during law school but had also used the drug as a faculty member at Harvard. Ginsburg returned to his post on the appeals court. *See also* KENNEDY, ANTHONY MCLEOD.

*GLASNOST.* A Russian word (гласность) that connotes transparency or openness, the term was a part of Soviet leader **Mikhail Gorbachev**'s efforts at political and economic reform. Gorbachev used the term to promote public dialogue on his economic policies as a means to circumvent opposition among party elites. *See also PERESTROIKA.*

**GOLDWATER–NICHOLS ACT (1986).** This legislation, signed by President **Ronald Reagan**, substantially revamped the organizational chain of command of the U.S. military. The bill was aimed at minimizing rivalries between branches of the armed services and streamlining operations. Among the changes was the centralization of military advice in the chairman of the Joint Chiefs of Staff, shared procurement among the different branches, and a greater unity in command at lower levels with the objective of increasing efficiency.

**GORBACHEV, MIKHAIL SERGEYEVICH (1931– ).** Gorbachev was born near Stavropol, Russia, and studied law at Moscow University. He later graduated from the Agricultural Institute, where he was trained in agronomy and economics. He advanced quickly up the ranks of the Soviet Communist Party structure. In 1970 he became first secretary for agriculture; a year later he became a member of the Communist Party's Central Committee, and in 1974 he was appointed to the Supreme Soviet. By 1979 he was made a member of the Politburo. He became party leader in 1984, and was essentially second-in-command to General Secretary **Yuri Andropov**. He traveled extensively abroad and was responsible for restructuring personnel in government ministries. In 1985, following the death of **Konstantin Chernenko**, Gorbachev became general secretary of the Communist Party.

Two years later he embarked on an ambitious reform agenda. *Glasnost* was aimed at democratization through greater governmental transparency; *perestroika* involved reforming and restructuring the Soviet economy with liberalizing measures. Gorbachev sought **détente** with the West, and President **Ronald Reagan** found him an entirely different type of Soviet leader. In October 1986, Reagan and Gorbachev met in Iceland for the **Reykjavík Summit,** and both agreed in principle to eliminate vast categories of nuclear weapons from their arsenals. The summit paved the way for the **Intermediate-Range Nuclear Forces (INF) Treaty,** signed a year later. Gorbachev withdrew Soviet troops from **Afghanistan** after a decade of occupation. He also repealed the **Brezhnev Doctrine** vis-à-vis the **Warsaw Pact** nations in Eastern Europe. Those countries would be able to decide their own futures without Soviet interference—the so-called **Sinatra Doctrine** of allowing the countries to "do it their own way." Domestically, however, the Soviet economy continued to decline in the late 1980s, despite Gorbachev's measures. As inflation mounted dramatically, public unrest increased. The "openness" that Gorbachev had championed began to take its toll on national unity as constituent republics of the **Soviet Union** stirred toward independence.

Although Gorbachev survived a coup attempt in 1991, his authority had diminished significantly relative to Russian President **Boris Yeltsin**. By late 1991, the **Baltic States** had declared independence, and Russia, Belarus, and the Ukraine agreed to form a **Commonwealth of Independent States** (CIS) to replace the Soviet federation. The agreement was a de facto dissolution of the Soviet Union. Gorbachev recognized it as such and resigned as general secretary on 24 December 1991, officially terminating the Soviet Union. Gorbachev established his own foundation in 1992, and later an environmentalist organization called Green Cross International. His autobiography *Memoirs* was published in 1997.

**GORE, ALBERT, JR. (1948– ).** A native of Carthage, Tennessee, Gore grew up in Washington, D.C., and is the son of veteran U.S. senator Albert Gore, Sr. He served as the 45th vice-president from 1993 to 2001, during the presidency of **William J. Clinton**. A graduate of Harvard (1969), Gore was a military journalist briefly during the Vietnam War. Upon his return to Tennessee, he was a reporter for the Nashville-based *Tennessean*. Gore began his political career in 1976 when he was elected to represent the fourth district for Tennessee in the House of Representatives. He was reelected thrice, and in 1984 won the Senate seat held by Republican **Howard Baker**. Gore was reelected to the Senate in 1990, but resigned in 1992 when he was elected vice president.

Early in his candidacy for the vice presidency, Gore debated **Reform Party** candidate **H. Ross Perot** on the Cable News Network (CNN). The memorable exchanges over the potential economic impact of the **North American Free Trade Agreement (NAFTA)** accentuated Gore's dispassionate, academic style—in contrast to Perot's prickly temperament. Gore headed the National Performance Review, or "Reinventing Government" initiative, aimed at making the federal bureaucracy more efficient. He was also heavily involved in Internet and technology issues in Clinton's second term, including federal efforts to encourage school and public library access to the Internet. In 2000, after beating back a primary challenge from former basketball player Bill Bradley, Gore won the Democratic Party nomination and chose as his running mate Connecticut Senator Joe Lieberman. The general election pitted the Gore/Lieberman ticket against Republican standard-bearer and Texas Governor **George W. Bush** and running mate **Richard (Dick) Cheney**.

For months the polls showed the race too close to call. The election was ultimately decided in Florida following 36 days of post-election court battles over voting irregularities in that state. Although Gore had received over a half million more votes nationwide than Bush, the U.S. **Supreme Court** ultimately put a halt to the recount of votes in Florida. Bush's victory—with a margin of 537 votes—was certified by the Florida secretary of state, Katherine Harris, giving the Bush/Cheney ticket all of the state's 25 electoral votes and a total of 271 to Gore's 266. Harris was appointed by George W. Bush's brother, **John Ellis "Jeb" Bush**, who was governor of Florida. Following the election, Gore taught journalism at Columbia University and several other universities. In summer 2005, he launched his own television network, Gore TV.

**GORSUCH, ANNE.** *See* ENVIRONMENT; ENVIRONMENTAL PROTECTION AGENCY (EPA).

**GRAHAM–LATTA II (1981).** This bill, named for Senator Bob Graham and Ohio Representative Delbert Latta, is also known as the Omnibus Budget Reconciliation Act of 1981. The budget bill contained many of President **Ronald Reagan**'s core agenda items, including an increase in military spending and a $5 billion reduction to entitlements such as **Social Security** and welfare. A coalition of Republicans and southern Democrats in the House of Representatives defeated the Democratic leadership's preferred budget by substituting Graham–Latta II, giving Reagan one of his most spectacular legislative victories. *See also* ECONOMIC RECOVERY TAX ACT.

**GRAMM–RUDMAN–HOLLINGS ACT (1985).** Named for senators Phil Gramm (Texas), Warren Rudman (New Hampshire), and Ernest "Fritz" Hollings (South Carolina), this legislation mandated that any new government spending be offset by budget cuts or **taxes**. The bill was a response to the growing national deficits of the 1980s and an attempt to balance the federal budget. The legislation was ruled unconstitutional in 1987, and another version of the bill was passed that year. The framework of Gramm–Rudman–Hollings was extended by President **George H. W. Bush** in the 1990 **Budget Enforcement Act**.

**GRAY, C. (CLAYLAND) BOYDEN (1943– ).** A native of North Carolina, Gray is a graduate of Harvard University (1964) and the University of North Carolina (1968), where he graduated first in his class with his law degree. He was a law clerk for U.S. **Supreme Court** Justice Earl Warren before joining the law firm of Wilmer, Cutler, Pickering in 1969. Gray became legal counsel to Vice President **George H. W. Bush** in 1981, and was also counsel to the **Presidential Task Force on Regulatory Relief**, which Bush chaired. He served as counsel to President Bush from 1989 to 1993, and is credited with the controversial policy of arguing that the president had the right to **pocket veto** legislation any time Congress goes out of session— against the general interpretation that pocket vetoes apply only when Congress adjourns at the end of a regular session. Gray returned to Wilmer, Cutler, Pickering in 1993, and presently serves as chair of Citizens for a Sound Economy. He also served on the Bush–Cheney Transition Department of Justice Advisory Committee from 2000 to 2001. He is a recipient of the Presidential Citizens Medal.

**GREENSPAN, ALAN (1926– ).** A New York City native, Greenspan earned B.A., M.A., and doctoral degrees (1977) from New York University. He served an unprecedented five terms as chair of the **Federal Reserve System** (Fed). First appointed by President **Ronald Reagan** in 1987, Greenspan was reappointed by presidents **George H. W. Bush**, **William Clinton**, and **George W. Bush**. He retired as Fed chair in January 2006.

Greenspan began his career as an economic consultant in the 1940s. He served as chair of President Gerald R. Ford's Council of Economic Advisors from 1974 to 1977. He later took directorship positions for various private corporations, including Alcoa, General Foods, and the investment firm J. P. Morgan.

As Fed chair, Greenspan was known for his steadfast commitment to managing the money supply to promote economic growth. He successfully handled the **stock market** crash of 9 October 1987 by reassuring investors that the Federal Reserve System would ensure the availability of funds. By the 1990s, his status as chief manager of the national economy worried some observers, who contended that he wielded too much influence. In December 1996, when Greenspan suggested that some stocks were overly valued due to "irrational exuberance," international markets closed sharply lower. Upon his retirement, Greenspan was awarded an honorary position on the Treasury of the United Kingdom. *See also* VOLCKER, PAUL ADOLPH.

**GRENADA.** President **Ronald Reagan** ordered the invasion of this tiny Caribbean island-nation on 26 October 1983, just several days after a deadly bombing of U.S. Marine barracks in **Beirut, Lebanon**. The military intervention, dubbed **Operation Urgent Fury**, included troops from several Caribbean nations concerned about the pro-Communist government and the presence of Cuban advisors in Grenada. Marxist Maurice Bishop had come to power in Grenada in 1979, following a coup d'état that ousted former prime minister Eric Gairy. Bishop subsequently refused to call elections and became embroiled in conflicts with a more extreme Stalinist faction in the ruling "New Jewel Movement." Bishop was executed six days before the invasion. Reagan moved to preclude Bernard Coard, a hard-line Communist, from retaining power. Nineteen of approximately 7,000 U.S. troops were killed in the invasion, which featured the safe return of about 600 U.S. nationals studying at the medical school of St. George's University. The invasion strained relations with the United Kingdom for a brief period. British Prime Minister **Margaret Thatcher** had opposed the invasion on grounds that Grenada was part of the British Commonwealth.

**GROMYKO, ANDREI ANDREYEVICH (1909–1989).** Gromyko was Soviet foreign minister during **Ronald Reagan**'s presidency until 1985. He was appointed Soviet ambassador to the United States in 1943, and later served as the Soviet representative in the **United Nations** Security Council and as ambassador to the United Kingdom. As foreign minister, Gromyko was a key figure throughout the **Cold War**, including the Cuban Missile Crisis under President John F. Kennedy. He played an important role in negotiating the reduction of nuclear weapons between the United States and **Soviet Union**, including the **Anti–Ballistic Missile (ABM) Treaty**, the Nuclear Test Ban Treaty, the Strategic Arms Limitation Treaty (SALT I and II), the **Intermediate-Range Nuclear Forces (INF) Treaty**, and the **Strategic Arms Reduction Treaty (START)**. *See also* ARMS CONTROL; DÉTENTE; DETERRENCE.

*GROVE CITY V. BELL* **(1984).** *See* CIVIL RIGHTS.

# – H –

**HAIG, ALEXANDER MEIGS, JR. (1924– ).** Born in Philadelphia and a graduate of West Point, Haig had an impressive military career and served as President **Ronald Reagan**'s first secretary of state from

1981 to 1982. Haig served in **Japan** as an aid to General Douglas MacArthur. During the Vietnam War he was an architect of bombings in Cambodia. He became a military advisor to Henry Kissinger during President Richard Nixon's first term. He also served as Nixon's **chief of staff** from 1973 to 1974, and is credited with facilitating Gerald Ford's transition to the White House. He left the White House a four-star general and acted as Supreme Allied Commander Europe of the **North Atlantic Treaty Organization (NATO)** from 1974 to 1979.

In the 18 months he served as President Ronald Reagan's secretary of state, Haig was known for his tough stance against the **Soviet Union**, confrontations with Reagan's **national security advisor** Richard Allen and Defense Secretary **Caspar Weinberger**, and his shuttle diplomacy during the **Falkland Islands War** between the United Kingdom and Argentina. Haig was roundly criticized in the press for his misunderstanding of presidential succession and his assertion to reporters that "I'm in control here" when President Reagan was shot by would-be assassin John Hinckley Jr. in 1981. He resigned as secretary of state abruptly in 1982 as a result of ongoing disputes about his authority in **foreign policy**, which he recounts in his memoir *Caveat: Realism, Reagan, and Foreign Policy* (1984). He is also author of *How America Changed the World* (1992).

**HAMAS.** *Hamas* is the Arabic acronym for *Harakat al-Muqawamah al-Islamiyyah*, or "Islamic Resistance Movement." The movement was founded in 1987 during the Palestinian "intifada," or uprising, against **Israel** in the Gaza Strip and occupied West Bank. Hamas is regarded by the United States as a **terrorist** organization. The movement is known for its suicide bombings in Israel and is considered more radical than the **Palestinian Liberation Organization (PLO)** since it continues to call for the destruction of the Jewish state of Israel.

**HART, GARY WARREN (1936– ).** A graduate of Yale Law School, Hart worked for the Department of the Interior in Colorado before taking up private practice in Denver in the 1960s. He managed Democratic nominee George McGovern's failed bid for the presidency in 1972. He won election to the U.S. Senate in 1974 from Colorado, and was reelected in 1980. He entered the crowded Democratic presidential primaries in 1984, but ultimately lost to **Walter Mondale**. In 1987 he was considered an early frontrunner for the Democratic primaries to follow in the spring of 1988. In April 1987, however, allegations of womanizing emerged against Hart. He denied the rumors and challenged the news **media** to follow him. A month later the *Miami Herald* observed a **woman** other than his wife leaving his townhome in Washington, D.C., and then caught photos of him with the woman aboard a boat in the Bahamas. The woman was identified as Donna Rice. Hart remained in the early primary races but did not get more than 7.5 percent of the vote in any state. He consequently withdrew and returned to private law practice.

**HAVEL, VÁCLAV (1936– )**. A native of Prague and a writer and playwright, Havel is a Czech dissident who spent five years in prison for his critiques of the state after Soviet forces put down a rebellion in **Czechoslovakia** in 1968. In 1989 he was a pivotal leader following the student demonstrations that ultimately toppled the Communist regime in the **Velvet Revolution**. He was appointed to the presidency of Czechoslovakia in 1989, and won the subsequent election in 1990. He later resigned in 1992 when Slovakia declared independence and ended the Czechoslovakian federation. Havel was subsequently elected to the presidency of the new Czech Republic in 1993 and reelected in 1998. He left office in 2003. *See also* BERLIN WALL; BREZHNEV DOCTRINE; COLD WAR; DUBČEK, ALEXANDER; SINATRA DOCTRINE.

**HECKLER, MARGARET MARY O'SHAUGHNESSY (1931– )**. A graduate of Albertus Magnus College (1953) and Boston College Law School (1956), Heckler won election to the Massachusetts Governor's Council in 1962—the first **woman** to do so. She was elected to eight terms to the U.S. House of Representatives from the 10th district of Massachusetts beginning in 1966. An independent voice in Congress and a strong supporter of women's issues and health care concerns, Heckler was chosen by President **Ronald Reagan** as secretary of Health and Human Services (HHS) in 1983. She had lost her House seat one year earlier because of redistricting by the Massachusetts legislature. In the wake of a highly public divorce and conservatives' critiques of her moderate views and controversial management style at HHS, she resigned her cabinet position in 1985 to become ambassador to Ireland, a post she kept from 1985 to 1989.

**HERRINGTON, JOHN STEWART (1939– ).** A California native and a graduate of Stanford (1961) and the University of California School of Law (1964), Herrington served in the U.S. Marine Corps and then worked in private law practice from 1965 to 1981. He served as assistant secretary of the navy from 1981 to 1983, and then as White House presidential personnel assistant to President **Ronald Reagan** from 1983 to 1985. He served as secretary of energy from 1985 to 1989. He received the Distinguished Service Medal from the Department of Defense in 1983 and the Presidential Citizens Medal in 1989. He returned to California following Reagan's presidency and served briefly as chair of the state Republican Party. He is also a trustee of the Ronald Reagan Presidential Foundation.

**HEZBOLLAH.** *Hezbollah* means "party of God" in Arabic and is a Shiite Muslim fundamentalist organization founded in Lebanon to combat the 1982 **Israeli** invasion of that country. The United States considers Hezbollah a **terrorist** organization. In the 1980s, the organization received financial support from Iran, whose aim was to spread the Iranian Revolution to other countries in the Middle East. Hezbollah was blamed for the October 1983 attacks on the U.S. Marine barracks in **Beirut, Lebanon**, which killed 241 Americans.

**HILL, ANITA (1956– ).** A graduate of Yale Law School (1980), Anita Hill was a star witness in the Senate confirmation hearings for President **George H. W. Bush**'s nomination of **Clarence Thomas** to the **Supreme Court** in 1991. Hill worked with Thomas when he was chair of the U.S. Equal Employment Opportunity Commission. During the confirmation process she gave sensational testimony to the Senate Committee on the Judiciary. She accused Thomas of making provocative sexual advances and attempting to force her to watch pornography with him. Thomas, who flatly denied such allegations, was narrowly confirmed by a Senate vote of 52–48. Although Hill's accounts were not corroborated, her testimony raised the specter of sexual harassment in the workplace and brought the issue to the forefront of **media** attention. Hill teaches at Brandeis University in Boston, Massachusetts. She published her memoirs of the Thomas confirmation hearings in *Speaking Truth to Power* (1997). *See also* WOMEN.

**HINCKLEY, JOHN WARNOCK, JR. (1955– ).** On 30 March 1981, just 69 days after **Ronald Reagan** had taken the oath of office, Hinckley fired six shots at the president as he and his entourage left the Washington Hilton. Reagan survived the assassination attempt but was shot in the chest. Three other members of the entourage, including Press Secretary **James Brady**, were gravely wounded. Although Reagan recovered quickly and his public approval soared, Secretary of State **Alexander Haig**'s misunderstanding of presidential succession caused the White House embarrassment immediately following the shooting. Hinckley was tried for attempted murder and found not guilty by reason of insanity. His defense attorneys argued that he had become obsessed with killing President Reagan after watching the popular 1976 film *Taxi Driver*, which featured an assassination attempt against the president. Hinckley was remanded to a psychiatric hospital in Washington, D.C. In 2005 he was granted limited visits outside the hospital to visit his parents.

**HIROHITO (1901–1989).** The longest-reigning Japanese emperor died from complications from cancer on 7 January 1989. He had assumed the throne in 1926. President **George H. W. Bush** and First Lady **Barbara Bush** attended the funeral. *See also* JAPAN.

**HODEL, DONALD PAUL (1935– ).** A graduate of the University of Oregon Law School, Hodel was president of the National Electric Reliability Council and deputy administrator and administrator of the Bonneville Power Administration. He served as secretary of energy (1982–85) and then secretary of the interior (1985–89) under President **Ronald Reagan**. As interior secretary, he articulated a policy that unused roads and paths were government right-of-ways, which had far-reaching implications for federal lands policy and wilderness areas. Hodel received the Presidential Citizens Medal from President Reagan in January 1989. He currently serves on several boards, including Integrated Electrical Services and Salem Communications

Corporation. In the 1990s he was president of the **Christian Coalition**, a conservative grassroots organization, but resigned over disputes with **Pat Robertson** about the impeachment and trial of President **William J. Clinton**. Hodel was also president of Focus on the Family, an evangelical Christian organization, from 1996 to 2003. He is author of *Crisis in the Oil Patch* (1994). *See also* ENVIRONMENT.

**HONECKER, ERICH (1912–1994).** A German Communist activist imprisoned by the Nazis until the end of **World War II**, Honecker became a central figure in the postwar government of East Germany (Deutsche Demokratische Republik). He became a member of the Central Committee of the Communist government in 1953 and oversaw the construction of the **Berlin Wall** in 1961. In 1971 he won a power struggle against his mentor, Walter Ubricht, to become general secretary. Honecker was known as a hardline ideologue. He was opposed to Soviet leader **Mikhail Gorbachev**'s reforms in the **Soviet Union** and **Warsaw Pact** nations. By 1989, as demonstrations raged in Germany, Honecker was ousted by **Egon Krenz**. Honecker fled to the Soviet Union but was extradited back to Germany to face charges of war crimes in 1992. He was released by the German authorities in 1993 and went into exile in Chile, where he died from cancer a year later.

**HORTON, WILLIAM R. (WILLY) (1951– ).** Horton was the subject of a controversial televised advertisement that supported **George H. W. Bush**'s presidential campaign in 1988. Convicted of a 1974 murder and sentenced to life in prison in Massachusetts, Horton gained release in 1986 as part of a weekend-furlough program and escaped custody. Ten months later, in April 1987, he assaulted a Maryland couple and repeatedly raped the man's fiancée. **Michael Dukakis**, the Democratic presidential candidate in 1988, was governor of Massachusetts when the incidents took place. Dukakis did not start but did support the furlough program. The National Security Political Action Committee, a group independent from Bush's campaign, produced an advertisement that portrayed a picture of Horton and recounted the events of 1987 to undermine Dukakis's record on crime. The narrative ended with "Weekend passes . . . Dukakis on crime." Some Democratic groups filed lawsuits against the ad and called it racist. The Federal Elections Commission found no evidence of malfeasance or violations of election laws. The advertisement ran for approximately two weeks, from late September until early October 1988. The Bush campaign later used an advertisement criticizing Dukakis for the furlough program by depicting a group of incarcerated criminals entering and exiting prison through a revolving door but did not specifically cite Horton.

**HUDSON, ROCK (1925–1985).** Born Roy Harold Scherer Jr., Rock Hudson starred in dozens of movies in the 1950s and 1960s. A friend of President **Ronald Reagan** from his days in Hollywood, Hudson announced that he had **Acquired Immune Deficiency Syndrome (AIDS)** just a year before he died—and was the first major movie star to make a public announcement about contracting the disease. Marc Christian, Hudson's homosexual partner, sought to dispel rumors that President Reagan and First Lady **Nancy Reagan** were homophobic. When the Columbia Broadcasting Service (CBS) planned a movie on Reagan's life that portrayed them in such a light, Christian "went public" in 2003 and detailed how the Reagans spoke to Hudson at length before his death and showed him kindness and compassion.

**HURRICANE ANDREW.** A category-five storm on the Saffir–Simpson scale when it passed over south Florida on 24 August 1992, Andrew was the most destructive and costliest hurricane to strike the United States up to that point in time. The storm devastated Dade County, Florida, and produced $25 billion in damage. After drifting over the Gulf of Mexico, the hurricane then took aim at central Louisiana as a category-three storm and caused an additional $1 billion in damage. Twenty-six deaths were reported from the hurricane. In the wake of slow and uncoordinated state and **Federal Emergency Management Agency** disaster relief efforts, President **George H. W. Bush** appointed Transportation Secretary **Andrew Card** to oversee the federal aid to south Florida.

**HUSSEIN, SADDAM (1937– ).** A native of Tikrit, Iraq, Hussein acceded to the presidency of that country in 1979 under the banner of the secular pan-Arab Ba'ath Party. Following a war with Iran (*see* IRAN–IRAQ WAR) that lasted from 1980 to 1988, Hussein ordered the Iraqi Army to invade the tiny but oil-rich country of **Kuwait** in 1990, which brought about the first **Persian Gulf War** in early 1991. The impressive international coalition assembled by President **George H. W. Bush** with the support of the **United Nations** (UN) pushed Iraqi forces out of Kuwait but stopped short of removing Hussein from power. Critics charge that President Bush failed to take advantage of a key opportunity to bring greater stability to the Middle East. However, the UN mandate to the international coalition did not include Hussein's capture or removal. For over a decade following the Persian Gulf War, the United States and the United Kingdom enforced "no-fly zones" in the north and in the south of Iraq to contain Hussein's military.

The Iraqi dictator was ultimately ousted by U.S.-led forces that invaded Iraq in spring 2003 when President **George W. Bush** claimed, incorrectly, that Hussein had developed weapons of mass destruction that he planned on using against the United States and its allies. Hussein had repeatedly denied access to United Nations weapons inspectors—a condition of the end of the 1991 conflict. As of early 2006, Hussein is on trial in Iraq for war crimes and murder during his two and a half decades in power. He was ruthless in his repression of opposition, particularly among the Kurdish population in the north of Iraq. At the end of the Iraq–Iran conflict in 1988, approximately 5,000 Kurds were killed when Hussein's army used poison gas to put down a revolt.

– I –

**INDEPENDENT COUNSEL.** Passed by Congress in 1978 in the wake of the Watergate scandal and President Richard Nixon's firing of special prosecutor Archibald Cox, the Ethics in Government Act provided for an independent counsel—beyond the reach of the president's authority—to investigate allegations of misconduct in the federal government. The law was reauthorized twice under President **Ronald Reagan** (1983, 1987), but lapsed under President **George H. W. Bush** (1992). It was again reinstituted in 1994, and expired in 1999. There were seven investigations by independent counsels during the Reagan–Bush presidencies. The most publicized was the investigation by **Lawrence Walsh** into the **Iran–Contra** affair beginning in 1986. *See also* MEESE, EDWIN, III.

**INTERCONTINENTAL BALLISTIC MISSILES (ICBMs).** ICBMs formed the bedrock of U.S. and Soviet nuclear weapons during the **Cold War.** Launched from either silos in the ground or submarines at sea, these long-range missiles can travel a minimum of 3,000 miles, exit the earth's atmosphere, and then reenter en route to their target. ICBMs were equipped with single or multiple nuclear warheads. President **Ronald Reagan**'s plans for a space-based defense system (*see* STRATEGIC DEFENSE INITIATIVE [SDI]) would have destroyed ICBMs while in space and before their final descent. *See also* ARMS CONTROL; DETERRENCE; MUTUALLY ASSURED DESTRUCTION (MAD).

**INTERMEDIATE-RANGE NUCLEAR FORCES (INF) TREATY.** This treaty between the United States and the **Soviet Union** was signed in December 1987 and ratified by the U.S. Senate in May 1988. It was the culmination of several years of negotiations between President **Ronald Reagan** and Soviet General Secretary **Mikhail Gorbachev.** The agreement grew out of a meeting between Reagan and Gorbachev in **Reykjavík, Iceland,** in October 1986, when the two leaders agreed, in principle, to scrap short-range nuclear weapons positioned in **North Atlantic Treaty Organization (NATO)** and **Warsaw Pact** nations. The treaty called for the elimination of a variety of arms, including Soviet **SS-20 missiles** and U.S. **Pershing II** and **cruise missiles** with ranges of approximately 300 to 3,000 miles. Both countries agreed to reciprocal inspections to guarantee the destruction of the weapons, and scrapped over 2,600 missiles by the deadline of June 1991. *See also* ANTI–BALLISTIC MISSILE (ABM) TREATY; ARMS CONTROL; DETERRENCE; MUTUALLY ASSURED DESTRUCTION (MAD).

**INTERNATIONAL PHYSICIANS FOR THE PREVENTION OF NUCLEAR WAR.** This transnational grouping of medical organizations was created in 1980 by Harvard doctor Bernard Lown and doctor Evgueni Chazov of the Soviet Cardiological Institute. The group advocated the prevention of nuclear war and the abolition of nuclear weapons. American and Soviet doctors belonging to the organization won the Nobel Peace Prize in December 1985.

**IRAN AIR FLIGHT 655.** *See* USS *VINCENNES*.

**IRAN–CONTRA.** The Iran–Contra scandal shook the presidency of **Ronald Reagan** beginning in late 1986. The Lebanese newspaper *al-Shiraa* contended that the administration had, at the behest of **Israel**, secretly sought Iranian assistance for the release of American hostages held by **terrorist**s in Lebanon. Exchanging arms for hostages violated the president's stated policy. Attorney General **Edwin Meese** revealed soon after the story broke that profits from the arms sales had been clandestinely channeled to the U.S.-backed **Contras** in **Nicaragua**, in violation of congressional legislation. The 1982 **Boland Amendment** specifically proscribed the administration from funding covert activities in Nicaragua. Assistant to the president for national security affairs **Robert McFarlane** and Defense Secretary **Caspar Weinberger** coordinated the arms deal with Iran. Colonel **Oliver L. North**, a military advisor on the **National Security Council**, and Admiral **John M. Poindexter**, Reagan's **national security advisor**, hatched the plan to divert the proceeds from the arms sales to the Contras. Their plan was inconsistent with White House policy under **Operation Staunch**, which sought to isolate Iran and slow the flow of weapons into the Persian Gulf.

Under public and congressional pressure, Reagan created a special, independent review board to investigate the matter. The **Tower Commission** issued its report in late February 1987, and ultimately found that Reagan was not explicitly linked to the affair. However, the commission scolded Reagan for failing to properly oversee the activities of his National Security Council. On 4 March 1987, Reagan made a televised address to the nation in which he accepted responsibility for the "mistakes" and outlined changes he would implement in the National Security Council and advisory process, as recommended by the Tower Commission. The **independent counsel** appointed by Congress to investigate Iran–Contra, **Lawrence Walsh**, won convictions for Colonel Oliver North and Admiral John Poindexter, but the convictions were overturned on appeal. In 1992 President **George H. W. Bush** pardoned Defense Secretary Caspar Weinberger and five others involved in the scandal, including former national security adviser Robert McFarlane and assistant to the president **Elliott Abrams**.

**IRANIAN HOSTAGE CRISIS.** The crisis began on 4 November 1979 when a mob of protestors and revolutionaries loyal to **Ayatollah Ruhollah Khomeini** stormed the U.S. embassy in Teheran, Iran, and took 66 Americans hostage. The hostages were held 444 days and were released on 20 January 1981—the day **Ronald Reagan** was sworn in as the 40th president of the United States. The protestors putatively took the hostages in retaliation for American support of the deposed **shah of Iran**, Mohammad Reza Pahlavi, who had come to the United States for medical treatment. They demanded the extradition of the shah for trial, which the United States refused. The hostages were routinely blindfolded and marched around the embassy in front of television cameras, and they endured both physical and psychological torture. When neither economic sanctions nor third-party negotiations with Khomeini's regime secured the release of the hostages, President **Jimmy Carter** ordered a military rescue in late April 1980. Dubbed Operation Eagle Claw, the mission ended in disaster when a helicopter and an aircraft collided, killing eight. Iranians discovered the crash site, took sensitive documents, and paraded the dead bodies through Teheran. The failed rescue attempt prompted Secretary of State Cyrus Vance, who opposed the mission, to resign. Carter's inability to bring closure to the hostage crisis was a factor in Ronald Reagan's election in 1980. The Reagan campaign had accentuated Carter's alleged weakness on **foreign policy**. In a final insult to Carter, Khomeini's regime freed the hostages the day Carter left office. President Reagan toasted their return to the United States, via Germany, at an inaugural reception.

**IRAN–IRAQ WAR.** The armed conflict between the two nations spanned 1980 to 1988. The conflict was the culmination of years of hostility and mistrust, but was deliberately initiated by Iraqi dictator **Saddam Hussein**. Each country hoped to establish dominance in the region. Following a number of border clashes, Iraq attempted a full-scale invasion in September 1980. When the invasion was rebuffed, military skirmishes continued and the two nations attacked each other's oil tankers in the Persian Gulf. It is for this reason that the United States sent the **USS *Vincennes*** to the region to protect shipping interests. In 1983 President **Ronald Reagan** launched **Operation Staunch**, which was aimed at isolating Iran and precluding a defeat of Iraq, while simultaneously attempting to curtail the flow of arms into the region. Iraqi dictator **Saddam Hussein** used chemical weapons during the war, while Iran sent guided missiles to targets in major cities, including Baghdad. A cease-fire was finally concluded in August 1988, and the antebellum Iraq–Iran border was reestablished. *See also* USS *STARK*.

**ISRAEL.** Israel was founded on 15 May 1948 as a Jewish state. Partition of the former British Mandate of Palestine into Arab and Jewish components had been approved by the **United Nations** a year earlier. An ensuing civil war between Palestinian Arabs and Jews in 1948 prompted military intervention from Israel's Arab neighbors. Following a cease-fire in 1949, Jordan occupied what become known as the West Bank, Egypt the area known as the Gaza Strip, and Israel expanded the reaches of its western borders. The West Bank and Gaza Strip became a refuge for Palestinians within the Jewish state and a bone of contention between Israel and its Arab neighbors for decades to come.

President **Ronald Reagan**, despite a somewhat tumultuous relationship with Israeli Premier Menachem Begin, was a steadfast ally of Israel. Begin had opposed the 1981 sale of **AWACs** planes to Saudi Arabia, which Reagan supported. When Israeli forces attacked **Palestinian Liberation Organization (PLO)** strongholds in Lebanon in 1982, Reagan undertook a peace initiative in the region and sent U.S. troops to Lebanon as part of an international peacekeeping effort, which resulted in the bombing of the marine barracks in **Beirut**. Reagan also pressured the **Soviet Union** to allow Jews to emigrate to Israel, increased direct foreign and military aid to Israel, and oversaw a bilateral free trade agreement.

At the end of the **Persian Gulf War,** President **George H. W. Bush** saw an opportunity to launch an international effort to resolve the ongoing dispute between Israel and Arab states in the Middle East over the Palestinian question. With the **Soviet Union**, the United States sponsored the Madrid Conference in October 1991 to bring Israel, Jordan, Lebanon, Syria, and the Palestinians to the negotiating table. Secretary of State **James Baker** led the bilateral and multilateral effort, which eventually led to the signing of a peace treaty between Israel and Jordan, improved relations between Israel and Syria, and paved the way for a peace process undertaken by President **William Clinton**. *See also* FOREIGN POLICY.

## – J –

**JAKES, MILOS (1922– ).** A longtime Czechoslovakian Communist apparatchik and party leader, Jakes supported the Soviet invasion of **Czechoslovakia** in 1968. As a member of the Czech Communist Party's Central Committee, he oversaw the subsequent elimination of reformist leaders from party ranks. He became general secretary two decades later, in 1987. In the midst of pro-democracy demonstrations in 1989, he was forced to resign, ultimately making way for reformer **Václav Havel**'s accession to power. *See also* DUBČEK, ALEXANDER; VELVET REVOLUTION.

**JAPAN.** With the second-largest economy in the world after the United States, Japan has been a key ally of the United States in the post–**World War II** era. Nonetheless, the country's successful economic expansion on the heels of strong exports of automobiles and electronics sparked a rivalry between the two countries that spanned the presidencies of **Ronald Reagan** and **George H. W. Bush**. Both presidents struggled to convince the Japanese to scuttle barriers to the import of U.S. goods—primarily nontariff barriers linked to Japan's complex internal distribution system.

Although Reagan professed an allegiance to free trade, he was buffeted by protectionist forces in Congress that took aim at Japan as the domestic economy struggled in the 1980s. Reagan convinced the Japanese to set voluntary quotas on automobile exports to lessen the United States' bilateral trade deficit. Reagan also prodded the Japanese government to reduce steel exports and impose price controls on semiconductors as the steel and computer electronics industries in the United States struggled to compete in international markets.

Trade disputes formed an important component of the U.S.–Japanese bilateral relationship during the administration of George H. W. Bush as well. A major controversy erupted in 1989 when the United States and Japan agreed to co-develop the **FSX fighter** aircraft. The

Senate placed restrictions on technology transfer pertaining to the project, drawing a veto from Bush. A year later, Mitsubishi Industries and General Dynamics decided to push forward with the aircraft's development, with the latter controlling 40 percent of the project.

Bush's visit to Japan in January 1992 stirred controversy and concern when he collapsed at a state dinner. Japanese **media**, which broadcast the event live, recorded Bush vomiting, passing out, and falling to the ground. Japanese Prime Minister Kiichi Miyazawa went to Bush's aid until the president was taken for medical treatment. The illness was apparently caused by the flu, and Bush recovered without delay. However, the incident caused public relations difficulties for Bush's reelection campaign. With the economy faltering and Bush fighting a challenge by fellow Republican **Patrick Buchanan** in the New Hampshire primary the following month, some questioned Bush's health and age in his bid for a second term. (*See also* HIROHITO).

**JARUZELSKI, WOJCIECH WITOLD (1923– ).** A Polish Communist military and political leader, Jaruzelski led the Soviet invasion of **Czechoslovakia** in 1968. He became the Polish Communist Party secretary and prime minister in 1981. He confronted **Lech Wałęsa**'s **Solidarity** labor and reform movement with an iron fist, imposing martial law in Poland on 13 December 1981. Jaruzelski used the pretext of an impending Soviet invasion of Poland to justify his actions, though there was little evidence that the **Soviet Union** was willing to resort to a military solution to quash Solidarity. After the fall of the **Berlin Wall** and the enacting of institutional reforms in Poland, the Communist Party lost its monopoly on power. Jaruzelski resigned in 1990 and was succeeded by Lech Wałęsa. *See also* BREZHNEV DOCTRINE; GORBACHEV, MIKHAIL SERGEYEVICH; SINATRA DOCTRINE; WARSAW PACT.

**"JUNK BONDS."** Junk bonds are high-yield, noninvestment-grade financial instruments of companies with very high credit or default risks. They became the preferred strategy for many financiers in the 1980s, including **Michael Milken**, who violated securities laws and used them to acquire companies. *See also* DREXEL, BURNHAM, LAMBERT.

## – K –

**KACZYNSKI, THEODORE (TED) (1942– ).** Kaczynski was known as the "Unabomber," an acronym derived by the **Federal Bureau of Investigation (FBI)** for "university and airline bomber." Between 1978 and 1996, Kaczynski sent dozens of bombs to unsuspecting faculty and students at various universities, as well as airline employees, killing three and wounding 29. By all accounts, Kaczynski was a gifted individual. He entered Harvard as a mathematics major at the age of 16. He received a doctoral degree in mathematics from the University of Michigan. He taught for two years at the University of California, Berkeley, but resigned abruptly in 1969. He became a recluse and took up residence in a remote Montana cabin. He was apprehended in 1996 when his brother David recognized his writing in a "manifesto" he wrote entitled "Industrial Society and Its Future." Kaczynski mailed the manuscript, which detailed the putative evils of technological advancement, to former victims, and newspapers published it. In January 1998, Kaczynski was sentenced to life in prison without the possibility of parole. The FBI manhunt was the most expensive in the history of the agency.

**KEATING FIVE.** The Keating Five scandal is named for Charles Keating, the chair of California-based Lincoln Savings and Loan, which failed in 1989. Keating was being investigated by the Federal Home Loan Bank Board for allegations that Lincoln had been engaging in risky investments. The board's head, Edwin Gray, alleged that several senators had asked him to back away from investigating Keating. Investigations by the California government, the Department of Justice, and the Senate Ethics Committee revealed that the five senators—Alan Cranston of California, Dennis DeConcini of Arizona, John Glenn of Ohio, John McCain of Arizona, and Donald Riegle of Michigan—together received over $1 million in campaign contributions from Keating. The Senate Ethics Committee stood poised to censure Cranston and was particularly critical of DeConcini and Riegle. Each of these three finished out his term of office but did not seek reelection.

**KEMP, JACK FRENCH (1935– ).** Kemp was born in Los Angeles, California, and graduated from Occidental College in 1957. He served in the army reserve from 1958 to 1962. A professional football player in the 1960s, Kemp was quarterback for the San Diego Chargers and the Buffalo Bills. He co-founded the American Football League's players association and was elected its president five times. After retiring from professional sports, he ran successfully for Congress in 1970, and served nine terms in the House of Representatives as a Republican member from the Buffalo, New York, area. He was appointed secretary of Housing and Urban Development (HUD) by President **George H. W. Bush** and served four years. Kemp unsuccessfully sought the vice presidency on the 1996 Republican ticket headed by Kansas Senator **Robert J. (Bob) Dole**. In 1993 he co-founded Empower America, a public-policy and advocacy organization devoted largely to economic growth. *See also* BENNETT, WILLIAM JOHN (BILL).

**KENNEDY, ANTHONY MCLEOD (1936– ).** Kennedy was the last of four **Supreme Court** appointments made by President **Ronald Reagan**. The U.S. Senate confirmed Kennedy as an associate justice in February 1988. Prior to Kennedy's eventual nomination, Reagan had chosen **Robert Bork** in 1987—but the Democratic-controlled Senate voted him down. Reagan's second choice, **Douglas Ginsburg**, withdrew from consideration. A California native, Kennedy received his law degree from Harvard Law School. For 23 years (1965–88) he taught constitutional law at the University of the Pacific while also serving in the Army National Guard and accepting positions in other judicial commissions and boards. Considered a moderate, Kennedy's positions as a justice paralleled Reagan's stances on issues such as states' rights and affirmative action. But he has also been an important swing vote on social issues such as **abortion** alongside another Reagan appointee, **Sandra Day O'Connor**.

**KGB.** The acronym is Russian for *Komitet Gosudarstvennoy Bezopasnosti*, or "Committee for State Security," in the **Soviet Union**. Like the American **Central Intelligence Agency** (CIA), the KGB was involved in foreign intelligence gathering and espionage. Unlike the CIA, however, it also gathered intelligence and prosecuted internal threats and dissidents in the Soviet Union. *See also* COLD WAR.

**KHOMEINI, AYATOLLAH SEYYED RUHOLLAH (1900–1989).** The spiritual leader of Iran, Khomeini spent 15 years in exile at the orders of the **shah of Iran,** Mohammed Reza Pahlavi, in the 1960s and 1970s. The Shiite cleric plotted the Iranian Revolution of 1979, which ousted the shah in 1979. Khomeini is best remembered for his anti-American rhetoric, his characterization of the United States as the "Great Satan," and the **Iranian hostage crisis** from 1979 to 1980. Khomeini reinstituted Islamic law in Iran and also presided over Iranian resistance during the eight-year-long **Iran–Iraq War** that began in 1980. He died in June 1989.

**KING, MARTIN LUTHER, JR. (1929–1968).** The slain African American **civil rights** leader and Baptist minister was honored with a federal holiday in January 1986. President **Ronald Reagan** signed a bill on 18 January of that year that observes King's birthday on the third Monday of January. Not all states celebrated the holiday until 1993.

**KING, RODNEY GLEN (1965– ).** This African American driver (no relation to **Martin Luther King Jr.**) was at the center of a police beating videotaped by a bystander in Los Angeles, California, on 3 March 1991. Four police officers were charged with using excessive force but were acquitted in 1992 by a largely white jury. Their acquittal sparked outrage among African Americans around the country and precipitated the **race riots** in Los Angeles that erupted on 29 April 1992 and lasted approximately four days. President **George H. W. Bush** toured the devastation left in the wake of the riots and recommended that the officers involved in the beating stand trial in federal court for **civil rights** violations. Two of the four officers, Stacey Koon and Lawrence Powell, received 30 months in federal prison in 1993.

**KIRKPATRICK, JEANE DUANE JORDAN (1926–2006).** Born in Oklahoma and a doctoral graduate from Columbia University, Kirkpatrick was the first **woman** to serve as U.S. ambassador to the **United Nations.** President **Ronald Reagan** appointed her in 1981, and she remained in the post until early 1985. A disillusioned Democrat whose political transition to the Republican Party began after

George McGovern's failed bid for the White House in 1972, Kirk-patrick caught Reagan's attention with her 1979 article in the journal *Commentary* entitled "Dictatorships and Double-Standards." She was highly critical of President **Jimmy Carter**'s **foreign policy**. She contended it was often better to have dictators in countries support-ive of the United States rather than leaders sympathetic with leftist or Communist causes. Kirkpatrick was a staunch advocate of President Reagan's anti-Communist policies in Latin America.

She and Secretary of State **Alexander Haig** engaged in a high-pro-file conflict over the **Falkland Islands War** between Britain and Ar-gentina in 1982, which ultimately precipitated Haig's resignation after she vetoed a United Nations resolution condemning the British mili-tary action. As a member of Reagan's national security team, she was accused of falsifying tapes that implicated Soviet forces in the shoot-ing down of a South Korean passenger jet, **Korean Airlines Flight 007**. After leaving the Reagan administration, Kirkpatrick taught at Georgetown University; became a fellow at the American Enterprise Institute, a conservative think tank; and in 1993 co-founded with **William J. Bennett** Empower America, a public-policy organization. *See also* COLD WAR; CONTRAS; EL SALVADOR; NATIONAL SECURITY DECISION DIRECTIVE (NSDD) 32; NICARAGUA; ORTEGA SAAVEDRA, DANIEL; SOVIET UNION.

**KISSINGER COMMISSION.** Headed by former secretary of state Henry Kissinger, the National Bipartisan Commission on Central America produced a 1984 report on Central America that contended Soviet and Cuban influence was growing in the region, and that Communism must be resisted through economic and military aid. *See also* CONTRAS; EL SALVADOR; KGB; NATIONAL SECURITY DECISION DIRECTIVE (NSDD) 32; NICARAGUA; ORTEGA SAAVEDRA, DANIEL; SOVIET UNION.

**KLINGHOFFER, LEON (1916–1985).** A disabled retiree from New York confined to a wheelchair, Klinghoffer was an American Jew killed by **terrorist**s who hijacked the Italian cruise ship *Achille Lauro* in 1985. The terrorists, who had connections with the Pales-tinian **Abu Abbas**, shot Klinghoffer and threw him off the side of the cruise ship to his death.

**KOHL, HELMUT JOSEF MICHAEL (1930– ).** Chancellor of Germany from 1982 to 1998 and leader of the Christian Democratic Union (CDU) Party from 1973 to 1998, Kohl was a central figure in **Cold War** politics during the presidencies of **Ronald Reagan** and **George H. W. Bush**. Kohl drew much criticism in his home country for his support of President Reagan's decision to deploy **Pershing II** short-range missiles on German soil. He stood by Reagan again in 1987 when both were at the **Berlin Wall** and Reagan called on **Mikhail Gorbachev** to "tear down this wall." In 1987 Kohl became the first West German chancellor to meet his counterpart from East Germany since the end of **World War II**. Kohl also oversaw the reunification of Germany (*Wiedervereinigung* in German), a process that began with the fall of the Berlin Wall in 1989 and ended on 3 October 1990. Along with French President **François Mitterrand**, he worked tirelessly toward greater economic and political integration in Europe and the development of the institutions of the European Union. Kohl left politics under a cloud when revelations of campaign finance abuses ousted his party from power in 1999.

**KOOP, C. (CHARLES) EVERETT (1916– ).** A graduate of Cornell Medical School (1941) and a specialist in pediatrics, Koop served as surgeon general under President **Ronald Reagan** from 1982 to 1989. Koop was a controversial and outspoken figure who raised the profile of the surgeon general's office. On many social issues he was quite conservative. He was staunchly opposed to **abortion**. As the federal government confronted the **Acquired Immune Deficiency Syndrome** (AIDS) epidemic in the 1980s, Koop accentuated the risks of gay sex in spreading the disease, and placed less emphasis on intravenous drug use. Yet his belief that sex education was paramount in public schools angered some conservatives. Koop also attacked the tobacco industry by publishing a report that contended that nicotine was addictive—and thereby set up many of the court battles over cigarettes that would arise in years to come.

**KOREAN AIRLINES FLIGHT 007.** This Boeing 747 left New York's Kennedy Airport en route to the Gimpo Airport in Seoul, South Korea, on 31 August 1983 with 240 passengers and 29 crew. The flight refueled in Anchorage, Alaska, before making the final leg of the voyage. When the flight was over international waters near Sakhalin Island in Eastern Russia on 1 September 1983, Soviet fighters shot a single missile at the plane and decimated it. All passengers and crew died, including 61 Americans. The official Soviet account was that the military did not know that the aircraft was commercial. Pilot navigation error caused the plane to enter Soviet airspace. Experts suggest that the Soviets mistook the Boeing for a U.S. Air Force intelligence-gathering mission. The pilots of KAL 007 apparently did not realize that the plane was off course and veering toward the Kamchatka Peninsula in a much more westerly direction than the flight path assumed. The error may have been caused when pilots entered wrong data into the onboard autopilot computer. The downing of the aircraft sparked worldwide condemnation. President **Ronald Reagan** denounced the incident as a "crime against humanity." *See also* SOVIET UNION.

**KOSOVO.** This province of Serbia in the former Yugoslavia was the site of a Kosovar Albanian uprising in early 1981. Under leader Slobodan Milosevic, Serbian forces increased their presence in Kosovo and ultimately occupied the territory in 1989.

**KRENZ, EGON (1937– ).** Born in Kolberg, Germany (now part of Poland), Krenz was the East German Communist leader who replaced **Erich Honecker** in October 1989, following widespread protests. Krenz himself resigned on 3 December 1989, shortly before the fall of the **Berlin Wall** and the collapse of East Germany. A hardline Communist, Krenz first joined the party in 1955. He was convicted by a German court in 1997 for his role in the killing of people attempting to flee over the Berlin Wall during the **Cold War**. He served three years of a six-and-a-half-year sentence. *See also* BREZHNEV DOCTRINE; GORBACHEV, MIKHAIL SERGEYEVICH; KOHL, HELMUT JOSEF MICHAEL; SINATRA DOCTRINE.

**KRISTOL, WILLIAM (BILL) (1952– ).** A doctor of philosophy in political science from Harvard University (1979), William Kristol is the son of conservative writer Irving Kristol. Before serving as chief of staff to secretary of education **William Bennett** in the administration of **Ronald Reagan** and chief of staff to Vice President **Dan Quayle** in the administration of **George H. W. Bush** (1990–93), Kristol taught at the University of Pennsylvania and the Kennedy School of Government (Harvard). An influential conservative writer and activist, Kristol headed the Project for the Republican Future in 1994, which shaped congressional Republicans' successful electoral strategy. He founded and edits the conservative magazine *The Weekly Standard* (1995–), and in 1997 co-founded the neoconservative Project for the New American Century, a think tank that has influenced President **George W. Bush**'s approach to defense policy and **foreign policy,** and whose membership includes **Richard (Dick) Cheney**.

**KUWAIT.** The former British protectorate is one of the Middle East's largest oil producers and has direct access to the Persian Gulf. Kuwait proclaimed its independence in 1961. Neighboring Iraq claimed that Kuwait was part of its territory, but for several decades Iraq was dissuaded from military adventurism. Iraqi dictator **Saddam Hussein** made good on threats to invade Kuwait and annex the country on 2 August 1990, just two years after the end of the **Iran–Iraq War**. In the lead-up to the **Persian Gulf War**, on 6 August 1990 the **United Nations** imposed economic sanctions on Iraq. In the following two days, President **George H. W. Bush** ordered troops to Saudi Arabia, a move dubbed **Operation Desert Shield**, to protect the Saudis from any aggression by Hussein. On 29 November 1990, the United Nations passed a resolution demanding that Hussein withdraw from Kuwait by 15 January 1991, and authorized the use of force to remove Iraqi forces if he did not comply. With the aid of Secretary of State **James Baker**, President Bush assembled an impressive international coalition of 34 nations, led by approximately 660,000 U.S. troops, which joined to push the Iraqis out of Kuwait and restore the country's monarchy and independent status. The military operation, known as **Operation Desert Storm**, began on 17 January. The allied air campaign was quickly successful, though the ground fighting continued for six weeks. As Iraqi forces left Kuwait, they set oil rigs on fire, creating an unprecedented ecological disaster. The damage to key infrastructures in Kuwait exceeded $5 billion.

# – L –

**LEBANON.** *See* BEIRUT, LEBANON.

**LEWIS, ANDREW LINDSAY, JR. (1931– ).** A Pennsylvania native, Lewis graduated from Haverford College (1953) and earned a master of business administration degree from Harvard (1955). After working his way to the position of director at Henkels and McCoy, Inc., he became director of American Olean Tile Company. Lewis was vice president and assistant chairman of National Gypsum Co. from 1969 to 1970, and chairman of Simplex Wire and Cable Co. from 1970 to 1972. He was president and CEO of Snelling and Snelling, Inc. (1972–74) and then of Lewis and Associates (1974–81). Lewis was deputy director of **Ronald Reagan**'s presidential campaign in 1980, and also deputy director of the transition team following the election. President Reagan appointed him transportation secretary in 1981, and he remained in that post until 1983. He left the administration to chair Warner Amex Satellite Entertainment Co. He was chairman and CEO of Union Pacific Railroad from 1986 to 1987, and was appointed to the board of directors of American Express, Ford Motor Co., and SmithKlein Beckman Corp.

**LIBYA.** The North African country has been ruled by Colonel **Muhammar Qaddafi**, widely viewed as a dictator, since a 1969 coup against the Libyan monarchy. In May 1981, President **Ronald Reagan** accused Libya of being a state sponsor of international **terrorism**. Diplomatic relations between the two countries were subsequently suspended. By 1982 the United States embargoed the import of Libyan oil and prohibited transfer of technology. The United States took military action twice against Libya in 1986. Early that year, naval forces engaged in several skirmishes with Libyan patrol boats in the Gulf of Sidra, which Qaddafi claimed belonged to Libya (but which is regarded as international waters). In April 1986, President Ronald Reagan ordered air raids on sites in Tripoli and Benghazi thought to be **terrorist** training sites (*see* OPERATION EL DORADO CANYON). The bombings were in retaliation for Libyan complicity in the bombing of a West Berlin nightclub frequented by U.S. military personnel. Libyan terrorists were also suspected in the bombing of **Pan Am Flight 103** over **Lockerbie, Scotland,** in December 1988. Two hundred and seventy died in the bombing, including 189 Americans. Under President **George H. W. Bush,** the United States pushed for and won international sanctions against Libya under the auspices of the **United Nations** in 1992. The sanctions were not lifted until September 2003, when Libya agreed to compensate the families of Pan Am Flight 103.

**LOCKERBIE, SCOTLAND.** The small Scottish town 20 miles north of the English border was the site of the bombing of **Pan Am Flight 103**, which exploded on 21 December 1988. The attack, perpetrated by **terrorist**s from **Libya,** killed 11 on the ground and all 259 people on the aircraft.

**LOS ANGELES, CALIFORNIA.** *See* RACE RIOTS (LOS ANGELES).

**LUJAN, MANUEL (1928– ).** Born in San Ildefonso, New Mexico, Lujan graduated from the College of Santa Fe in 1950. While working in his family's insurance business, he became vice-chairman of the New Mexico Republican Party and served as a delegate to the Republican National Convention in 1972, 1976, 1986, 1988, 1992, 1996, 2000, and 2004. A 10-term member of the House of Representatives for Albuquerque who was first elected in 1968, Lujan served as secretary of the interior for President **George H. W. Bush** from 1989 to 1993.

**LYNG, RICHARD EDMUND (1918–2003).** Lyng served as President **Ronald Reagan**'s second secretary of agriculture from 1986 to 1989. A native of California and a graduate of Notre Dame, he had prior ties to presidents Reagan and Richard Nixon. From 1967 to 1969 he served under Governor Reagan as associate director of the California Department of Agriculture. He later served as assistant secretary of agriculture during President Nixon's first term, after which he joined the American Meat Institute as a lobbyist. He was active in President Reagan's 1980 campaign, and was deputy secretary of agriculture from 1981 to 1985. He died in his Modesto, California, home on 1 February 2003.

# – M –

**MADIGAN, EDWARD RELL (1936–1994).** A businessman and native of Lincoln, Nebraska, Madigan entered local politics in 1965. He served in the Illinois state house from 1967 to 1972. He ran for Congress in 1963 and was elected to 10 terms in the House of Representatives. President **George H. W. Bush** appointed him secretary of agriculture in 1991. He died on 7 December 1994 in Springfield, Illinois, and is buried at Holy Cross Cemetery in Lincoln, Nebraska.

**MANDELA, NELSON ROLIHLAHLA (1918– ).** A South African anti-**apartheid** activist and 1993 Nobel Peace Prize winner, Mandela was released from prison after 27 years on 11 February 1990. In 1994 he was elected as the first black president of South Africa. He was regarded by President **Ronald Reagan** as a **terrorist** for his leadership of anti-apartheid activities as head of the African National Congress, including sabotage and armed resistance against the South African government. *See also* SOUTH AFRICA SANCTIONS.

**MARTIN, LYNN MORLEY (1939– ).** Born in Chicago and a graduate of the University of Illinois, Martin was a teacher and school board member in Winnebego County, Illinois, from 1972 to 1976. From 1977 to 1979, she served in the Illinois statehouse. She successfully ran for the Illinois state senate in 1979. Beginning in 1980, she won five terms to the House of Representatives. After being defeated for a seat in the U.S. Senate in 1990, President **George H. W. Bush** appointed her secretary of labor to replace **Elizabeth Dole** in 1991. She joined the faculty of Northwestern University in 1993, and has served as chair of the **tax** and consulting firm Deloitte & Touche's Council on the Advancement of Women.

**MARTINEZ, ROBERT (BOB) (1934– ).** A native of Tampa, Florida, Martinez became the United States' first Hispanic governor in 1987. After earning a bachelor's degree from the University of Tampa, he taught in the Hillsborough County public schools (1957–62, 1964–66). He earned a master's degree in labor and industrial relations from the University of Illinois in 1964. He represented the Hillsborough County Classroom Teachers Association from 1966 to

1975. Governor Ruben Askew named him vice-chairman of the Southwest Florida Water Management District in 1975, a post in which he earned valuable experience in environmental affairs. He successfully ran for mayor of Tampa in 1979, and he held that position until 1986, despite having changed his party affiliation from Democrat to Republican in 1983. He won the open-seat governor's race to replace the outgoing Democrat Bob Graham in 1986. As governor, Martinez earned a solid reputation for **environmental** and drug programs, as well as fiscal responsibility, but fell from Republicans' grace when he supported **taxes** on services. Although he lost his reelection bid to the governor's mansion in 1990, President **George H. W. Bush** tapped him to direct the **Office of National Drug Control Policy** in 1991, and he remained in that position until the end of Bush's term. He left national politics in 1992 to head a Tampa-based business consulting company. *See also* ANDEAN INITIATIVE; COLOMBIA; DRUG TRAFFICKING; MEDELLÍN CARTEL; "WAR ON DRUGS."

**MCAULIFFE, SHARON CHRISTA CORRIGAN (1948–1986).** A native of Framingham, Massachusetts, Christa McAuliffe was the first schoolteacher to be chosen for a space shuttle mission. She was chosen for the *Challenger* mission in 1984 and began training shortly thereafter. Her inclusion on the mission, and the **media**'s affinity to her, drew intense coverage of her preparations. McAuliffe had planned to teach lessons from space. As a result, thousands of children in the United States and around the world were in classrooms observing the launch of the *Challenger*, which ended in a tragic explosion just moments after takeoff on 28 January 1986. All aboard the shuttle perished. McAuliffe received much posthumous praise, including scores of public schools named for her.

**MCFARLANE, ROBERT CARL (BUD) (1937– ).** A marine lieutenant and a graduate of the Naval Academy, McFarlane served as an assistant to **national security advisor**s Henry Kissinger and **Brent Scowcroft** under presidents Richard Nixon and Gerald Ford, respectively. McFarlane served as an assistant to President **Ronald Reagan**'s secretary of state **Alexander Haig** beginning in 1981. He was a central architect of President Reagan's policies in **Nicaragua** and of U.S. support for the **Contras**. He became Reagan's national security advisor in October 1983, and remained in that post until December 1985. McFarlane supervised Lieutenant Colonel **Oliver North** and was implicated in the **Iran–Contra** scandal. McFarlane lied to Congress about the arms-for-hostages deal with Iran and the diversion of the proceeds to the Contra insurgency. When revelations of the scandal broke, he attempted suicide in February 1987, saying he had failed his country. McFarlane was investigated and charged by **independent counsel Lawrence Walsh**, who investigated the Iran–Contra affair. He pled guilty to several misdemeanors, was fined $20,000, and was given probation. He received a pardon from President **George H. W. Bush** in 1992. *See also* BOLAND AMENDMENT.

**MCLAUGHLIN, ANN DORE (1941– ).** A graduate of Marymount College (1963) and the Wharton School of Business, McLaughlin had a long career in communications in the private and public sectors. She was network communications supervisor for the American Broadcasting Corporation from 1963 to 1966, and an account executive at Myers–Infoplan International from 1969 to 1971. She entered government as director of communications for the Presidential Election Commission (1971–72) and director of the Office of Public Information at the **Environmental Protection Agency** between 1973 and 1974. Under President **Ronald Reagan**, McLaughlin served as assistant secretary for public affairs in the Department of the Treasury (1981–84) and as undersecretary of the Department of the Interior (1984–87). She left the Reagan administration briefly to manage **Robert Dole**'s failed campaign for the Republican presidential nomination in 1987. She returned as Reagan's secretary of labor in 1987, and finished out the rest of his term. As labor secretary she was particularly active on workers' quality-of-life issues, and headed a presidential commission on the subject in 1989.

**MEDELLÍN CARTEL.** Named for the Colombian city where it originated, the Medellín cartel was a **drug trafficking** ring founded by Pablo Escobar. The cartel operated throughout Latin America. During the presidencies of **Ronald Reagan** and **George H. W. Bush,** the United States sent military and financial assistance to Colombia as part of the "**war on drugs**" to stop the inflow of illegal narcotics to the United States. By the early 1990s, many of the cartel's leaders, including Escobar and the Ochoa brothers, surrendered to Colombian authorities following a decade-long effort by authorities to capture them. *See also* ANDEAN INITIATIVE; COLOMBIA; OFFICE OF NATIONAL DRUG CONTROL POLICY.

**MEDIA.** The centrality of the mass media in American politics grew tremendously during the presidencies of **Ronald Reagan** and **George H. W. Bush**. Reagan's mastery of televised speeches and press conferences earned him the title of "Great Communicator." His April 1981 nationally broadcast speech to Congress for his budget and economic package is often cited as one of the greatest contemporary victories for a president in the bid to marshal public support for his policies. Bush, on the other hand, was criticized for a perceived inability to curry favor with the print or broadcast media. His attempt to rally public support for the **Budget Agreement (1990)** backfired, and mass opinion actually dropped following his televised plea. Bush's reversal of his "**read my lips, no new taxes**" pledge in the address prompted immediate and long-lasting negative media coverage. Negative coverage of Bush during the 1992 campaign led supporters to argue that he had been unfairly treated by the press, and they posted "Annoy the Media—Reelect Bush" bumper stickers on their cars.

The 1980s and 1990s were also a time of significant change in communications. The advent of cable television and then the Cable News Network (CNN) provided increasing choice to television viewers. CNN, and later other channels dedicated to full-time news coverage such as Fox News and MSNBC, also changed the nature of news coverage of the presidency. An emerging 24-hour news cycle challenged the White House's ability to control stories and respond to spontaneous coverage of events. Moreover, national broadcast networks' coverage of presidential speeches dropped, making it more difficult for presidents to reach a broad audience.

The development of the **World Wide Web** and later the Internet revolutionized communications by the early 1990s. The Internet, like cable television, offers individuals expanded access to instantaneous news coverage. President **William Clinton** was the first president to have a Web page for the White House, on which readers could find information on the president's policies, travels, and accomplishments. The Internet has also broadened the ability of political parties and candidates to raise funds for campaigns, mobilize voters, and maintain contact with party activists.

**MEDICARE.** Adopted by Congress in 1965 as an amendment to **Social Security**, Medicare is a federal program that provides health insurance to elderly, retired, and disabled Americans. Workers finance the program with payroll **taxes**, which are matched by their employers. Like Social Security, Medicare's portion of the federal budget increased dramatically in the 1980s and 1990s and was targeted by deficit-reduction legislation such as **Gramm–Rudman–Hollings (1985)** and the **Budget Enforcement Act (1990)**.

**MEESE, EDWIN, III (1931– ).** Meese was undoubtedly one of the most controversial and criticized members of President **Ronald Reagan**'s cabinet. He served as attorney general from 1985 to 1988, during which time he was the subject of two **independent counsel** investigations. The first stemmed from allegations that a New York–based military contractor, WedTech, had attempted to bribe government officials to obtain contracts. The second concerned Meese's involvement in the **Iran–Contra** affair. Although in neither case was Meese brought before a grand jury, the **Tower Commission** that investigated the Iran–Contra arms-for-hostages scheme criticized him for failing to keep records and blocking access to the office of **Oliver North** during the initial investigation into the matter. Meese won acclaim, however, for the arrests and convictions of spies **John Walker** and **Jonathan Pollard**, as well as for his law enforcement focus on child pornography and **drug trafficking**.

A graduate of Yale and the University of California, Berkeley, Law School, Meese traces his relationship with President Reagan to Sacramento. After working in private law practice and as a state attorney in northern California, Meese became a member of Governor Reagan's staff in 1967, and was later named **chief of staff**. He left public service in 1975 to head an aerospace corporation, and then joined the law faculty of the University of San Diego. In the first Reagan administration, Meese headed the transition team in the White

House, was counselor to the president, and advised on domestic affairs. Meese is now a member of the Heritage Foundation, a conservative think tank, and chair of the George Mason University governing board. He is also author of *With Reagan: The Inside Story* (1992).

**MELLENCAMP, JOHN "COUGAR" (1951– ).** A native of Indiana, Mellencamp is a popular rock singer and songwriter who had numerous hits in the 1980s. With fellow singers **Willie Nelson** and **Neil Young**, Mellencamp co-organized a 1985 concert known as **Farm Aid**, which was aimed at bringing public attention to the plight of farmers. *See also* AGRICULTURAL CREDIT ACT; BLOCK, JOHN RUSLING.

**MICHEL, ROBERT HENRY (1923– ).** A decorated veteran who won two Bronze Stars and a Purple Heart for his infantry service in Europe during **World War II**, Michel went to Washington to work for Illinois Congressman Harold Velde. He won election in his own right in 1956 and was reelected 18 times. He served as the Republican minority whip under presidents Gerald Ford, **Jimmy Carter**, and **Ronald Reagan**. He became minority leader in 1987, and retained that position until his retirement in 1994. The soft-spoken Michel was criticized by some in the Republican Party, including **Newt Gingrich**, for not being more confrontational with the Democratic majority.

**MILKEN, MICHAEL (1946– ).** An executive at the financial firm of **Drexel, Burnham, Lambert**, Milken made millions in the **"junk bond"** market in the 1980s. He was convicted of federal securities and racketeering charges in 1990 and sentenced to 10 years in prison—a sentence that was later reduced to three years. *See also* STOCK MARKET.

***MIR* SPACE STATION.** The **Soviet Union** began constructing the first permanently occupied research space station on 19 February 1986 with the launch of the first module. Over the next decade, additional modules were added. *Mir* orbited the Earth until 23 March 2001, when it disintegrated in the Earth's atmosphere upon reentry. The word *mir* in Russian translates as both "world" and "peace."

**MITTERRAND, FRANÇOIS MAURICE ADRIEN (1916–1996).** Born in Jarnac, France, Mitterrand became the first Socialist president of the Fifth French Republic (1958– ) in 1981. He was reelected in 1988 and left office in 1995. He had twice before lost his bid for the presidency, once in 1965 against Charles de Gaulle, and again in 1974 against Valéry Giscard d'Estaing. His relations with President **Ronald Reagan** were sometimes cool. In 1986, Mitterrand refused to grant the United States permission to fly over France to take military action against **Muhammar Qaddafi** in **Libya**. Mitterrand took a different stance toward Muslim nations of the Middle East, and evidenced less support for **Israel** as France struggled with **terrorism** on its own soil. With German chancellor **Helmut Kohl**, Mitterrand was a major architect of European integration and rapprochement in Franco–German relations. Mitterrand died of cancer in November 1995. His legacy remains controversial, including revelations about his role in the Vichy government during the Nazi occupation of France in **World War II**, his alleged ordering of the sinking of the Greenpeace ship *Rainbow Warrior* in 1986, and a mistress with whom he fathered a daughter.

**MONDALE, WALTER FREDERICK (FRITZ) (1928– ).** Born in Ceylon, Minnesota, and a graduate of the University of Minnesota Law School (1956), Mondale entered Democratic Party politics in 1960 when he managed the reelection campaign of incumbent Minnesota governor Orville Freeman. Freeman returned the favor by appointing Mondale state attorney general. Mondale was appointed to the U.S. Senate from Minnesota in 1964 when Hubert Humphrey became President Lyndon Johnson's vice president. He was elected in his own right in 1966 and again in 1976. During his years in the Senate, Mondale gained publicity for his critique of the National Aeronautics and Space Administration (NASA) while investigating the *Apollo I* spacecraft fire that killed the crew of three in 1967 during a training exercise. **Jimmy Carter** chose Mondale as his running mate in 1976, and he became the 42nd vice president upon his inauguration in January 1977. Mondale returned to private law practice following Carter's unsuccessful reelection bid in 1980 against **Ronald Reagan**.

He returned to the forefront in 1984 by winning the Democratic nomination for the presidency. He chose Representative **Geraldine**

**Ferraro** as his vice-presidential candidate. By most accounts, the Mondale ticket ran a general campaign that was left of center, emphasizing his support for a **nuclear freeze** and criticizing incumbent president Ronald Reagan for foreign and economic policies. Mondale admitted during his acceptance speech at the Democratic convention that he would raise **taxes**—and claimed that Ronald Reagan would too, but would not admit it. The claim may have been true, but Mondale's admission dogged his campaign and enabled Republicans to paint him as a tax-and-spend liberal. In the 1984 election, Mondale won only a single state—his home state of Minnesota. His defeat was the worst Electoral College rout of any Democrat. Mondale again left the public eye for private law practice, but returned to government service as ambassador to **Japan** under President **William Clinton** from 1993 to 1996. In 2002 he made a failed effort to replace incumbent Minnesota Democratic senator Paul Wellstone on the ballot when Wellstone was killed just days before the election. Mondale narrowly lost the statewide race to Republican Norm Coleman.

**"MORNING AGAIN IN AMERICA."** This refrain was the unofficial title of Reagan's reelection campaign in 1984. The themes of economic growth and patriotism were portrayed in several television spots that sounded the phrase. *See also* "REAGANOMICS".

**MOSBACHER, ROBERT ADAM (1927– ).** Born in New York, Mosbacher made his fortune in Texas in the 1950s when he discovered a multimillion-dollar natural gas field. In the 1960s and 1970s, he earned a reputation as an invaluable fundraiser for Republican presidential candidates Richard Nixon and Gerald Ford. Under President **Ronald Reagan,** Mosbacher served as a member and chair of the National Petroleum Council (1984–85) and of the Governor's Energy Council for Texas. Mosbacher raised $75 million for **George H. W. Bush**'s 1988 campaign. President Bush tapped him to serve as secretary of commerce from 1989 to 1992. Following his public career, Mosbacher returned to Texas to chair Mosbacher Energy Company and the Mosbacher Power Group.

**MUJAHADEEN.** A derivative of the Arabic word for "struggle," the term *mujahadeen* was used by the **media** in the 1980s primarily to describe the Muslim resistors who engaged in guerrilla warfare against Soviet forces that invaded **Afghanistan** in 1980.

**MULRONEY, MARTIN BRIAN (1939– ).** Born in Québec, Canada, Mulroney is often referred to in French as "*le petit gars de Baie-Comeau*" ("the little guy from Baie-Comeau"), a reference to his hometown. A graduate of the Université Laval in law, Mulroney was prime minister of Canada from 1984 to 1993 under the Tory (Conservative) Party banner. He forged a particularly close relationship with presidents **Ronald Reagan** and **George H. W. Bush**, which paved the way first for a free trade accord with the United States and later for the trilateral **North American Free Trade Agreement (NAFTA)**. Mulroney's government also provided Canadian troops as part of the international coalition against Iraq in the **Persian Gulf War**. Internal politics—particularly his inability to seal constitutional change twice—contributed to Mulroney's decision to step down as prime minister in 1993. He returned to law and business consulting in Montréal, Québec.

**MUTUALLY ASSURED DESTRUCTION (MAD).** During the **Cold War**, the doctrine of Mutually Assured Destruction guided U.S. and Soviet strategy on nuclear weapons. Because each country had enough weapons to destroy the other's society many times over, the doctrine posits that neither side would have an incentive to attack the other or launch a first strike. Moreover, even if a first strike were successful in destroying one or the other country's land-based **intercontinental ballistic missiles (ICBMs)**, submarine-based nuclear forces guaranteed mutual destruction in a second strike. **Deterrence** hinges on this stalemate, whereby neither side has an advantage to commence a nuclear exchange. Critics charge that the theory makes too many assumptions, including the rationality of actors in decision making. The logical flaw of the theory is that it cannot be falsified unless it fails and nuclear war breaks out.

Practically, MAD ensured that the United States and **Soviet Union** could not directly confront each other in warfare. Counterintelligence, propaganda, and "wars of proxy" in the developing world where Marxist and anti-Communist forces squared off, such as **Angola**, **Nicaragua**, and **El Salvador**, became the superpowers' focus.

The doctrine also spawned an expensive arms race for both countries that extended over four decades.

President **Ronald Reagan**'s plan to develop a space-based anti-missile defense system called the **Strategic Defense Initiative (SDI)** represented a direct challenge to the doctrine of MAD. Critics argued that SDI would violate the **Anti–Ballistic Missile (ABM) Treaty**, the purpose of which was to avert either side's ability to gain a first-strike advantage. The United States' deployment of space-based missiles capable of destroying incoming Soviet missiles would destabilize the delicate balance of the nuclear standoff. Soviet General Secretary **Mikhail Gorbachev** vehemently opposed SDI when he met with Reagan at the **Reykjavík Summit** in 1986. *See also* ARMS CONTROL; DÉTENTE.

**MX MISSILES.** Short for "missile experimental," President **Ronald Reagan** pushed for the deployment of 100 MX missiles in land-based silos. Congress approved the move in 1983 to enhance the United States' nuclear deterrent and demonstrate resolve vis-à-vis the **Soviet Union**'s nuclear stockpile. Like other **intercontinental ballistic missiles (ICBMs)**, MX missiles may be armed with multiple warheads. *See also* ARMS CONTROL; COLD WAR; DETERRENCE; FOREIGN POLICY; GORBACHEV, MIKHAIL SERGEYEVICH; MUTUALLY ASSURED DESTRUCTION (MAD).

– N –

**NAMIBIA.** After two decades of war between the Marxist South-West Africa People's Organization (SWAPO) and the **apartheid** regime of South Africa, Namibia gained independence from South Africa on 20 March 1990. *See also* FOREIGN POLICY; SOUTH AFRICA SANCTIONS.

**NATIONAL SECURITY ADVISOR.** Also known as the assistant to the president for national security affairs, the national security advisor is appointed at the president's discretion and does not require Senate approval. He or she serves at the president's pleasure, is a member of the **National Security Council**, and is the president's principal advisor on national security matters. *See also* CARLUCCI, FRANK CHARLES, III; CLARK, WILLIAM PATRICK; IRAN–CONTRA; MCFARLANE, ROBERT CARL (BUD); NORTH, OLIVER LAURENCE; PERSIAN GULF WAR; POINDEXTER, JOHN MARLAN; POWELL, COLIN LUTHER; SCOWCROFT, BRENT.

**NATIONAL SECURITY COUNCIL.** The National Security Council was established by Congress in the National Security Act of 1947. The purpose of the council is to provide **foreign policy** and military advice to the president, who chairs the proceedings, and coordinate policy with other departments and agencies. Current members (as of 2006) include the vice president; secretaries of state, treasury, and defense; the president's **national security advisor**; chairman of the Joint Chiefs of Staff; and the director of national intelligence (before the creation of the latter post in 2005, the director of the **Central Intelligence Agency** was a member of the council).

**NATIONAL SECURITY DECISION DIRECTIVE (NSDD) 32.** On 28 May 1982, President **Ronald Reagan** outlined a strategy aimed at prevailing in the **Cold War** with the **Soviet Union**. The document called for relying on nuclear **deterrence**, bolstering the U.S. military, strengthening allied relationships around the globe, and containing Soviet influence and propaganda in the developing world. *See also* ARMS CONTROL; FOREIGN POLICY; NORTH ATLANTIC TREATY ORGANIZATION (NATO); WARSAW PACT.

**NATIONAL SECURITY DECISION DIRECTIVE (NSDD) 138.** Elaborated in April 1984 by President **Ronald Reagan**, NSDD 138 set forth the administration's **terrorism** policy. The directive called for better protection of foreign officials in the United States, antiterrorism training, and the ratification of, or enabling legislation by Congress for, dealing with international situations such as aircraft sabotage, hostage taking, and rewarding information on **terrorist** acts, and prohibitions against training or supporting terrorist organizations. *See also* BEIRUT, LEBANON; LIBYA; OPERATION EL DORADO CANYON; PAN AM FLIGHT 103; QADDAFI, MUHAMMAR; TERRORIST.

**NELSON, WILLIE HUGH (1933– ).** A native of east-central Texas, Nelson is a country music singer-songwriter. With fellow singers **John Mellencamp** and **Neil Young**, Nelson coproduced a 1985 concert known as **Farm Aid**, which was aimed at bringing public attention to the plight of farmers. *See also* AGRICULTURAL CREDIT ACT; BLOCK, JOHN RUSLING.

**"NEW WORLD ORDER."** President **George H. W. Bush** used this phrase to suggest that the end of the **Cold War** would have a positive effect on international cooperation. President Woodrow Wilson had used the same phrase following World War I, during his unsuccessful bid to ratify the League of Nations. Conservative critics feared that Bush used the phrase to imply a "world government" led by the **United Nations**. The phrase is also associated with television evangelist **Pat Robertson**, who adopted it as the title of a book in which he explains the historical forces culpable for the decline of Christianity in modern times.

**NICARAGUA.** The largest country in Central America, Nicaragua was ruled by the Somoza family beginning the in 1930s. **Anastasio Somoza Debayle** was deposed as leader in 1979, and the left-wing revolutionary **Sandinista** government took the reigns of power. Sandinista leader **Daniel Ortega** emerged as the principal leader and embarked on a campaign of economic "reform," which included nationalization of industries and confiscation of land held by the wealthy. Deeply concerned about events in Nicaragua, the administration of **Ronald Reagan** secretly funded the right-wing **Contras** in their civil war against the Sandinistas. The revelations that the Reagan administration had traded arms for hostages with Iran and then used the proceeds to fund the Contras resulted in the **Iran–Contra** scandal. *See also* BOLAND AMENDMENT; COLD WAR; NORTH, OLIVER LAURENCE; POINDEXTER, JOHN MARLAN; TOWER COMMISSION.

**NIDAL, ABU (1937–2002).** Nidal was a left-wing Palestinian **terrorist** who formed his own political organization (the Fatah, or Revolutionary Council, also known as the Abu Nidal Organization) after breaking away from the **Palestinian Liberation Organization**

**(PLO)** in 1974. He was a ruthless mercenary known for the brutality of his attacks and assassinations, which killed or injured hundreds around the world. Of particular note were the 1985 attacks in Rome and Vienna on passengers at the ticket counters of Israel-based El Al Airlines. Gunmen associated with Nidal opened fire on bystanders, killing 18 and wounding 120. Nidal's organization is also suspected to have played a part in the bombing of **Pan Am Flight 103** over **Lockerbie, Scotland**, in 1988. Nidal was shot and killed in Baghdad, Iraq, in August 2002. The circumstances of his death are unclear. Palestinians believe he was killed on the orders of Iraqi dictator **Saddam Hussein**, but Iraqi authorities claim he committed suicide. *See also* FOREIGN POLICY; ISRAEL; NATIONAL SECURITY DECISION DIRECTIVE (NSDD)138; TERRORISM; TERRORIST.

**NOFZIGER, FRANKLYN C. (LYN) (1924– ).** Born in Bakersfield, California, Republican political consultant Lyn Nofziger worked as an aide to **Ronald Reagan** when he was governor of California. He also worked as Richard Nixon's deputy assistant and campaigned for Nixon's reelection in 1972. Nofziger joined Reagan's presidential campaign in 1980, and joined the White House staff briefly as an assistant to the president for political affairs. He left in 1982 to start his own lobbying and consulting firm. In 1988 Nofziger was indicted and convicted of violating the 1978 Ethics Act, which proscribes former White House staff from lobbying elected officials for 12 months. For his involvement in what became known as the Wedtech scandal, Nofziger was fined and sentenced to 90 days in prison. However, an appeals court overturned the judgment, arguing the government had failed to show that Nofziger had any knowledge of matters pending before the agency he was lobbying. In 1992 he published his memoir of his years with Reagan, entitled *Nofziger*, and has since turned attention to writing Western novels.

**NOONAN, PEGGY (1950– ).** Noonan worked as a speechwriter for presidents **Ronald Reagan** and **George H. W. Bush**. A former producer for CBS News, Noonan was assistant to Ronald Reagan from 1984 to 1986. She became the principal communications advisor to George H. W. Bush during his presidential campaign in 1988. Known for her eloquent prose, Noonan wrote Reagan's *Challenger* disaster speech. She is also attributed with Bush's use of the phrase "kinder, gentler" nation, and is reputed to have urged the president to go against his **"read my lips, no new taxes"** pledge, both of which upset conservatives. She is a contributor to the *Wall Street Journal*, and is author of *What I Saw at the Revolution: A Political Life in the Reagan Era* (1990) and *When Character Was King: A Story of Ronald Reagan* (2001). *See also* POINTE DU HOC, FRANCE.

**NORIEGA MORENO, MANUEL ANTONIO (1938– ).** Army general, *caudillo* or "strongman," and political leader of Panama from 1983 to 1989, Noriega was removed from power by U.S. forces in 1989 during **Operation Just Cause**, ordered by President **George H. W. Bush**. Noriega had previously been viewed favorably by the administration of **Ronald Reagan** for his role in supplying intelligence on the Nicaraguan **Sandinistas** and getting arms to the **Contras,** until it was learned he was also selling Cuban arms to the left-wing insurgency in **El Salvador**. For his duplicity, the United States levied economic sanctions on Noriega's regime, but the strategy failed to oust him. As retaliation, Noriega threatened to expose alleged money launderers and drug smugglers among U.S. officials while George H. W. Bush had been director of the **Central Intelligence Agency** (CIA). Noriega refused to accept the outcome of the 1989 Panamanian presidential elections. Protestors were assaulted by his forces, sparking outrage in the United States and internationally. President George H. W. Bush worried about Noriega's choice of administrator for the Panama Canal, and used these concerns over the impending turnover of the canal to Panama in 1999 as a pretext for military action. After a standoff that featured U.S. Army forces surrounding his compound and blaring rock music for several days, Noriega was later captured by U.S. forces, brought to the United States for trial, and convicted on cocaine-trafficking, racketeering, and money-laundering charges. He is serving a 40-year sentence in prison in Miami, Florida, and was ordered to pay back $44 million to the Panamanian government. *See also* DRUG TRAFFICKING; "WAR ON DRUGS."

**NORTH, OLIVER LAURENCE (1943– ).** A military officer, political advisor, and political commentator, North was a lieutenant colonel in the U.S. Marine Corps who gained notoriety during the **Iran–Contra**

scandal. A decorated veteran in the Vietnam War, his awards include a Bronze Star for valor and two Purple Hearts for injuries sustained in combat. He joined the administration of **Ronald Reagan** in 1981 as part of the **National Security Council** (NSC) staff for counterterrorism. He played instrumental roles in coordinating the invasion of **Grenada** in 1983 and the air raids on **Libya** in 1986 (*See* OPERATION EL DORADO CANYON). He later became deputy director for political-military affairs in the NSC. North's downfall occurred after he secretly coordinated the sale of weapons to Iran—the profits of which were diverted to support the **Contras** in **Nicaragua**. His activities contravened the 1982 **Boland Amendment** passed by Congress, which prohibited such covert financial support. President Reagan fired North in November 1986. He was subpoenaed by Congress to testify during televised hearings, and claimed he had been authorized by superiors to undertake his actions. The independent **Tower Commission** created by President Reagan to investigate the affair implicated both North and Admiral **John Poindexter** in the scandal. North was indicted on multiple counts, including destroying key documents, but his convictions were overturned upon concerns that his Fifth Amendment rights had been violated. North had made comments to Congress under a grant of immunity, yet statements from his congressional testimony were admitted into evidence during his trial.

North left the public eye until 1994, when he launched an unsuccessful campaign for a U.S. Senate seat in Virginia that split the state Republican establishment. He later became affiliated with cable television's Fox News as a political commentator and host of *War Stories*, a weekly program on military affairs and history. He is author of *Under Fire: An American Story* (1992), *War Stories: Operation Iraqi Freedom* (2003), and a novel entitled *The Jericho Sanction* (2003). North remains a controversial figure. To his supporters, he is a hero who broke the law to defend "freedom fighters" in Central America. To his detractors, his disregard for congressional authority nearly provoked a constitutional crisis.

**NORTH AMERICAN FREE TRADE AGREEMENT (NAFTA).** The North American Free Trade Agreement is an accord between Canada, Mexico, and the United States that liberalizes trade relations and gradually eliminates duties on most consumer, agricultural, and commercial goods by 2009. NAFTA was an expansion of the bilateral U.S.–Canada Free Trade Accord negotiated by President **Ronald Reagan** and Canadian Prime Minister **Brian Mulroney** in 1987. In September 1990, President **George H. W. Bush** notified Congress of his intention to pursue bilateral negotiations for a free trade accord with Mexico following President Carlos Salinas's commitment to privatization plans and an economic reform agenda. Canada entered the negotiations in February 1991 as a precursor to the continent-wide accord, which was signed in October 1992. The U.S. Congress approved the agreement in 1993. President **William Clinton** marshaled sufficient congressional support for the agreement, but a majority of Democrats failed to support passage in the House of Representatives due to labor and environmental concerns. The treaty was implemented effective 1 January 1994.

NAFTA was a major issue in the 1992 presidential election. President George H. W. Bush faced intense criticism from fellow Republican **Patrick Buchanan** in early primary election battles. Buchanan contended that the agreement would compel American companies to seek cheaper labor in Mexico, resulting in massive job losses in the United States. **Reform Party** candidate **H. Ross Perot** made similarly dire forecasts of American jobs being exported to Mexican *maquiladoras*, American multinational factories located just across the southern border between the United States and Mexico. **Environmental** and human rights groups also opposed the agreement, contending that disparities in U.S. and Mexican environmental and labor laws would lead to increased pollution and abuse of workers. Some "side agreements" were reached in the early 1990s that addressed elements of these concerns. While there is no consensus on the overall effects of NAFTA, most economists posit that the agreement has resulted in a significant increase in the exchange of goods and services between the member countries.

**NORTH ATLANTIC TREATY ORGANIZATION (NATO).** The North Atlantic Treaty Organization was founded in 1949 to promote military cooperation among North American and European countries in the aftermath of **World War II**. The initial signatories included Belgium, Canada, Denmark, France, Great Britain, Iceland, Italy, Luxembourg, Netherlands, Norway, Portugal, and the United States.

France withdrew from the organization in 1966, but remained committed to the defensive posture of NATO. Germany, Greece, and Turkey became members in the 1950s; Spain joined in 1982. The organization played a particularly important role during the **Cold War**, as member states pledged that if any other member state were attacked, they would come to the member's defense. The framework is similar to that of the **Warsaw Pact** nations. As such, NATO was an important component of **deterrence** theory aimed at precluding Soviet aggression—either through conventional or nuclear weaponry. With the disintegration of Communist regimes in Eastern Europe and the fall of the **Soviet Union** by 1991, many former Warsaw Pact nations have since joined NATO, including the Czech Republic, Hungary, and Poland (1999) and Bulgaria, Estonia, Latvia, Lithuania, Romania, Slovakia, and Slovenia (2004). With the end of the Cold War confrontation, NATO's mission and future have been called into question. *See also* ARMS CONTROL; DÉTENTE; INTERCONTINENTAL BALLISTIC MISSILES (ICBMs); MUTUALLY ASSURED DESTRUCTION (MAD); PERSHING II MISSILES; STRATEGIC DEFENSE INITIATIVE (SDI); ZERO OPTION.

**NOVELLO, ANTONIA COELLO (1944– ).** Born in Fajardo, Puerto Rico, Novello earned a medical degree from the University of Puerto Rico (1970) and joined the National Institutes of Health in 1978, where she focused on pediatrics and **Acquired Immune Deficiency Syndrome** (AIDS). President **George H. W. Bush** appointed her surgeon general on 9 March 1990. She became the first Hispanic and first **woman** to hold the position. During her tenure as surgeon general, Novello focused on children's and women's health issues, including AIDS and smoking. Novello later served with the **United Nations** Children's Fund (1993–96), and became commissioner of health for New York in 1999.

**NUCLEAR FREEZE.** Peace and antinuclear weapons activists in the West during the 1980s advocated terminating, or "freezing," production of new nuclear weapons as a means to halt the arms race between the United States and **Soviet Union**. The notion ran counter to President **Ronald Reagan**'s position that peace was best achieved through strength or parity in the number of nuclear weapons between the two countries. Reagan's stance was based on the doctrine of **Mutually Assured Destruction**, whereby neither country would have a strategic advantage in launching a first strike on the other. *See also* ARMS CONTROL; DÉTENTE; DETERRENCE; FOREIGN POLICY.

# – O –

**O'CONNOR, SANDRA DAY (1930– ).** Born in El Paso, Texas, and raised in Arizona, O'Connor received her law degree at Stanford University (1952), where she served on the law review and graduated in only two years. She worked as a deputy attorney for San Mateo County, California, and was in private practice in Phoenix, Arizona, in the 1950s. She served as assistant attorney general for the state of Arizona from 1965 to 1969 before being appointed to fill a vacancy in the Arizona senate. She was subsequently elected twice in her own right. She successfully ran for a judgeship in Maricopa County before being appointed to the Arizona Court of Appeals in 1979. President **Ronald Reagan** chose her as his first appointment to the **Supreme Court** of the United States in 1981 to fill the vacancy left by retiring justice Potter Stewart. O'Connor became the first **woman** in U.S. history to serve on the high court, and was unanimously confirmed by the Senate. Regarded as a moderate justice, O'Connor was the pivotal vote on many cases to come before the high court, including controversial decisions about **abortion** such as *Webster v. Reproductive Health Services* (1989). In 2005 she announced that she would retire from the Supreme Court as soon as the Senate confirmed a nominee chosen by President **George W. Bush**.

**OFFICE OF INFORMATION AND REGULATORY AFFAIRS (OIRA).** Housed within the **Office of Management and Budget (OMB)**, OIRA was strengthened by President **Ronald Reagan**. Executive Order 12291, which Reagan signed in early 1981, required that federal agencies assess the costs and benefits of rules that they planned to promulgate. The order further gave the OMB substantial authority to deny proposed rules based on the office's own analysis. *See also* COUNCIL ON COMPETITIVENESS; ENVIRONMENT.

**OFFICE OF MANAGEMENT AND BUDGET (OMB).** Housed in the **Executive Office of the President**, OMB boasts a staff nearly as large as the White House staff—over 500. Among its many functions, OMB provides economic analysis and forecasts to the president and oversees regulations in the departments and agencies of the federal government. The office plays a pivotal role in the budget process. All departments and agencies must first submit their budget requests to OMB for review to ensure priorities are consistent with the president's agenda—a process known as "central clearance"—before appropriations requests are sent to Congress. Formerly known as the Bureau of the Budget, OMB takes its current name from the 1970 reorganization of its functions, spearheaded by President Richard Nixon.

**OFFICE OF NATIONAL DRUG CONTROL POLICY.** This White House agency, housed in the **Executive Office of the President**, was created by Congress in the Anti–Drug Abuse Act of 1988. The office sets national policies on illegal drug control, **drug trafficking**, and interdiction efforts. The office was established under President **George H. W. Bush** on 29 January 1989. Bush had vowed a "**war on drugs.**" The first director of the office, often referred to as the "drug czar," was **William J. Bennett**. The office was raised to cabinet-level status under President **William Clinton** in 1993. *See also* MARTINEZ, ROBERT (BOB).

**OLYMPIC GAMES (1984).** The 1984 Summer Olympic Games were held in Los Angeles, California. The **Soviet Union** boycotted the games in retaliation for President **Jimmy Carter**'s decision not to participate in the Moscow Olympic Games in 1980. Carter made the decision four years earlier to protest the Soviet Union's invasion of **Afghanistan**.

**OPERATION DESERT SABRE.** Desert Sabre was the military offensive on the ground during the **Persian Gulf War**. Following the air campaign of **Operation Desert Storm**, on 24 February 1990, U.S. armed forces entered Iraq and **Kuwait**, captured Iraqi prisoners of war, and recaptured key cities and military positions. Two days later, most Iraqi troops began fleeing Kuwait, but set oil wells on fire as they left, creating a devastating ecological disaster. *See also* OPERATION DESERT SHIELD.

**OPERATION DESERT SHIELD.** Four days after Iraqi dictator **Saddam Hussein**'s invasion of **Kuwait** on 2 August 1990, President **George H. W. Bush** ordered 230,000 troops and two naval battalions to the Persian Gulf to protect Saudi Arabia. The military operation, dubbed Operation Desert Shield, was a defensive move aimed at deterring Hussein from any plans for further aggression in the region. President Bush subsequently ordered an additional 200,000 troops to the gulf in preparation for eventual offensive military operations to drive Hussein's army out of Kuwait. *See* OPERATION DESERT STORM; PERSIAN GULF WAR.

**OPERATION DESERT STORM.** Desert Storm was the offensive military operation by a multinational coalition, led by the United States and sanctioned by the **United Nations**, to drive Iraqi dictator **Saddam Hussein**'s troops out of **Kuwait** during the **Persian Gulf War**. Hussein invaded Kuwait on 2 August 1990. Four days later, President **George H. W. Bush** sent U.S. troops to protect Saudi Arabia, in what was known as **Operation Desert Shield**. Desert Shield was transformed into the offensive mission dubbed Desert Storm when Hussein refused to comply with United Nations Resolution 678, which called for the complete withdrawal of Iraqi forces from Kuwait by 15 January 1991. Two days later, the United States and coalition forces mounted a massive air campaign that effectively decimated the Iraqi air force and command-and-control facilities. The offensive enabled ground forces to enter Kuwait, recapture Iraqi-held positions, and drive Iraqi troops back into Iraq. *See* OPERATION DESERT SABRE; SCHWARZKOPF, H. NORMAN.

**OPERATION EL DORADO CANYON.** El Dorado Canyon was the name given to the offensive air strikes ordered by President **Ronald Reagan** against **Libya** on 14 April 1986. Reagan suspected Libyan complicity in the bombing of the La Belle discotheque in West Berlin—a nightclub frequented by U.S. service personnel—several weeks earlier. In addition, intelligence suggested Libya's dictator, **Muhammar Qaddafi**, had been sponsoring the **Abu Nidal** terrorist organization, which had attacked the Rome and Vienna airports in December 1985. Reagan could not win approval from French President **François Mitterrand** to allow U.S. planes to fly over France en route to Libya. Mitterrand's refusal strained U.S.–French relations. Reagan did win the support of British Prime Minister **Margaret Thatcher** to launch jets from U.S. bases in England, even if those jets were forced to fly an additional 1,300 miles around French airspace to reach their targets. F-111 aircraft based at Lakenheath, England, joined aircraft from aircraft carriers in the Mediterranean Sea and hit targets in Tripoli and Benghazi. Qaddafi's adopted daughter was killed during a raid on his compound. Two of his sons sustained injuries. Several civilian targets were also struck in the raids, killing 30 Libyans. One U.S. aircraft was shot down, killing both men on board. Qaddafi was unharmed and ordered missile attacks on U.S. military installations in Italy, which failed. Whether the downing of **Pan Am Flight 103** by Libyan terrorists on 21 December 1988, over **Lockerbie, Scotland**, was in retaliation for the raids on Tripoli and Benghazi remains an open question.

**OPERATION JUST CAUSE.** Just Cause was the code name given to the U.S. military invasion of the Central American nation of Panama ordered by President **George H. W. Bush** on 20 December 1989. Nearly 28,000 U.S. troops were involved in the invasion, which overwhelmed the tiny Panamanian Army and ousted **Manuel Noriega** from power. President Bush justified the invasion by alleging that Noriega was responsible for **drug trafficking**, had violated human rights, and posed a threat to the security of the Panama Canal. Bush also argued that a state of war existed between the United States and Panama following the killing of four U.S. servicemen by Panamanian forces. Within several days after the invasion, the U.S. military took over the main airport and quickly dominated Noriega's Panama Defense Force of approximately 3,000, and **Guillermo Endara** was sworn in as president of Panama. The United States believed Endara would have won the presidency had Noriega not cancelled regularly scheduled elections a year earlier. Noriega fled to the Vatican's diplomatic compound in Panama City, which was surrounded by U.S. troops. After days of blaring rock-and-roll music around the compound to increase the psychological pressure on Noriega, he surrendered to U.S. troops on 3 January 1990, was extradited to the United States, and was convicted on charges relating to drug trafficking. United States troops remained in Panama as part of the invasion force until late February 1990. Twenty-three U.S. troops were killed and 320 were wounded during the mission. It is estimated that between 500 and 1,000 Panamanians died during the invasion. Most countries in Central and South America condemned the invasion as unjustified, noting that Noriega had formerly been considered an ally of the United States.

**OPERATION STAUNCH.** President **Ronald Reagan** put into place a policy of stemming the flow of arms into the Persian Gulf during the **Iran–Iraq War**. The White House viewed Iran's revolutionary regime under **Ayatollah Khomeini** as a greater threat to stability in the region than Iraq. Although Reagan did not want Iraq to lose the military confrontation, he nevertheless sought to limit Iraqi access to weapons—which were readily provided by European and Middle Eastern governments. Colonel **Oliver North** and Admiral **John Poindexter** violated the stated policy when they masterminded the sale of arms to Iran in exchange for hostages in the **Iran–Contra** scandal. *See also* BOLAND AMENDMENT.

**OPERATION URGENT FURY.** *See* GRENADA.

**ORTEGA SAAVEDRA, DANIEL (1945– ).** At an early age, Ortega joined the **Sandinistas** (Frente Sandinista de Liberación Nacional, or FSLN, in Spanish), a leftist political organization opposed to **Nicaragua**'s president **Anastasio Somoza**. Ortega was imprisoned for guerrilla activities in the late 1960s but released in 1974. When the Sandinistas overthrew Somoza in 1979, Ortega joined the five-member junta that ruled the country. A schism among the junta members forced two to resign, effectively giving Ortega the most powerful position. Ortega won the election of 1984 and assumed the presidency, though opposition parties refused to take part. Ortega remained in office until 1990. For much of the 1980s, his authority was challenged by the Catholic Church and the **Contras**, the U.S.-backed insurgents supported by President **Ronald Reagan**. Ortega's close ties to Cuba, property seizures of the Somoza regime, and nationalizations were of particular concern in the closing decade of the **Cold War**. Years of de facto civil war contributed to Ortega's downfall, as he lost reelection in 1990. His subsequent efforts to win the presidency also failed. As of 2005, he remains the leader of the Sandinistas, which has continued representation in the Nicaraguan legislature.

## – P –

**PALESTINIAN LIBERATION ORGANIZATION (PLO).** Founded in 1964, the Palestinian Liberation Organization is a secular movement that is devoted to the establishment of a sovereign Palestinian state. **Abu Nidal** broke away from the PLO in 1974 to establish an Islamic-based organization that championed Palestinian independence. Yasser Arafat headed the PLO from 1969 until his death in 2004. Basing many of its paramilitary operations in Lebanon, the PLO used guerrilla warfare tactics to challenge **Israel**'s dominance in the occupied territories in the West Bank and Gaza Strip. The PLO was driven from Lebanon in 1982, following the Israeli occupation of that country. From 1985 to 1988, during the Lebanese civil war, Syrian-backed troops drove Palestinian refugees out of the country and brought mass suffering and death. In a watershed development in 1988, Arafat accepted Israel's right to exist in exchange for Palestinian statehood, as part of a set of **United Nations** resolutions aimed at resolving the Israeli–Palestinian conflict. *See also* TERRORISM; TERRORIST.

**PAN AM FLIGHT 103.** The downing of Pan Am Flight 103 by **Libyan** terrorists was the deadliest terrorist attack on U.S. citizens up to that point in time. Pan Am 103 began its journey in Frankfurt, Germany, on 21 December 1988, en route to its final destination in Detroit, Michigan, with stopovers in London and New York. On the London–New York leg of the commercial jet's flight, the aircraft exploded over the small town of **Lockerbie, Scotland**, killing everyone on board and an additional 11 people on the ground. One hundred and eighty-nine of those killed were Americans. British and American authorities determined that the explosion was caused by plastic explosives in the forward cargo hold. Joint investigations by the United

States and United Kingdom led to indictments for murder against Abdel Basset Ali al-Megrahi, a Libyan intelligence officer, and Lamin Khalifah Fhimah, a Libyan Arab Airlines station manager, both of whom were alleged to have connections to the **terrorist** organization of **Abu Nidal**. U.S. intelligence believed that the downing of Pan Am 103 was in retaliation for air strikes taken against Libya several years earlier in Benghazi and Tripoli, as part of **Operation El Dorado Canyon,** and the **USS** *Vincennes*'s accidental shooting down of Iran Air Flight 655. Investigators cited a phone call to the U.S. embassy in Helsinki, Finland, during which a threat was made against Pan Am. Libyan leader **Muhammar Qaddafi** refused to hand over documents or the indicted suspects until 1999. Megrahi was convicted by a Scottish court in 2001 and sentenced to 27 years in prison. Fhimah was acquitted on all counts.

**PANAMA.** *See* DRUG TRAFFICKING; NORIEGA MORENO, MANUEL ANTONIO; OPERATION JUST CAUSE; "WAR ON DRUGS."

**PERESTROIKA.** A Russian word (Перестройка) that translates as "restructuring," the term came to represent Soviet leader **Mikhail Gorbachev**'s economic reform effort, begun in 1987. Gorbachev enabled state-owned industries to set production based on consumer demand, withdrew government subsidies for unprofitable industries, and allowed foreign investment. Although the reform effort was considered intrepid, the Soviet economy nevertheless continued to suffer and became further crippled by high inflation. *See also GLASNOST*; SOVIET UNION.

**PEROT, H. (HENRY) ROSS (1930– ).** A native of Texarkana, Texas, Perot graduated from the United States Naval Academy in 1953 as president of his class and battalion commander. He spent time in Korea, and left the navy in 1957. After a brief career in sales and administration with International Business Machines (IBM), Perot founded his own Dallas-based company, Electronic Data Systems, which served the insurance industry. Within just 10 years, Perot transformed a small operation into a thriving national business and became a billionaire. Perot established his own foundation in 1969, which he used to give money to public schools in Dallas and to award grants to the Boy Scouts of America. Perot earned the attention of President Richard Nixon with efforts to draw public attention to American prisoners of war (POWs) in Vietnam through his United We Stand organization.

After a series of business fiascos with General Motors and controversy surrounding his POW activities in the 1980s, Perot decided to run for the presidency in 1992. He launched a populist campaign under the newly formed **United We Stand America** campaign organization. He argued that he was in a unique position as an outsider to apply business principles to government in order to improve sagging economic conditions. His opposition to the **North American Free Trade Agreement (NAFTA)** and other policy stands were elaborated in his 1992 book, *United We Stand: How We Can Take Back Our Country*. With his use of "electronic town hall" meetings and memorable, if sometimes controversial, one-line sound bites and prickly temperament (which was revealed in a debate with Democratic vice-presidential candidate **Al Gore** on the Cable News Network's *Larry King Live*), Perot gained momentum early in the 1992 election period, only to withdraw from the race in summer, when the Democratic ticket headed by **William Clinton** and **Al Gore** began to surge. In October Perot nevertheless reentered the race and eventually polled 19 percent of the popular vote—the best showing for a third party since Theodore Roosevelt's Bull Moose Party in 1912.

Although Perot won no electoral votes, many Republicans contend that he robbed the incumbent **George H. W. Bush** of reelection by drawing votes away from him and enabling William Clinton to win the White House with a narrow plurality (43 percent) of the national vote. Perot formed the **Reform Party** in 1994, and announced his second candidacy for the presidency in 1996. Nomination politics within the new party proved controversial, however, and once Perot had received the nomination he was not allowed to participate in the presidential debates. The Presidential Debate Commission determined he did not have a reasonable chance of success. Perot gained only 8 percent of the popular vote in the 1996 election. He left the political scene in 1997 after briefly becoming interested in campaign finance reform. He was opposed to **Patrick J. Buchanan**'s bid to run for the presidency under the Reform Party banner in 2000.

**PERSHING II MISSILES.** Pershing II were intermediate-range ballistic missiles deployed by the United States in Germany in 1984 to counter Soviet **SS-20 missiles**. The Pershing IIs were armed with low-yield nuclear warheads and could reach a distance of over 1,000 miles. West German chancellor **Helmut Kohl** supported the move despite strong internal opposition. The missiles were dismantled following the signing of the **Intermediate-Range Nuclear Forces (INF) Treaty** in 1988. *See also* ARMS CONTROL; DETERRENCE; GORBACHEV, MIKHAIL SERGEYEVICH; MUTUALLY ASSURED DESTRUCTION (MAD); REYKJAVÍK (SUMMIT).

**PERSIAN GULF WAR.** The Persian Gulf War began on 16 January 1991. The United States, alongside 33 other nations that composed an international coalition approved by the **United Nations**, took decisive military action against Iraq to liberate **Kuwait**. The action took place after Iraqi dictator **Saddam Hussein** invaded the tiny emirate on 2 August 1990 and failed to comply with United Nations resolutions that demanded he withdraw troops by 15 January 1991. The military operation, dubbed **Operation Desert Storm**, included over 660,000 U.S. troops. General **Norman Schwarzkopf** oversaw the allied operation.

The conflict stemmed from Hussein's contention that Kuwait was an Iraqi province that had wrongly been separated from the motherland. Beneath his rhetoric, however, was a starker political and economic reality. During the **Iran–Iraq War**, Iraq had borrowed money from several Arab countries, including Kuwait and Saudi Arabia, to finance its military efforts. When Kuwait refused to raise oil prices, which would have enabled Hussein to pay off the debts more easily, Hussein charged the emirate with "economic warfare." Hussein further argued that Kuwait was illegally tapping into Iraqi oil fields through the process of "slant drilling," a technique that pumps oil from horizontal rather than strictly vertical drilling. Iraq had also sustained large-scale damage to many of its ports in the Persian Gulf during the Iran–Iraq War, and Kuwait's coastal access was highly desirable for oil exports.

President **George H. W. Bush** refused to negotiate with Hussein and demanded full and unconditional withdrawal of Iraqi troops from Kuwait to reestablish the *status quo ante*. Chairman of the Joint

Chiefs of Staff **Colin Powell** initially opposed military options and sought to persuade President Bush to isolate Iraq through economic sanctions, a plan dubbed the "Powell Doctrine." President Bush rejected the idea, and Powell, Secretary of State **James Baker**, and Secretary of Defense **Richard Cheney** worked tirelessly alongside the president through diplomatic channels to assemble the unprecedented international coalition against Hussein. Participating countries included **Afghanistan**, Argentina, Australia, Bahrain, Bangladesh, Canada, **Czechoslovakia**, Denmark, Egypt, France, Greece, Hungary, Honduras, Italy, Kuwait, Morocco, the Netherlands, Niger, Norway, Oman, Pakistan, Poland, Portugal, Qatar, Saudi Arabia, Senegal, South Korea, Spain, Syria, Turkey, the United Arab Emirates, and the United Kingdom.

The initial air-campaign component of the war was over within approximately 96 hours, as allied forces overwhelmed and destroyed Iraq's air force and bases with over 1,000 missions a day. The ground component of the mission, called **Operation Desert Sabre**, began on 24 February 1991. Two days later Iraqi troops began to flee Kuwait, setting fire to oil fields as they departed, which caused an unparalleled environmental disaster. On 27 February, President Bush called a cease-fire and declared that Kuwait had been liberated. On 10 March, U.S. forces began departing from the gulf. Less than 400 allied troops were killed in the conflict, while estimates put the number of Iraqis killed anywhere from 100,000 to 300,000. Although President Bush's approval rating skyrocketed during the Persian Gulf War, he was criticized for not having pressed for the capture and removal of Saddam Hussein. Bush and his advisors hoped that Hussein would be overthrown internally, but correctly pointed out that the United Nations mandate did not sanction regime change in Iraq. When Kurds in the north of Iraq rebelled against Hussein, he used brutal force and chemical weapons to put down any insurrection—and Bush was further criticized for failing to intervene militarily.

In the aftermath of the war, allied forces enforced a "no-fly zone" in the northern and southern areas of Iraq to prohibit Hussein from any aggression against neighboring countries and to protect Kurdish and Shiite minorities in the north and south of the country, respectively. The policy was continued under the administration of **William**

**Clinton**. The United Nations also imposed economic sanctions against Iraq and an embargo against oil exports, notwithstanding a limited amount in exchange for food and medicine (the "oil for food" program). In retrospect, the Persian Gulf War was remarkable for the instantaneous **media** coverage of military operations, including media personnel embedded in military units. Nevertheless, news coverage and site visits were heavily censored to avoid jeopardizing the mission's success and to avert comparisons to the unpopular Vietnam War three decades earlier. *See also* FOREIGN POLICY; OPERATION DESERT SABRE; OPERATION DESERT SHIELD.

**PHILIPPINES.** The archipelago in southeast Asia was first occupied by the United States in 1901 and became a commonwealth of the United States in 1935. The Republic of the Philippines was established in 1946 following **World War II**. In November 1992, U.S. military forces left the nation permanently.

**PIERCE, SAMUEL RILEY, JR. (1922–2000).** A veteran of the army during **World War II**, Samuel Pierce was the only African American to serve in President **Ronald Reagan**'s cabinet. He was secretary of Housing and Urban Development (HUD) for the entirety of Reagan's two terms. Pierce earned a law degree from Yale, and served as a New York City district attorney and a U.S. attorney. He worked in the administration of Dwight Eisenhower as undersecretary of labor, was active in President Richard Nixon's 1968 election campaign, and became general counsel at the Treasury Department under Nixon. Pierce was also active in **civil rights** affairs, founding the Freedom National Bank — a New York–based black-owned bank. As HUD secretary, Pierce sought to rationalize administration of the agency's programs. By 1987, however, Pierce was thrown into the spotlight for a broadening scandal concerning widespread kickbacks and corruption at HUD. At issue were loans on failed housing projects dating to the early 1980s that cost taxpayers some $3 billion. Pierce took the Fifth Amendment when called before Congress to testify about alleged conspiracies to defraud the government. Several of Pierce's colleagues at HUD were convicted in multiple investigations, though he ultimately escaped prosecution. He died of a stroke in 2000 at his suburban Maryland home.

**POCKET VETO.** Under the U.S. Constitution, presidents may "pocket veto" legislation by refusing to sign a bill within a 10-day period during which Congress adjourns. In this case, the bill does not take effect and Congress must repass the legislation. Controversy over the pocket veto erupted in the administrations of **Ronald Reagan** and **George H. W. Bush**. They interpreted adjournment to mean any time Congress goes out of session. In the administration of George H. W. Bush, assistant counsel **William Barr** argued before Congress that pocket vetoes are permissible any time Congress goes out of session for more than three days, since one chamber cannot do so without the permission of the other. This broad interpretation of the pocket veto power conflicts with more narrow interpretations held by members of Congress. The courts have not definitively settled the question to date. *See also* GRAY, C. BOYDEN.

**POINDEXTER, JOHN MARLAN (1936– ).** Poindexter earned notoriety for his involvement in the **Iran–Contra** scandal during the presidency of **Ronald Reagan**. A graduate of the U.S. Naval Academy and a nuclear physicist with a doctorate from Caltech, Poindexter served in the navy from 1958 until 1987, retiring with the rank of admiral. Among his notable service accomplishments were his command of a destroyer squadron and various high-level staff assignments, including executive assistant to the chief of naval operations and administrative assistant to the secretary of the navy. Poindexter joined the Reagan administration in 1981 when he became a military advisor. In 1983 he rose to deputy national security advisor, and from 1985 to 1986 was **national security advisor** to the president. He played an important role in developing Reagan's foreign and national security policies, including the **Strategic Defense Initiative** and the **Reykjavík** Summit with Soviet General Secretary **Mikhail Gorbachev**. He is best remembered for his role in the Iran–Contra affair. Special prosecutor **Lawrence Walsh**'s investigation led to Poindexter's indictment and ultimate conviction for conspiracy, obstruction of justice, and lying to Congress. Particularly egregious was his destruction of documents and e-mail correspondence involving the Iran–Contra scandal. However, as with his colleague Colonel **Oliver North**, Poindexter's conviction was overturned in 1991 when a court decided that a previous grant of immunity in testimony before Congress constituted a violation of procedure.

From 1988 to 2002, Poindexter worked in the private sector as a consultant and executive at several high-technology and defense firms. He briefly returned to public service in 2002 to head the Defense Advanced Research Projects Agency, which was charged with developing information technologies to prevent future **terrorist** attacks. The project came under severe criticism from civil libertarians, and Congress scrapped it in 2003.

**POINTE DU HOC, FRANCE.** Pointe du Hoc is the site of the **World War II** allied invasion of Normandy on 6 June 1944. **Ronald Reagan** visited Pointe du Hoc on the 40th anniversary of D-Day in 1984 after a ceremony at Utah Beach with French President **François Mitterrand**, Canadian Prime Minister Pierre Trudeau, Queen Elizabeth of Britain, and the heads of other European nations. Reagan's speech at Pointe du Hoc, written by speechwriter **Peggy Noonan**, was among his most memorable. Reagan stood before a group of veterans and brought tears to their eyes as he recalled the bravery of the soldiers who disembarked a British carrier to wage battle in Nazi-occupied France: "We stand on a lonely, windswept point on the northern shore of France. The air is soft, but 40 years ago at this moment, the air was dense with smoke and the cries of men, and the air was filled with the crack of rifle fire and the roar of cannon. . . . These are the boys of Pointe du Hoc. These are the men who took the cliffs. These are the champions who helped free a continent. These are the heroes who helped end a war . . ."

**POLLARD, JONATHAN (1954– ).** Pollard worked as an intelligence officer for the U.S. Navy. He was convicted of spying for **Israel** in 1986, and received a life sentence in prison. The extent of classified material he handed over to the Israelis was never revealed. His punishment was the subject of great controversy, as the sentencing judge was given a detailed memorandum by Secretary of Defense **Caspar Weinberger** on the impact of Pollard's activities that defense attorneys were not allowed to review. In addition, Israel has repeatedly demanded that Pollard, a Jew, be released and allowed to come to

Israel. Those pleas were rejected by presidents **Ronald Reagan**, **George H. W. Bush**, and **William Clinton**.

**POPE JOHN PAUL II (1920–2004).** Born Karol Józef Wojtyła in Poland, John Paul became pope of the Catholic Church in October 1978. He was the first non-Italian to reign as pope in over 400 years, and his tenure was the third longest in church history. He survived two assassination attempts in the early 1980s. On 13 May 1981, he was shot twice in St. Peter's Square by a Turk named Mehmet Ali Ağca. The pope visited Ağca in prison and pardoned him. Ağca first claimed that he had been hired by the Soviet **KGB** through Bulgarian intermediaries to kill the pope because of his support of the **Solidarity** movement in Poland. John Paul II survived a second attempt on his life in Portugal on 12 May 1982. A Spanish priest named Juan María Fernández y Krohn attempted to stab the pope with a bayonet, but was captured by guards before he could carry out his attack. Pope John Paul II died in 2004 of natural causes, and in 2005, his successor, Pope Benedict XVI, initiated the process to have John Paul II beatified.

**POWELL, COLIN LUTHER (1937– ).** A decorated veteran born in New York City, Powell was a central figure in the administrations of presidents **Ronald Reagan**, **George H. W. Bush**, and **George W. Bush**. He graduated from the City College of New York with a degree in geology, and later earned a master of business administration from George Washington University. Powell entered military service in 1958 as a second lieutenant, served in Korea, and during his 35-year military career was promoted to the rank of four-star general. He served as **national security advisor** to President Reagan from 1987 to 1989. He became chairman of the Joint Chiefs of Staff under President George H. W. Bush in 1989, and remained in that post until 1993. He was an integral part of President Bush's **foreign policy** team during **Operation Desert Storm** and the **Persian Gulf War** following Iraqi dictator **Saddam Hussein**'s invasion of **Kuwait**. Though Powell generally advocated military solutions as a last resort to international disputes, he is attributed with the success of the strategy in Operation Desert Storm, whereby massive air strikes effectively disabled Hussein's defenses and enabled a successful allied invasion of Iraq.

Following George H. W. Bush's defeat in the presidential election of 1992, Powell retired from the army, returned to private life, and wrote an autobiography entitled *My American Journey* (1995). A popular figure and moderate Republican, Powell was urged by some to run for the presidency in 1996, but declined. He returned to public service in 2001 when President **George W. Bush** nominated him to the post of secretary of state. Powell earned the distinction of becoming the highest-ranking African American in the history of U.S. government. His initial opposition to the invasion of Iraq in 2003 ran counter to the stances of many in Bush's cabinet. Powell subsequently led the diplomatic charge to build international support for an invasion, however dubious the evidence was that Hussein had weapons of mass destruction that threatened neighboring countries or the United States. Powell resigned as secretary of state in late 2004, and returned to private life with his wife. His civilian awards include a Congressional Gold Medal and two presidential Medals of Freedom.

**PRESIDENTIAL TASK FORCE ON REGULATORY RELIEF.** On 17 February 1981, President **Ronald Reagan** signed Executive Order 12291. The order sought to "reduce the burdens of existing and future regulations, increase agency accountability for regulatory actions, provide for presidential oversight of the regulatory process, minimize duplication and conflict of regulations, and ensure well-reasoned regulations." The order also set up a task force on regulatory relief, headed by Vice President **George H. W. Bush**. Reagan's focus on regulation enhanced significantly the authority of the **Office of Management and Budget** to review regulatory proposals by agencies and departments of the federal government. *See also* COUNCIL ON COMPETITIVENESS; OFFICE OF INFORMATION AND REGULATORY AFFAIRS (OIRA).

**PRICE WATERHOUSE V. HOPKINS (1989).** *See* CIVIL RIGHTS.

**PROFESSIONAL AIR TRAFFIC CONTROLLERS ORGANIZATION (PATCO).** On 3 August 1981, the labor union representing air traffic controllers went on strike, despite an earlier warning by President **Ronald Reagan** that such a strike would violate federal law and jeopardize air transportation safety. The union sought higher wages, an improvement in working conditions, and a reduction in work-week schedules. Reagan used his authority under the Taft–Hartley labor relations legislation of 1947 to order the air traffic controllers back to work. When they refused to return to their jobs by the president's deadline of 5 August, Reagan summarily fired over 11,000 controllers. Reagan's decision remains controversial. His supporters applauded his decisiveness. Detractors contend that he used the strike as a pretext to deal a significant blow to organized labor.

# – Q –

**QADDAFI, MUHAMMAR (1942– ).** Libyan military dictator Qaddafi seized power in 1969 by overthrowing pro-Western monarch King Idris. Although he has no formal title in government, Qaddafi is heralded as the leader of the revolution and is de facto leader of **Libya**. In the 1980s and 1990s, the United States considered Qaddafi a state sponsor of **terrorism**, with connections to the **Palestinian Liberation Organization**, the Iranian Revolution of **Ayatollah Khomeini**, and worldwide **terrorist** incidents dating to the 1970s, including the bombing of a West Berlin nightclub frequented by U.S. service personnel and the downing of **Pan Am Flight 103** over **Lockerbie, Scotland**. In 1986 Qaddafi claimed waters in the Gulf of Sidra were territorial and not international. Several skirmishes between U.S. naval vessels and Libyan patrol boats ensued. In April 1986, President **Ronald Reagan** ordered the bombing of targets in Tripoli and Benghazi (**Operation El Dorado Canyon**) in retaliation for alleged Libyan involvement in the West Berlin nightclub bombing. Qaddafi has recently moderated his stances, offering public apologies for the Lockerbie bombing, renouncing terrorism, and seeking conciliation with the West. President **George W. Bush** lifted the embargo and travel restrictions on Libya, in place since the 1980s.

**QUAYLE, JAMES DANFORTH (DAN) (1947– ).** A native of Indianapolis, Indiana, Quayle was born on 4 February 1947. He graduated with a degree in political science from De Pauw University (1969). He served in the Indiana National Guard from 1969 to 1975, and earned a law degree from Indiana University in 1974. He got his start in politics at the state level as an investigator for the attorney general's office. He later served as an assistant to Indiana Governor Edgar Whitcomb (1973–74) and became director of the Inheritance Tax Division of the Indiana Department of Revenue. From 1974 to 1976, Quayle was associate publisher and general manager of his family-owned newspaper, the *Huntington Herald Press*. He entered national politics in 1976, winning two terms to the U.S. House of Representatives. He successfully ran twice for the U.S. Senate (1980, 1986), and resigned his seat to join **George H. W. Bush**'s presidential ticket. He served as vice president of the United States from 1989 to 1993.

Quayle was often mocked by the **media** for his reputation for bizarre quotations and frequent verbal mistakes, including his insistence at a student spelling bee that the word *potato* was spelled "potatoe." He was nonetheless an integral part of the Bush White House, serving as chair of the National Space Council and as head of the **Council on Competitiveness**, a body tasked with applying cost-benefit analyses to congressional regulatory efforts. Quayle is author of *Standing Firm: A Vice-Presidential Memoir* (1994) and *Worth Fighting For* (1999). He considered a run for the Republican presidential nomination in 2000, but withdrew after placing eighth in the Iowa caucuses.

**QUAYLE COUNCIL.** *See* COUNCIL ON COMPETITIVENESS.

**QUIGLEY, JOAN (1927– ).** An astrologer, Quigley came into the public eye in 1988 when former White House **chief of staff Donald Regan** revealed in his memoir, *For the Record*, that First Lady **Nancy Reagan** regularly consulted an astrologer about President **Ronald Reagan**'s schedule. Quigley had become acquainted with Mrs. Reagan a decade earlier when television celebrity Merv Griffin introduced them. The extent of Quigley's involvement in White House affairs is disputed. In her book *My Turn*, Mrs. Reagan contends that consultations were of limited importance. Quigley argues that her counsel influenced President Reagan's travel and meeting schedules, particularly after the 1981 assassination attempt by **John Hinckley Jr.**

**– R –**

**RACE RIOTS (LOS ANGELES).** The race riots that swept Los Angeles, California, beginning on 29 April 1992, stemmed from the acquittal by an all-white jury of four police officers on all but one count in the beating of suspect **Rodney King**. King, who had been convicted previously of drunk driving, had been stopped by the police on 3 March 1991, and was believed to be under the influence of drugs. When he refused to cooperate with police, the officers beat and restrained King with taser guns. The beating was videotaped by a bystander and broadcast nationally. Critics of the officers charged that the beating was excessive and typical of racism and racial profiling perpetrated by the Los Angeles Police Department, headed by Commissioner Daryl Gates. The officers and their supporters contended that King had refused to comply, and the amount of force was necessary given his demeanor and alleged drug use.

When the nationally covered trial ended in the officers' acquittal, rioting broke out all over Los Angeles. Stores were looted, buildings set ablaze, and police and firefighters shot at by residents. Bystanders and shopkeepers were killed or beaten, and many of the horrific events were captured on live television from helicopters circling the city. Perhaps the most stunning was the beating of Reginald Denny, a truck driver who had stopped at a traffic light, was pulled from his vehicle and beaten, and then received a blow to the head with a brick by his assailant. The rioting spread outward from central Los Angeles over the next two to three days. California Governor Pete Wilson ordered National Guard troops to the city and later requested federal troops to restore order. In a plea for calm on the third day of the riots, King himself was televised asking, "Can't we all get along?" On 1 May, President **George H. W. Bush** addressed the nation and condemned the violence, vowed to restore order, and promised that federal authorities would investigate the acquittal of the police officers. Fifty-eight people were killed during the mob violence, which lasted nearly a week. A year later, two of the officers were convicted of violating federal **civil rights** in the beating of King.

**"READ MY LIPS, NO NEW TAXES."** During his acceptance speech for the presidential nomination at the Republican Convention in

1988, **George H. W. Bush** made the pledge that if elected, he would reject any new **tax** increase. The sound bite became an integral part of his general-election campaign. Critics charge that Bush reneged on this pledge in the **Budget Agreement of 1990**. Faced with a large Democratic majority in Congress and a mounting federal deficit, Bush accepted some tax increases to avoid congressionally mandated automatic cuts in entitlement programs such as **Social Security** and **Medicare**. During his reelection effort in 1992, Bush met intense criticism from Republican primary challenger **Patrick Buchanan** on the issue. Similarly, in the general campaign Democratic candidate **William Clinton** used the phrase to demonstrate the president's alleged duplicity. *See also* GRAMM–RUDMAN–HOLLINGS ACT.

**REAGAN DOCTRINE.** The so-called Reagan Doctrine was the president's pledge to support anti-Communist insurgencies against Soviet-backed regimes around the world, including **Afghanistan, Angola**, and Central America. Reagan elaborated his view in his State of the Union address in 1985, in which he stated, "Support for freedom fighters is self-defense." The Reagan Doctrine was aimed at countering Soviet General Secretary **Leonid Brezhnev**'s claim (the **Brezhnev Doctrine**) that the **Soviet Union** had the right to intervene militarily in countries in its sphere of influence. *See also* COLD WAR; CONTRAS; EL SALVADOR; GORBACHEV, MIKHAIL SERGEYEVICH; NATIONAL SECURITY DECISION DIRECTIVE (NSDD) 32; NICARAGUA; SINATRA DOCTRINE.

**REAGAN, NANCY DAVIS (1921– ).** Born on 6 July 1921 in New York City and raised in Chicago, First Lady Nancy Reagan is a graduate of Smith College (1943), where she studied drama. She returned to New York after college and worked for six years as a stage performer on Broadway and other shows, including the musical *Lute Song*. She moved to Hollywood, California, in 1949 to work for Metro-Goldwyn-Mayer, and starred in 11 films over the following seven years, including *East Side, West Side* (1949), *Shadow on the Wall* (1950), and *The Next Voice You Hear* (1950). She met her husband, **Ronald Reagan**, in 1951 when he was president of the Screen Actors Guild, and they were married a year later. In 1956 she starred opposite her husband in the film *Hellcats of the Navy*. She is mother to Patti and Ronald Jr., and stepmother to President Reagan's children Maureen (1941–2001) and Michael from his first marriage, to **Jane Wyman**.

Nancy Reagan's preparation for the role of first lady began when Ronald Reagan won the California governor's race in 1966. While in Sacramento she was particularly active on Vietnam veterans' issues, including prisoners of war. Following her husband's victory in the 1980 presidential election, Nancy spent the next eight years focusing on drug abuse, and became an advocate for the Foster Grandparent program, which places disadvantaged children with senior citizens. Her tireless campaign against drug and alcohol abuse among America's youth was on behalf of the "Just Say No" Foundation. She was not without controversy as first lady, however. She was criticized for allegedly consulting an astrologer to aid her husband's policy decisions (*see* QUIGLEY, JOAN) and for lavish renovations and redecorations in the White House. After leaving Washington in 1989, she established the Nancy Reagan Foundation, which continues to promote drug abuse awareness. She has written four books, including *To Love a Child*, the proceeds of which were donated to the Foster Grandparent program. Her biography *My Turn: The Memoirs of Nancy Reagan* was published in 1989, and in 2002 she released *I Love You, Ronnie: The Letters of Ronald Reagan to Nancy Reagan*.

**REAGAN, RONALD WILSON (1911–2004).** The 40th president of the United States was born on 6 February 1911 in Tampico, Illinois, to Nelle and John Reagan. He attended high school in Dixon, Illinois, during which time he worked part-time as a lifeguard. He graduated from Eureka College, a small Christian liberal arts school, in 1932. He was an avid swimmer and football player, and earned degrees in both sociology and economics. Reagan began a broadcasting career shortly thereafter, announcing Chicago Cubs baseball games for WOC (later WHO) radio in Davenport, Iowa. In 1937 Warner Brothers Studios offered him a seven-year movie contract. He starred in *Love Is in the Air* (1938), *Brother Rat* (1938), and *Brother Rat and a Baby* (1940). His heartrending role as Notre Dame football player George "The Gip" Gipper opposite Pat O'Brien in *Knute Rockne All American* (1940) won him widespread acclaim—and gave him an unforgettable phrase he would resurrect decades later, as president, when he squared off with Congress: "Win one for the Gipper."

Reagan married actress **Jane Wyman** in 1940. Their first daughter, Maureen, was born in 1941. That same year Reagan was elected president of the Screen Actors Guild (he would serve five terms, until 1960) and was also drafted into the U.S. Navy. Due to vision problems that kept him from the battlefield, Reagan was assigned to the Motion Picture Army Unit in Culver City, California—dubbed "Fort Roach"—where he made **World War II** training and propaganda films. The 1942 release of *Kings Row*, in which Reagan starred as Drake McHugh, represented the acme of his film career. Reagan nearly won an Academy Award for his portrayal of a wounded young man who wakes up to find his legs amputated, and cries out, "Where's the rest of me?" After adopting a son, Michael Edward, in 1945, Ronald Reagan and Jane Wyman divorced in 1948. Wyman charged Reagan with "mental cruelty," but many factors—including Reagan's deepening interest in politics and allegations of an affair between Wyman and a fellow actor—have been speculated as responsible for the breakup.

In 1952 Reagan married **Nancy Davis (Reagan)**, an actress under contract with MGM. Their daughter Patricia was born later that same year, during which time Reagan campaigned for Republican presidential nominee Dwight D. Eisenhower. In 1954 Reagan became the host of *General Electric Theater*, a Sunday-evening television show. For the next eight years he made appearances at General Electric facilities around the country and developed his political ideas. Reagan costarred with Nancy in the 1957 production *Hellcats of the Navy*, and their son, Ronald Prescott, was born in 1958. In 1960 Reagan campaigned earnestly for "Democrats for Nixon"; in 1962 he officially changed his party affiliation to Republican. General Electric Theater fired Reagan in 1962 for a speech in which he criticized the Tennessee Valley Authority, an icon of the New Deal, as an example of "big government." His final acting job was as host of *Death Valley Days* (1964); that same year he starred in his last film, *The Killers*.

His transformation from Roosevelt Democrat to conservative Republican was an evolutionary process. Reagan's championing of limited government and concern with the threat of Communism were undoubtedly influenced by his experiences as president of the Screen

Actors Guild. He had testified in front of the House Un-American Activities Committee (HUAC) in 1947 about the alleged infiltration of Communists in Hollywood. He became increasingly skeptical of the Conference of Studio Unions, an amalgam of labor unions representing the film industry, which he believed had become a front organization for Communists. In 1964, as cochair of California Republicans for Barry Goldwater's presidential candidacy, Reagan made one of his most important speeches. In "A Time for Choosing," he lambasted the growth of "big government" and threats to individual liberty. Although Goldwater lost the election to Lyndon Johnson in a landslide, Reagan's stances struck a chord with California voters, who elected him governor in 1966 and again in 1970. In 1969, when rioting students at the University of California, Berkeley, took over a parking lot (the People's Park protests), Reagan ordered National Guard troops to occupy the campus. One student was killed and several were injured in scuffles with authorities.

Reagan was widely hailed for his fiscal policies while governor of California. He balanced the state budget and turned a record deficit of $200 million into a surplus by trimming government expenditures. Leaving Sacramento in 1974, Reagan mounted a failed effort to challenge incumbent president Gerald Ford for the Republican nomination in 1976. He was particularly critical of Ford's efforts at **détente** with the **Soviet Union**. Reagan won 47 percent of the delegates at the Republican convention, and laid the groundwork for his 1980 campaign in an impassioned convention speech on the dangers of Communism.

Reagan successfully won the 1980 Republican presidential nomination, chose **George H. W. Bush** as his running mate, and campaigned vigorously against Democratic incumbent **Jimmy Carter**. The campaign proceeded against the backdrop of the **Iranian hostage crisis**. Reagan criticized Carter for weak leadership in **foreign policy**, high **taxes**, and a national economic slump linked to high interest rates and high energy prices. During the presidential debates, Reagan emphasized these points by asking voters, "Are you better off today than you were four years ago?" Reagan won the election with 50.7 percent of the popular vote; he swept the Electoral College with 489 votes to Carter's 49. A 12-seat gain for Senate Republicans gave the GOP the majority for the first time since 1954, though Democrats retained control of the House of Representatives. At 69 years of age, Reagan was the oldest president to enter the Oval Office.

On 30 March 1981, just 69 days after Reagan had taken the oath of office, **John Hinckley Jr.** fired six shots at the president as he and his entourage left the Washington Hilton. Reagan survived the assassination attempt, but was shot in the chest. Three other members of the entourage, including press secretary **James Brady**, were wounded. Although Reagan recovered quickly and his public approval soared, Secretary of State **Alexander Haig**'s misunderstanding of presidential succession caused the White House embarrassment immediately following the shooting. Haig told the White House press corps that he was "in charge."

Reagan's most important first-term legislative victories in the domestic realm included the **Economic Recovery Tax Act (1981)** and the Omnibus Budget Reconciliation Act of 1981, which were core components of **Reaganomics**—the president's supply-side approach (sometimes referred to as "trickle-down economics") to economic management. The strategy was aimed at lowering inflation and interest rates to spur economic growth. Reagan won reelection in 1984 with nearly 60 percent of the popular vote in a landslide victory over Democratic standard-bearer **Walter Mondale**. Mondale publicly acknowledged he would raise taxes, and the Reagan campaign skillfully exploited that misstep with television ads that portrayed the rebirth of American prosperity and jobs ("**Morning Again in America**"). In 1986 Reagan prompted Congress to simplify the tax code with passage of the **Tax Reform Act (1986)**.

In the foreign policy realm Reagan advocated "peace through strength," and won significant increases in defense spending to compete with the Soviet Union's military and nuclear warfare capability. Because these increases were not offset by reductions in domestic social spending, Reagan's budget policies contributed to massive federal deficits and a tripling of the national debt over his two terms, even as unemployment and inflation lessened. Reagan's more confrontational approach to the Soviets and his insistence on increasing the United States' capability for **deterrence** against the Soviet nuclear arsenal marked a break with the policy of détente, dating to the presidency of Richard Nixon. Reagan's strategy, outlined in **National Security Decision Directive (NSDD) 32**, was aimed at undermining the Soviet Union through economic, military, and covert means, but arguably heightened **Cold War** tensions. Reagan also proposed the **Strategic Defense Initiative (SDI)**, dubbed "Star Wars" by the press. The space-based defense system to shield the United States from Soviet **intercontinental ballistic missiles (ICBMs)** would have violated the 1972 **Anti–Ballistic Missile (ABM) Treaty** with the Soviet Union, and many experts believed such a system to be unworkable. Nonetheless, Soviet General Secretary **Mikhail Gorbachev** apparently believed the Soviet Union could not sustain the economic costs of attempting to compete with the United States, and instead pursued a series of **arms control** agreements, including the **Intermediate-Range Nuclear Forces (INF)** and **Strategic Arms Reduction Treaty (START)** treaties. The conclusion of these treaties also followed Reagan's decision to deploy **Pershing II** and land-based Tomahawk **cruise missiles** in Western Europe to counter the Soviets' installation of short-range **SS-20 missiles**.

Reagan also supported anti-Communist movements and insurgencies in the 1980s, including **Solidarity** in Poland, the **mujahadeen** in Soviet-occupied **Afghanistan**, factions loyal to **Jonas Savimbi** in **Angola**, and the **Contras** in **Nicaragua**. The administration's activities in Nicaragua led to revelations of the **Iran–Contra** affair in 1987, which was subsequently investigated by **independent counsel Lawrence Walsh** and the **Tower Commission** appointed by the president. The **Boland Amendment** adopted by Congress prohibited military aid to the **Contras**. Between 1984 and 1986, the administration traded arms for hostages being held by Iran, and diverted the profits to the Contras. Although Reagan was never directly implicated in the scandal, **Oliver North** and Admiral **John Poindexter** were convicted, but they were acquitted on appeal. Defense Secretary **Caspar Weinberger**, also implicated in the scandal, resigned in 1987; he was later pardoned by President **George H. W. Bush**.

U.S. forces were also involved in multinational peacekeeping efforts in Lebanon, where 241 Marines were killed in a car bombing of their barracks in **Beirut** in 1982. Reagan also took unilateral military action in **Grenada (Operation Urgent Fury)** to rescue medical students under alleged threat from the country's pro-Cuban government, as well as in **Libya** on leader **Muhammar Qaddafi**'s compound in retaliation for the bombing of a nightclub frequented by U.S. soldiers in West Berlin.

Reagan left office in 1989 with a popularity rating of 63 percent—higher than for any president since Franklin D. Roosevelt. In February 1994, Reagan announced that he had Alzheimer's disease. He died at the age of 93 on 5 June 2004 at his ranch in Santa Barbara, California. His 1981 autobiography is entitled *Where's the Rest of Me?* The Ronald Reagan Presidential Library opened in 1991 in Simi Valley, California, and houses archival holdings for his administration.

**"REAGANOMICS."** President **Ronald Reagan**'s economic program was often referred to as "Reaganomics" and called "trickle-down economics" by some. Reagan supported a "supply-side" approach to encourage economic growth and control inflation by cutting government spending and supporting across-the-board **tax** cuts to individuals and corporations. Supply-side economics theorizes a specific amount of money should be available in the economy regardless of demand, and that individuals and corporations will use tax savings to invest in and create new businesses. Tax cuts would then be offset later by higher government revenues. When running against Reagan in the 1980 primaries, **George H. W. Bush** had referred to Reagan's call for tax cuts combined with higher military expenditures as **"voodoo economics**," a phrase he came to regret as vice president. The consequences of Reagan's early economic policies did increase the national deficit dramatically over the course of his two terms. The federal debt was $930 billion in early 1981 and reached $2.6 trillion when Reagan left office. Detractors contend that Reaganomics slowed economic growth and contributed significantly to greater income inequality. Supporters contend that Reagan's economic policies cut government waste, trimmed federal domestic spending, and reinvigorated the economy. Increased military spending with which the **Soviet Union** could not compete, they argue, was a factor in precipitating the collapse of the Communist regime and ending the **Cold War**. *See also* ECONOMIC RECOVERY TAX ACT (1981); GRAMM–RUDMAN–HOLLINGS ACT.

**REFORM PARTY.** Having run for the presidency in 1992 as an independent who garnered 19 percent of the popular vote, millionaire businessman **H. Ross Perot** formed the Reform Party in 1994 and announced his second candidacy for the presidency in 1996 under the party's banner. The party drew support from voters disillusioned with the Democratic and Republican Parties. The Reform Party's platform under Perot emphasized fiscal responsibility and an adversity to free trade, in addition to a reform of campaign finance laws.

Perot's 1996 campaign was hampered by his late entry into the presidential race and the decision by the Federal Elections Commission (FEC) to not allow him to participate in the presidential debates between Democratic incumbent **William Clinton** and Republican standard-bearer **Robert Dole**. Perot had taken part in the 1992 presidential debates as an independent and made compelling arguments about the economy and his opposition to the **North American Free Trade Agreement**. However, between 1992 and 1996 the FEC changed the rules governing presidential debates, which effectively shut out Perot and other third-party candidates. Perot won 8 percent of the national vote in 1996 and no Electoral College votes.

**Patrick Buchanan**, a conservative Republican who challenged incumbent President **George H. W. Bush** for the GOP nomination in 1992 and lost after a bitter primary campaign, gravitated toward the Reform Party in the late 1990s. Buchanan advocated tougher policies on immigration, abortion, and tax reductions—and his social conservatism was at odds with Perot's prior platform. Much to Perot's chagrin, Buchanan attempted to capture the Reform Party nomination for the presidency in 2000. He was ultimately unsuccessful, and pro- and anti-Buchanan demonstrators clashed at the party's national committee meeting; the ensuing infighting dashed any chances of electoral success. Buchanan attempted to attract registered voters by running under the "Freedom Party" banner in various states, which he claimed was the "real" party of rank-and-file Reform Party activists. But he ultimately lost the Reform Party nomination when he and his supporters were unable to obtain the requisite two-thirds of delegates at the party convention. The party remained in disarray through the 2004 presidential elections, throwing its support to Ralph Nader rather than fielding a candidate of its own.

**REGAN, DONALD THOMAS (1918– ).** A graduate of Harvard Law School (1940) and a Marine Corps veteran for his service during **World War II** in the Pacific, including combat at Guadalcanal and

Okinawa, Regan joined the investment firm of Merrill Lynch in 1946. Over the course of the next several decades, he worked his way to the top of the firm, becoming chairman and chief executive in 1971. At Merrill Lynch Regan was responsible for diversifying the brokerage house's products and services, and in the process he tripled the firm's earnings and accrued a personal fortune himself. President **Ronald Reagan** tapped him to serve as his first secretary of the treasury. Regan supported **tax** reform and became the primary advocate of the administration's economic policy until 1985, when he exchanged positions with **James A. Baker III** and became **chief of staff** in Reagan's second term. Regan resigned in early 1987 as disagreements with First Lady **Nancy Reagan** and revelations of the **Iran–Contra** scandal eroded his position. The **Tower Commission** reproved Regan for applying excessive personal influence over the White House staff and for failing to ensure the integrity of the policy/advisory process surrounding the decision to sell arms for hostages, while others suggested Regan had not gone far enough to insulate the president from the scandal. In his memoirs, *For the Record: From Wall Street to Washington* (1989), Regan stirred ample controversy by accusing Nancy Reagan of his ouster. He also alleged that she was obsessed with astrology, soliciting the advice of astrologist **Joan Quigley** to the point that it interfered with the president's schedule. Regan retired to Virginia following his White House service.

**REHNQUIST, WILLIAM HUBBS (1924–2005).** A native of Milwaukee, Wisconsin, Rehnquist was a **World War II** veteran who later received degrees from Harvard and a law degree from Stanford, where he graduated first in his class. He clerked for **Supreme Court** Justice Robert Jackson before taking up private practice in Arizona from 1953 to 1969. Rehnquist worked in President Richard Nixon's Office of White House Counsel from 1969 to 1971. Nixon nominated him to associate justice of the Supreme Court to replace John Marshall Harlan in 1971. The Senate confirmed Rehnquist 68–21, and he took up his post in January 1972.

Rehnquist evidenced a conservative voting record as an associate justice, writing critical opinions on desegregation and opposing the *Roe v. Wade* decision of 1973, which legalized **abortion**. When Chief Justice Warren Burger retired in 1986, President **Ronald Reagan** nominated Rehnquist to take his place. Rehnquist was confirmed by a Senate vote of 65–25, and **Antonin Scalia** was later tapped by Reagan to fill the associate justice position created by Rehnquist's elevation to chief justice. Rehnquist and Scalia were considered among the most conservative members of the high court during the administrations of Reagan, **George H. W. Bush**, and **William Clinton**. Rehnquist died of complications from thyroid cancer on 3 September 2005. His support for states' rights, particularly in reference to the wall separating church from state, is one of his most controversial legacies.

**REYKJAVÍK (SUMMIT).** On 11–12 October 1986, President **Ronald Reagan** and Soviet General Secretary **Mikhail Gorbachev** met in Reykjavík, Iceland. The two-day summit was held to discuss nuclear weapons and Reagan's **Strategic Defense Initiative (SDI)** or "Star Wars"—a space-based system to shoot down incoming missiles, which the **Soviet Union** contended would violate the 1972 **Anti–Ballistic Missile Treaty** signed by the United States and Soviet Union. Surprisingly, the meeting nearly produced a far-reaching reduction in nuclear weapons, despite observers' pessimism. Reagan proposed eliminating all offensive nuclear weapons in 10 years, and Gorbachev reciprocated by proposing to eliminate not only all offensive weapons but all *strategic weapons* in the Soviet arsenal. Any chances for agreement collapsed, however, when Reagan clarified that he was unwilling to scrap SDI. British Prime Minister **Margaret Thatcher** became particularly alarmed that Reagan was nevertheless willing to conclude such an agreement without consultation with **North Atlantic Treaty Organization (NATO)** allies. Although the summit failed, it succeeded in fostering a closer working relationship between Reagan and Gorbachev (who had only met once earlier). The summit laid the groundwork for the **Intermediate-Range Nuclear Forces (INF) Treaty**, concluded between the United States and Soviet Union in December 1987. *See also* ARMS CONTROL; DÉTENTE; DETERRENCE; FOREIGN POLICY; WARSAW PACT.

**ROBERTSON, MARION GORDON (PAT) (1930– ).** A Virginia native, Robertson is a prominent conservative television evangelist. He is host of the *700 Club*, and founded the Christian Broadcasting Network, the **Christian Coalition**, and Regent University. A Republican, Robertson entered the 1988 presidential primaries and emphasized conservative themes, including balancing the federal budget and allowing biblical teachings in public schools. His campaign was harmed by controversy over his statements about his military service during the Korean War. Robertson claimed he had been in combat, whereas men who served with him emerged to contend that he never saw combat. The controversy ended up in a lawsuit Robertson filed, and later dropped, against two Democratic members of Congress over the matter. Robertson's primary campaign never gained momentum, and he ultimately dropped out of the race and threw his support to **George H. W. Bush**. Robertson later founded the Christian Coalition as a means of influencing politics. The organization began as a voter-mobilization effort and became an important source of support for Republican candidates in the 1990s. Robertson left the Christian Coalition in 2001. His stances on homosexuality and the role of religion in government, and his focus on eschatology, in addition to staunch support for **Israel**, remain controversial. In 2005 he stirred ample controversy when he called for the assassination of Venezuelan leader Hugo Chávez. Robertson is author of over a dozen books, including *The New World Order* (1991) and *Courting Disaster: How the Supreme Court Is Usurping the Power of Congress and the People* (2004).

**ROE V. WADE (1973).** *See* ABORTION; REHNQUIST, WILLIAM HUBBS; SCALIA, ANTONIN; SUPREME COURT; WOMEN.

**RUBY RIDGE, IDAHO.** *See* WEAVER, RANDALL (RANDY).

**RUSHDIE, SALMAN (1947– ).** A British citizen born in India, Rushdie wrote a 1988 book entitled *The Satanic Verses*. The book is a fantasy account of two actors who survive a plane crash over the English Channel, and then become the incarnation of good and evil. The book's title references an account of the Prophet Muhammad's life, which many Muslims reject. The book was banned in a number of countries, including Rushdie's native India. On 14 February 1989, **Ayatollah Khomeini** of Iran called the book blasphemous and issued a *fatwa*, or decree calling for Rushdie's death. Khomeini later backed up the fatwa with a $3-million bounty. Rushdie took refuge in London, England, where he was guarded by authorities. The bounty against Rushdie was finally dropped by Iran in 1998.

– S –

**SADAT, ANWAR (1918–1981).** Imprisoned during **World War II** for attempting to expel the British from Egypt, Sadat became vice president to controversial Egyptian president Gamal Abdal Nasser in 1969. Sadat acceded to the presidency in 1970 following Nasser's death. Along with Syria, Sadat orchestrated the military victories in the Yom Kippur War with **Israel** in 1973, reclaiming lands in the Sinai Peninsula lost to Egypt in the 1967 Six-Day War. Sadat later won the Nobel Peace Prize, along with his Israeli counterpart Menachem Begin, after signing the Camp David Accords of 1978 brokered by President **Jimmy Carter**. Sadat's repression of pan-Islamist groups in Egypt led to significant internal unrest following the accords. On 6 October 1981, he was assassinated during a parade. Members of the Egyptian Army were responsible for coordinating his murder with a combination of grenades and gunfire. Sadat was succeeded by his vice president, Hosni Mubarak.

**SANDINISTAS.** The short name for the Frente Sandinista de Liberación Nacional (FSLN), the Sandinistas are a left-wing Marxist political and paramilitary organization in **Nicaragua** that succeeded in removing **Anastasio Somoza** from power in 1979 following a civil war. The name of the group is in memory of Augusto César Sandino, the leader of a rebellion against the United States in the 1920s. President **Ronald Reagan** was particularly concerned about Sandinista leader **Daniel Ortega**'s internal policies and Cuban involvement in Nicaragua in the 1980s. In 1981 Reagan ordered the **Central Intelligence Agency** (CIA) to provide military and organizational assistance to the **Contras**, or counterrevolutionary forces that had supported Somoza and opposed the Sandinistas. The Contras conducted nothing less than a civil war and armed resistance to Sandinista rule, staging military operations from Honduras and Costa Rica. With the **Boland Amendment** of 1983, the U.S. Congress prohibited covert activities and military support to the Contras. However, Colonel **Oliver North** hatched a scheme to secretly divert funds to the Contras from the sales of weapons to Iran, which evolved into the **Iran–Contra** scandal. Sandinista rule in Nicaragua ended in 1990 with the election of Violeta Barrios de Chamorro as president. *See also* COLD WAR; NATIONAL SECURITY DECISION DIRECTIVE (NSDD) 32; REAGAN DOCTRINE.

**SAVIMBI, JONAS MALHEIRO (1934–2002).** Savimbi was the leader of the forces opposed to the Marxist government in **Angola** during the civil war that raged in the country from 1976 to 2002. President **Ronald Reagan** called Savimbi a "freedom fighter." The United States provided military aid to Savimbi, and he was hailed by American conservatives. He was assassinated in an ambush in 2002. *See also* COLD WAR.

**SAVINGS AND LOAN BAILOUT.** By the late 1980s, a wave of failures in the savings and loan industry threatened the banking system. A combination of poor investment strategies, changes in the economy, and federal deregulation contributed to the crisis, which came to the fore in the **Keating Five** scandal. In 1989 President **George H. W. Bush** prompted Congress to pass legislation that gave the Treasury Department enhanced regulatory authority over the savings and loan industry and $30 billion over two years to oversee the industry's recovery and restabilization.

**SCALIA, ANTONIN (1936– ).** A Catholic and native of New Jersey, Scalia graduated from Georgetown University first in his class (1957) and Harvard Law School (1960). He entered private practice in Ohio in 1961 before taking a professorship in law at the University of Virginia in 1967. He served as general counsel to President Richard Nixon on telecommunications issues, and was assistant attorney general for the Office of Legal Counsel for President Gerald Ford. He returned to the academy in 1977 to teach at the University of Chicago Law School. In 1982 he was appointed to a judgeship on the U.S. Court of Appeals for the District of Columbia. President **Ronald Reagan** nominated him to the U.S. **Supreme Court** in 1986 when **William Rehnquist** was elevated to chief justice. He was confirmed unanimously by the Senate by a 98–0 vote. Scalia is the first Italian American justice to serve on the high court. He is widely considered among the most conservative contemporary judges, and takes a "strict constructionist," or literalist, position on interpretation of the Constitution.

**SCHWARZKOPF, H. NORMAN (1934– ).** Schwarzkopf's long military history, which began in 1956, includes two tours of duty in Vietnam. He was deputy commander of the invasion of **Grenada** ordered by President **Ronald Reagan** in 1983. He is best remembered for his command of the international coalition forces that expelled Iraqi dictator **Saddam Hussein**'s troops from **Kuwait** during the **Persian Gulf War** in 1991. A native of New Jersey, Schwarzkopf attended West Point and earned a graduate degree from the University of Southern California. A veteran wounded twice in battle and decorated with three Silver Stars, three Bronze Stars, and the Distinguished Service Medal, Schwarzkopf retired in 1992. His autobiography, *It Doesn't Take a Hero*, was published in 1992.

**SCHWEIKER, RICHARD SCHULTZ (1926– ).** A veteran of the navy during **World War II**, Schweiker graduated from Pennsylvania State University in 1950. The president of a leading ceramic tile manufacturer, he was elected to the U.S. House of Representatives in 1960, and served four terms for the 13th district of Pennsylvania. He won election to the U.S. Senate in 1968, and was reelected in 1974. Schweiker was **Ronald Reagan**'s vice-presidential candidate at the 1976 Republican nominating convention, which ultimately chose Gerald Ford to lead the GOP ticket. In 1976 he was appointed a member of the House Select Committee on Assassinations that investigated the deaths of President John F. Kennedy and the Reverend **Martin Luther King Jr.** He served as secretary of Health and Human Services during President Ronald Reagan's first term from 1981 to 1983. Schweiker left the administration in 1983 to head the American Council of Life Insurance, a position he held until 1994.

**SCOWCROFT, BRENT (1925– ).** Scowcroft graduated from West Point and later pursued master's and doctoral degrees from Columbia University in international relations. His first commission was with the air force, and he rose to the position of lieutenant general over the course of his 29-year career. He held positions in the Organization of the Joint Chiefs of Staff, Headquarters of the U.S. Air Force, and the Office of the Assistant Secretary of Defense for International Security Affairs before becoming a military assistant to President Richard Nixon. He was **national security advisor** to Republican presidents Gerald R. Ford and **George H. W. Bush**. Scowcroft is founder of the Forum for International Policy, a think tank, and is a member of the Council on Foreign Relations. He also served on the **Tower Commission**, which was charged with investigating the **Iran–Contra** scandal in the 1980s. President George H. W. Bush awarded him the Presidential Medal of Freedom in 1991. He was made an honorary knight of the British Empire by Queen Elizabeth in 1993. He is coauthor, with George H. W. Bush, of *A World Transformed* (1998). The book recounts the White House response to the fall of the **Soviet Union** and the end of the **Cold War**.

**SHAH OF IRAN (1919–1980).** Also known by his name, Mohammad Reza Pahlavi, the shah of Iran came to power in 1941 and ruled as an autocrat until 1979. He was known for nationalizing the Iranian oil industry and bringing great wealth to the nation. But as a secular leader with good relations with the United States and **Israel**, he was vilified by fundamentalist Muslims, which culminated in the Iranian Revolution led by **Ayatollah Khomeini**. The shah went into exile with his family and came to the United States to seek treatment for cancer. President **Jimmy Carter**'s decision to allow the shah to travel to the United States was putatively one of the reasons for the **Iranian hostage crisis** in which revolutionaries stormed the American embassy in Teheran. He died in Egypt and is buried in Cairo.

**SHEVARDNADZE, EDUARD AMVROSIYEVICH (1928– ).** Born in the Georgian Republic of the **Soviet Union**, Shevardnadze rose through the ranks of the Communist Party apparatus and was known for his tough stance on corruption. Soviet General Secretary **Mikhail Gorbachev** appointed him minister of **foreign policy** in 1985 when **Andrei Gromyko** resigned. A reformer, Shevardnadze helped formulate the **"Sinatra Doctrine"** vis-à-vis Eastern European countries in the late 1980s, and supported Gorbachev's economic agenda (*see*

*PERESTROIKA*). As the Soviet Union edged toward dissolution, however, Shevardnadze called for even more dramatic changes in the economy and parted ways with Gorbachev. He resigned in 1990. Five years later he was elected president of newly independent Georgia. Shevardnadze was chased from office in 2003 by mass demonstrations in protest of flawed elections that were also denounced by the international community.

**SHULTZ, GEORGE PRATT (1920– ).** A Princeton graduate (1938), **World War II** Marine Corps veteran in the Pacific theater, and a doctor of philosophy in industrial economics from the Massachusetts Institute of Technology, George Shultz has the distinction of having worked for four presidents. He was a consultant to President John F. Kennedy, and worked for President Dwight D. Eisenhower as part of the Council of Economic Advisors. He was President Richard Nixon's labor secretary from 1969 to 1970 before heading the **Office of Management and Budget**. In 1972 Nixon appointed him secretary of the treasury, a position in which he gained valuable experience in domestic and international economic policy. Shultz left Washington in 1974 after disagreements with Nixon over inflation policy to become an executive vice president of Bechtel Corporation, where he later became president.

He was summoned back to presidential service by **Ronald Reagan**, who appointed him secretary of state to replace **Alexander Haig** in 1983. He remained in the post until the end of Reagan's term, pursuing **arms control** agreements with the **Soviet Union**, which culminated in the **Intermediate-Range Nuclear Forces (INF) Treaty** in 1987 and the Soviet withdrawal of troops from **Afghanistan** in 1988. Shultz was also a major spokesman for the administration's anti-**terrorism** campaign following the bombing of the Marine barracks in **Beirut, Lebanon**, in 1983. Shultz was an opponent of the arms-for-hostages policy that ended in the **Iran–Contra** scandal, and criticized the policy in his 1986 congressional testimony. In 1989 Shultz became a senior fellow at the Hoover Institution, a conservative think tank linked to Stanford University. Shultz is author of *Economic Policy Beyond the Headlines* (1977, with Kenneth W. Dam) and *Turmoil and Triumph: My Years as Secretary of State* (1993).

**SIMPSON, ORENTHAL JAMES (O.J.) (1947– ).** A record-setting football player for San Francisco City College and later the University of Southern California in the 1960s, Simpson won the Heisman Trophy in 1969. He entered professional football with the Buffalo Bills that same year, and by the mid-1970s shattered records as a running back. A familiar face on national television in advertisements for Hertz Rent-a-Car, Simpson also appeared in several movies, including *Naked Gun* with co-star Leslie Nielson. In 1994 Simpson was thrown into the spotlight following the murders of his ex-wife Nicole Brown Simpson and her friend Ronald Goldman in Los Angeles. When police set out to arrest Simpson, he engaged them in a slow-speed freeway chase for hours, which was covered live by the **media**. Simpson stood trial for murder charges amid a veritable media frenzy. He was acquitted in 1995. However, the families of Goldman and Brown filed a civil action against Simpson, and won a wrongful death case. Simpson was ordered to pay $33.5 million to the families, which left the former football star in financial peril. The public attention surrounding the murder case is notable for the sharp divisions in opinions among whites and African Americans. Whites were much more likely to view Simpson as guilty; blacks were far more convinced of his innocence.

**"SINATRA DOCTRINE."** In December 1988 Soviet General Secretary **Mikhail Gorbachev** formally abandoned the **Brezhnev Doctrine** in favor of the "Sinatra Doctrine," so named for singer Frank Sinatra's song "My Way." The **Soviet Union** would no longer intervene in the affairs of **Warsaw Pact** nations, who would alone determine their own futures. The policy was key in the fall of the **Berlin Wall** and the subsequent crumbling of communist regimes in Eastern Europe. *See also* BREZHNEV, LEONID; COLD WAR; REAGAN, RONALD.

**SKINNER, SAMUEL KNOX (1938– ).** A graduate of DePaul University law school in 1966, Skinner was an assistant U.S. attorney for the Northern District of Illinois from 1968 to 1975. President Gerald Ford appointed him the U.S. attorney in 1975. Skinner resumed a private law practice from 1977 to 1989, serving as chair of the Regional Transportation Authority of northeastern Illinois and as vice chair of

President **Ronald Reagan**'s Commission on Organized Crime. He served as President **George H. W. Bush**'s secretary of transportation from 1989 until late 1992, and was particularly visible during the **Eastern Airlines strike** and the *Exxon Valdez* oil spill in Alaska. Skinner was the principal architect of the Bush administration's "open skies" policy, which relaxed regulation on international airline travel. He briefly served as White House **chief of staff** in 1992.

**SMITH, SAMANTHA (1972–1985).** A native of Maine, Smith became famous in 1982 after she wrote a letter to Soviet General Secretary **Yuri Andropov** to inquire about the state of relations between the United States and **Soviet Union**. Smith was particularly concerned about the possibility of nuclear war during the **Cold War**. Andropov was touched by the letter, and extended a personal invitation for the fifth-grader to visit the Soviet Union, which she did with great **media** fanfare. Smith wrote a book on her visit entitled *A Journey to the Soviet Union* (1985). She was killed in an airplane accident in 1985.

**SMITH, WILLIAM FRENCH (1917–1990).** Smith was born in the small town of Wilton, New Hampshire. He graduated from the University of California at Los Angeles in 1939, and earned a law degree from Harvard in 1942, after which he joined the navy and was sent to the Pacific theater during **World War II**. After two decades of private law practice, Smith became **Ronald Reagan**'s personal attorney in 1966. He campaigned for Reagan's successful bid for the California governorship and was an integral part of Reagan's informal set of advisors, or "kitchen cabinet," in Sacramento. Reagan appointed Smith to the board of regents of the University of California, where he served as a member from 1968 to 1976 and as chair (1970–72, 1974–76). Following Reagan's election to the White House in 1980, Smith served as attorney general in the president's first administration from 1981 to 1985. As attorney general, he was highly critical of judicial activism. The imprint he left on the Department of Justice was palpable, as he sought to align the organization's tasks with Reagan's conservative stances. Smith opposed racial quotas on **civil rights** matters and was less favorable to antitrust enforcement. After he resigned his post as attorney general, Smith returned to private law practice and to chair the board of trustees for the Ronald Reagan

Presidential Library. He died from cancer in Los Angeles in 1990. *See also* MEESE, EDWIN, III.

**SNOW, ROBERT ANTHONY (TONY) (1955– ).** Snow is a native of Kentucky and a graduate of Davidson College and the University of Chicago. In the 1980s, he worked variously as a columnist and editorial-page editor for the *Washington Times*, *Detroit News*, *The Daily Press* (Newport News, Va.), the *Virginian Pilot* (Norfolk, Va.), and the *Greensboro* (N.C.) *Record*. A host on the Fox News Network since 1996, he was director of speechwriting in the administration of **George H. W. Bush** from 1992 to 1993. President **George W. Bush** tapped him to be White House press secretary in April 2006.

**SOCIAL SECURITY.** Created in 1935, Social Security refers to the social insurance program known as Old Age, Survivors, and Disability Insurance managed by the Social Security Administration. American workers fund the program with payroll **taxes**, which are matched by their employers. Retirement and survivor benefits are paid according to how much workers have contributed to the program over their lifetime. In the 1980s and 1990s, Social Security became one of the fastest growing items in the federal budget. These increased outlays for Social Security prompted Congress to adopt several laws, including **Gramm–Rudman–Hollings (1985)** and the **Budget Enforcement Act (1990)** in an attempt to cap spending for the entitlement program and reduce the federal deficit. *See also* MEDICARE.

**SOLIDARITY.** Known as *Solidarność* in Polish, Solidarity is the trade union and sociopolitical movement in Poland headed by **Lech Wałęsa** in the 1980s and 1990s. Originally begun as a labor movement, Solidarity gained widespread support as an anti-Communist organization. Transformed into a quasi political party by 1989, Solidarity led democratization and economic reform efforts in Poland as Communist rule in **Warsaw Pact** nations crumbled with the fall of the **Berlin Wall**. *See* JARUZELSKI, WOJCIECH WITOLD.

**SOMALIA.** Civil war has ravaged the impoverished eastern African country since 1977. In 1981, the northern part of the country rebelled, precipitating a bloody, decade-long ethnic conflict that killed an estimated 40,000 and prompted some 400,000 refugees to flee for Ethiopia. Somalian bandits (Shifaa) also engaged in military actions against Ethiopia. In 1991 the northern part of the country declared its independence and took the name Somaliland. Other areas of the country declared independence in the late 1990s, and no central government exists at the time of writing.

**SOMOZA DEBAYLE, ANASTASIO (1925–1980).** Educated at Saint Leo University and West Point, Somoza Debayle was the third and final Somoza since 1936 to serve as president of **Nicaragua**. He headed Nicaragua from 1967 to 1979, including two years of civil chaos from 1973 to 1974, following a devastating earthquake in the capital, Managua. He was ousted in 1979 when the **Sandinistas** overthrew his government and forced him into exile in the United States. Although backed by the United States, Somoza was accused of human rights violations and brutality in the closing years of the civil war in Nicaragua, during which he ordered the military to kill civilians and bomb the country's major cities. Civilian casualties are estimated at 40,000–50,000. Somoza was assassinated in Asunción, Paraguay, on 17 September 1980, at the age of 54. *See also* COLD WAR; CONTRAS; ORTEGA SAAVEDRA, DANIEL; REAGAN DOCTRINE.

**SOUTER, DAVID HACKETT (1939– ).** Born in Melrose, Massachusetts, Souter is a Rhodes Scholar who graduated from Harvard Law School in 1966. He spent several years in private practice in Concord, New Hampshire, before becoming assistant attorney general of New Hampshire. He was promoted to deputy attorney general in 1971, and became attorney general in 1976. He was appointed associate justice on the Superior Court of New Hampshire in 1978, was elevated to the New Hampshire Supreme Court in 1983, and took a judgeship on the U.S. Court of Appeals for the First Circuit (New England) in 1990. That year President **George H. W. Bush** nominated Souter for the U.S. **Supreme Court** to fill the seat of retiring justice William J. Brennan. He was confirmed by the Senate by a vote of 90–9. Although considered a traditionalist in his interpretations of the Constitution, Souter has a record of jurisprudence that has varied from conservative positions in his early days on the high court to more moderate stances in recent years.

**SOUTH AFRICA SANCTIONS.** The issue of **apartheid** in South Africa—the minority white government's forced segregation of blacks and other nonwhite races—divided President **Ronald Reagan** and Congress during his second term. When Anglican bishop **Desmond Tutu** called on the West to impose economic sanctions on South Africa, Reagan opposed the move, believing that sanctions would only bring further hardship to black South Africans. The Anti-Apartheid Act of 1986, which prohibited imports from South Africa and business investment in that country, passed by large majorities in the House and Senate. President Reagan vetoed the bill on 26 September 1986. Within a week's time, both chambers of Congress overrode his veto and enacted the bill. Observers cited Reagan's failure to sustain his veto as the worst defeat for a president on **foreign policy** matters in Congress since the override of President Richard Nixon's veto of the War Powers Resolution. Whether the sanctions were responsible for the dismantling of the apartheid system in the 1990s remains a point of contention. *See* MANDELA, NELSON ROLIHLAHLA.

**SOVIET UNION.** The Soviet Union, also known as the Union of Soviet Socialist Republics (USSR), was the United States' principal military and ideological rival in the decades following **World War II** and during the **Cold War**, which spanned the 1940s through 1991. The Communist state was founded in 1922 after the 1917 Russian Revolution, spearheaded by Vladimir Ilych Lenin, which ousted Czar Nicholas II. The political structure of the country was a highly centralized federation of republics, most of which could be traced to Imperial Russia (Finland and Poland notwithstanding). The "command" economy was planned by political leaders, typically through five-year plans that dictated manufacturing and agricultural production goals. Private property was abolished for all intents and purposes. The only political party—the Communist Party—maintained a monopoly on power for seven decades.

By the 1980s, the Soviet Union was struggling to keep pace with U.S. technology, and the financial burden of military spending took a heavy toll on the economy. When **Mikhail Gorbachev** became general secretary of the Soviet Union in 1985, he advanced several reform notions—*glasnost* and *perestroika*—that were aimed at greater transparency in government and a revitalization of the economy, respectively. These reforms arguably paved the way for the eventual dissolution of the Soviet Union, though some suggest that **Ronald Reagan**'s proposal for the **Strategic Defense Initiative (SDI)** hastened the breakup by convincing Gorbachev that Soviet competition against the project would bankrupt that country's finances. The economic reforms caused deterioration in living standards, particularly because of high inflation. The "openness" championed by Gorbachev encouraged the public to express anger over the effects of the reforms.

By 1989, pressure for greater autonomy in the republics intensified. The Russian Republic held a congress in an attempt to usurp authority from the central government in Moscow. After a coup attempt against Gorbachev in 1991, power in Russia shifted definitively to **Boris Yeltsin**. That year the **Baltic States** declared independence. A meeting of Yeltsin and his counterparts from Belarus and Ukraine produced an agreement to disband the Soviet Union and create a new **Commonwealth of Independent States** (CIS). The Soviet Union formally came to an end on 25 December 1991 when Gorbachev resigned. *See also* ANTI–BALLISTIC MISSILE (ABM) TREATY; ARMS CONTROL; DÉTENTE; DOBRYNIN, ANATOLY FYODOROVICH; "EVIL EMPIRE"; NATIONAL SECURITY DECISION DIRECTIVE (NSDD) 32; REAGAN DOCTRINE.

**SPACE SHUTTLE.** *See CHALLENGER* (SPACE SHUTTLE); *COLUMBIA* (SPACE SHUTTLE).

**SPEAKES, LARRY MELVIN (1939– ).** A graduate of the University of Mississippi, Speakes worked for a number of Mississippi newspapers in the 1960s. He got his start in Washington politics as press secretary to Democratic senator James Eastland of Mississippi, for whom he worked from 1968 to 1974. Speakes then moved to the White House and served as assistant press secretary (1974–76) and later press secretary (1977) to President Gerald R. Ford. President **Ronald Reagan** chose Speakes as deputy press secretary in 1981. Speakes took over day-to-day press operations when press secretary **James Brady** was seriously injured by a bullet fired by **John Hinckley Jr.** in his attempt on the life of President Reagan on 30 March

1981. Speakes remained in the White House until 1987, at which time he left to serve as senior vice president of Merrill Lynch. He is author of *Speaking Out: Inside the Reagan White House* (1988).

**SS-20 MISSILES.** The **Soviet Union** deployed SS-20 intermediate-range ballistic missiles on its territory and in **Warsaw Pact** nations in the late 1970s and through the mid-1980s. The missiles could travel from 100 to 5,000 miles, and carried nuclear warheads up to one megaton. Improvements to the SS-20 model enabled the Soviets to arm the rocket with lower-yield, multiple warheads (multiple independently targetable reentry vehicles, or MIRVs). The United States deployed the **Pershing II** missile in Germany to counter the SS-20s. All SS-20 missiles were decommissioned following the **Intermediate-Range Nuclear Forces (INF) Treaty**, signed by President **Ronald Reagan** and Soviet General Secretary **Mikhail Gorbachev** in 1988. *See also* ARMS CONTROL; DETERRENCE; MUTUALLY ASSURED DESTRUCTION (MAD); REYKJAVÍK (SUMMIT).

**"STAR WARS."** *See* STRATEGIC DEFENSE INITIATIVE (SDI).

*STARK*, **USS.** *See* USS *STARK*.

**STEALTH BOMBER.** Sometimes described as a "flying wing," the Stealth Bomber (also known as the B-2 or B-2 Spirit) was developed during the administration of **Ronald Reagan**. The aircraft became operational in 1988. Its design enables long-range flights of up to 6,000 miles for the delivery of nuclear warheads. Advanced technology also allows the aircraft to avoid radar detection. **George H. W. Bush** scaled back production of the aircraft, though the Stealth has since been used in conflicts in **Kosovo** and **Afghanistan** under presidents **William Clinton** and **George W. Bush**. *See also* COLD WAR.

**STETHEM, ROBERT.** *See* TRANS WORLD AIRLINES (TWA) FLIGHT 847.

**STOCKMAN, DAVID ALAN (1946– ).** A Texas native, Stockman graduated from Michigan State University (1968) and did graduate work at Harvard in the 1970s. He got his start in Republican politics in 1970 when he served as an assistant to moderate Republican congressman John Anderson of Illinois. He left Anderson's office to become executive director of the House Republican Conference in 1972, and remained in that post until 1975. He ran for Congress in the fourth district of Michigan in 1976, and was elected thrice to the House of Representatives. He resigned from Congress in 1981 to become President **Ronald Reagan**'s director of the **Office of Management and Budget (OMB)**.

Stockman was derided in the press for proposing that ketchup be classified as a vegetable to reduce outlays for federally subsidized lunches for needy students. He ultimately became disillusioned with the failure of **Reaganomics** to reduce the largesse of the federal government and left the OMB in 1985. His 1986 book, *The Triumph of Politics: Why the Reagan Revolution Failed*, in which he argued that Reagan's supply-side purposefully ballooned the deficit to force domestic spending ceilings and cuts, was a scathing behind-the-scenes indictment of what he viewed as conservatives' ultimate unwillingness to sacrifice constituency interests for smaller government. The book caused an immediate stir among conservatives, many of whom viewed the book as a betrayal to Reagan. Stockman returned to the private sector, taking positions in various investment firms, including Salomon Brothers. *See also* GRAMM–RUDMAN–HOLLINGS ACT.

**STOCK MARKET.** In 1987 the stock market attained two contrary records. On 8 January 1987, the Dow Jones Industrial Average (DJIA) closed above 2,000 for the first time. For some time it was buoyed by enthusiasm and **tax** cuts in the early Reagan years. On 9 October, the bottom fell out of the market, sending the DJIA plummeting a record 508 points, a loss of over 20 percent. *See also* ECONOMIC RECOVERY TAX ACT; "REAGANOMICS."

**STRATEGIC ARMS REDUCTION TREATY (START).** START was a nuclear weapons limitation treaty between the United States and the **Soviet Union**. Proposed by President **Ronald Reagan**, the treaty limited the number of nuclear warheads each country could possess. The second round of the treaty, START II, was signed by

President **George H. W. Bush** on 31 July 1991, and ratified by the Senate on 1 October 1992. *See also* ARMS CONTROL.

**STRATEGIC DEFENSE INITIATIVE (SDI).** Popularly dubbed (and sometimes with pejorative intent) "Star Wars," the Strategic Defense Initiative was proposed by President **Ronald Reagan** in March 1983. He called for a space-based missile defense system that could shield the United States from a nuclear attack. The system would destroy incoming **intercontinental ballistic missiles (ICBMs)** before they reentered the atmosphere and descended toward their targets. When Reagan met Soviet leader **Mikhail Gorbachev** for the **Reykjavík Summit** in Iceland in October 1986, Soviet opposition to SDI postponed any agreement on a reduction in intermediate-range nuclear forces (**Intermediate-Range Nuclear Forces [INF] Treaty**). Critics contended that the deployment of such a space-based system would undermine the doctrine of **Mutually Assured Destruction (MAD)** by giving a strategic advantage to the United States. Moreover, such a system would have abrogated the U.S.–Soviet **Anti–Ballistic Missile (ABM) Treaty**. Reagan argued that the system would be purely defensive. Other proponents contended that the **Soviet Union** was probably already violating the ABM Treaty with weapons stationed in Krasnoyarsk, Siberia. Whether SDI was technologically feasible remains an open question. Some argue that Gorbachev's fear of being unable to compete with the weapons system helped precipitate the collapse of the Soviet Union, while others suggest internal dynamics were responsible. Research on SDI ended in 1993, though **George W. Bush** raised the issue of a national missile defense system in 2002, and experimental tests are ongoing as of 2006. Many of the ground-based tests have been unsuccessful. *See also* ARMS CONTROL; COLD WAR; DETERRENCE.

**SULLIVAN, LOUIS WADE (1933– ).** Founder of the Morehouse School of Medicine in Atlanta, Georgia, Sullivan served as secretary of Health and Human Services for the duration of President **George H. W. Bush**'s term. A graduate of Boston University's School of Medicine (1958), he taught at Harvard University and the New Jersey College of Medicine. From 1966 to 1975, he taught at Boston University before moving to Morehouse College. In the Bush administration he was active against the tobacco industry and was an advocate for victims of **Acquired Immune Deficiency Syndrome** (AIDS). He returned to Morehouse School of Medicine as president in 1993.

**SUNUNU, JOHN HENRY (1939– ).** Born in Havana, Cuba, where his father was working as a film distributor, Sununu was raised in New York. Educated at the Massachusetts Institute of Technology, Sununu worked as an engineer for Astro Dynamics, Inc., before joining the faculty at Tufts University in 1966, where he remained until 1982. Sununu entered local politics in Salem, Massachusetts. After moving to New Hampshire, he won a seat in the statehouse in 1972. Losing electoral bids for various state and federal offices in 1974, 1978, and 1982, he made a surprisingly successful run for the New Hampshire governor's office against the incumbent, Democrat Hugh Gallen, in 1982. Sununu campaigned on the themes of lowering **taxes** and government mismanagement. He was reelected twice in 1984 and 1986.

In 1988 **George H. W. Bush** made Sununu his chair for that year's presidential campaign in New Hampshire. Sununu's campaigning savvy and his organizational skills earned him the position of **chief of staff** in Bush's administration, a position in which he served from 1989 to 1991. He resigned in 1991 in the wake of allegations that he abused travel privileges and mismanaged White House affairs.

**SUPREME COURT.** The Supreme Court is the only court in the United States that is specifically mentioned in the Constitution. Congress created a framework for the federal district and appellate courts in the Judiciary Act of 1789.

The composition of the Supreme Court changed dramatically during the presidencies of **Ronald Reagan** and **George H. W. Bush**. As a result of retirements and new appointments, most observers contend that many of the high court's decisions marked a decidedly conservative shift. Nonetheless, both Reagan and Bush fought difficult and sometimes losing battles with Congress over their choice of appointments, and not all of the Court's opinions were consistent with the two presidents' stances.

Reagan's first appointment to the high court, **Sandra Day O'Connor**, met with almost universal praise in 1981. O'Connor became the first **woman** justice, and was confirmed by the Senate unanimously.

In 1986 Reagan nominated Associate Justice **William Rehnquist** to the position of chief justice when Warren Burger, appointed by Richard Nixon in 1969, decided to retire. Rehnquist's subsequent confirmation by a vote of 65–25 opened up another spot on the Court, for which Reagan nominated **Antonin Scalia**. Scalia was confirmed unanimously, but like Rehnquist, has been criticized for decisions based largely on an "originalist" doctrine that seeks to resolve current controversies by assessing the intentions of the founders. In 1987 Reagan suffered two major defeats. When Associate Justice Lewis Powell retired, the president nominated **Robert Bork** to replace him. A controversial figure for his role in the administration of Richard Nixon during the Watergate fiasco, Bork's nomination was defeated by a Senate vote of 42–58. His opposition to **abortion** rights and the 1973 decision in *Roe v. Wade* galvanized the opposition of women's groups. Reagan's subsequent nomination of **Douglas Ginsburg** was withdrawn when Ginsburg confirmed allegations that he had used marijuana while a faculty member at Harvard. Finally, in February 1988 the Democratic-controlled Senate confirmed Reagan's third choice, **Anthony Kennedy**, a moderate, to fill Powell's vacancy. Along with O'Connor, Kennedy proved a crucial swing vote on social issues, including abortion.

George H. W. Bush had the opportunity to nominate two associate justices to the Supreme Court. When William Brennan, who had been appointed by President Dwight D. Eisenhower in 1956, decided to retire in 1990, Bush nominated **David Souter**, a moderate from Massachusetts, to replace him. Souter was confirmed with relatively little controversy by a vote of 90–9. Bush's subsequent nomination of **Clarence Thomas** in 1991 to replace retiring justice Thurgood Marshall—the first African American justice and a key figure in the **civil rights** movement in the 1950s and 1960s—set the stage for dramatic confirmation hearings broadcast on television and a very narrow vote. Bush's choice to nominate Thomas, an African American, was viewed by some as disingenuous because of Thomas's highly conservative stances, including opposition to affirmative action, that conflict with the position of many in the black community. Further, Thomas's confirmation hearings were marred by allegations that he had engaged in sexual harassment of a female colleague, **Anita Hill**, while they were working together at the Equal Employment Opportunity Commission. The hearings ended with a Senate vote of 52–48 for Thomas's confirmation, the narrowest vote in decades.

Supreme Court decisions in the 1980s and 1990s had tremendous impacts on a range of issues that divided the country, and sometimes prompted Congress to challenge the high court's interpretations. Issues of discrimination and civil rights often plagued the Court. In the 1984 decision in *Grove City v. Bell*, the Court contended that only specific programs in colleges and universities receiving funds were required to comply with federal antidiscrimination laws. In 1988 Congress overturned the decision with passage of the Civil Rights Restoration Act, which clarified that if any program in an institution of higher learning receives federal funds, the entire institution must comply with antidiscrimination guidelines.

The *Wards Cove v. Atonio* and *Price Waterhouse v. Hopkins* cases in 1989 essentially shifted the burden of proof of workplace discrimination to the plaintiffs. The Democratic-controlled Congress passed the Civil Rights Act of 1991 to counter the Court's decisions, providing for jury trials and damages and shifting the burden of proof back to employers. The Rehnquist Court took a critical view of affirmative action programs that involved "set-asides" of government contracts for minority-owned businesses. In the 1989 case of *Richmond v. Croson*, the majority argued that societal discrimination, per se, was not a sufficiently compelling reason for set-asides. Instead, such programs were constitutional only insofar as they addressed specific cases of past discrimination by the governmental entity in question. In 1990, however, the high court held in *Metro Broadcasting v. FCC* that the Federal Communications Commission's promotion of minority-owned broadcasting stations was constitutional because the policy was consistent with congressional intent.

Abortion also drew the Court's attention in the **Webster v. Reproductive Health Services** (1989) and *Planned Parenthood v. Casey* (1992) cases. In *Webster* the Court affirmed the right of states to restrict public funds for abortion procedures. In *Planned Parenthood v. Casey*, the court modified *Roe*'s "right to privacy" rationale and emphasized the right to abortions based on the viability of the fetus outside the womb.

The Court was also not willing to extend the "right to privacy" to homosexuals. In the 1986 case *Bowers v. Hardwick*, a majority contended that Georgia's state sodomy laws did not violate the Constitution, and that homosexual acts, even between consenting adults, were not protected. The Court would not reverse its decision until 2003 in the *Lawrence v. Texas* case.

The Supreme Court overturned several key congressional statutes in the 1980s that challenged the doctrine of the separation of powers. In 1983 in *INS v. Chadha*, the Court found that Congress's use of the "legislative veto"—enabling the president to take actions contingent upon post-facto congressional approval or disapproval—was unconstitutional, though the practice still continues. In 1986 the majority ruled in *Bowsher v. Synar* that the **Gramm–Rudman–Hollings** anti-deficit legislation, which mandated automatic spending cuts, was unconstitutional because Congress cannot execute the laws. The legislation had provided for the comptroller general to enforce provisions, violating the separation of powers.

In the late 1980s, the Court clarified the constitutionality of the death penalty. In 1986 the majority decided in *Ford v. Wainwright* that a convicted murderer who was summarily denied clemency after developing delusions was entitled to a new hearing on his competence to stand for capital punishment. In 1988 the Court affirmed in *Thompson v. Oklahoma* that a minor who committed a capital crime when under age 16 was not eligible for the death penalty. In 1987, however, the Court refused to accept the argument that Georgia's administration of the death penalty was discriminatory to minorities.

The Court also wrestled with issues of free speech during the Reagan and Bush presidencies. In 1989 in **Texas v. Johnson**, the justices struck down a Texas law that forbade the burning of the American flag. Flag burning, the Court affirmed, was symbolic speech protected by the First Amendment. Similarly, when Congress passed a flag-burning statute, the Court struck down that law as a violation of First Amendment protections in *United States v. Eichman* in 1990. Finally, in *Hustler Magazine, Inc. v. Falwell* (1988), the Court contended that a magazine's portrayal of Jerry Falwell, a prominent evangelist, as a homosexual did not constitute libel. As a public figure, Falwell was not protected under the First or Fourteenth Amendments.

The intersection of religion and government was also brought to the high court for adjudication. In *Bob Jones University v. United States* (1983), the Court affirmed the Internal Revenue Service's retraction of tax-exempt status for a religious educational institution because of its discriminatory admissions policy. In 1992, the majority contended in *Lee v. Weisman* that prayers by clergy at graduation ceremonies crossed the line vis-à-vis the establishment clause, and prohibited such activities.

**SWAGGART, JIMMY (1935– ).** Assemblies of God television evangelist Jimmy Swaggart earned millions in the 1980s. In 1988 he was at the center of a scandal involving relations with a prostitute. The revelation came after Swaggart's condemnation of fellow televangelist **Jim Bakker** a year earlier. Swaggart promised his audiences he would repent, but instead was caught three more times with prostitutes over the next six years. Swaggart nonetheless kept his ministry, and as of 2006 continues to preach. The scandal surrounding Swaggart, as with Bakker, substantially tarnished the image of television evangelists in the 1980s–1990s.

## – T –

**TAX(ES).** Taxes imposed by the federal government on individuals' earnings comprise the largest share of revenue for the national budget, followed by taxes on corporations' earnings. In 1980 **Ronald Reagan** ran for the presidency on a platform that promised to reduce the income tax burden on individuals and corporations as one means of spurring economic growth. Reagan made good on his pledge in 1981 when he persuaded Congress to pass the **Economic Recovery Tax Act**, which cut taxes by $749 billion by reducing individual tax rates 25 percent over three years and accelerating business-depreciation write-offs. As early as 1982, however, federal deficits began to mount, and Congress forced Reagan to accept some tax increases to offset increased spending for defense programs he supported. Reagan was nevertheless successful in prompting Congress to simplify the tax code in 1986 with the passage of the **Tax Reform Act (1986)**. The bill phased out deductions of consumer credit card interest, increased personal and standard deductions, and enabled homeowners to deduct mortgage interest from their taxes.

As a presidential candidate in 1988, **George H. W. Bush** vowed to continue Reagan's legacy of holding the line on tax increases. At the Republican convention he solemnly pledged, **"read my lips, no new taxes**." However, when disagreements with Congress over the budget threatened to invoke automatic spending cuts under the antideficit **Gramm–Rudman–Hollings Act**, Bush reversed his position. He made a public plea for the **Budget Agreement of 1990**, which had the inverse effect of rallying public support against the bill and alienating conservatives. Bush's popularity fell dramatically, and he wound up vetoing the very budget agreement he had earlier supported. Bush had also consistently advocated a reduction of the capital gains tax throughout his presidency, but was unable to procure congressional support for the idea. *See also* "REAGANOMICS"; "VOODOO ECONOMICS."

**TAX REFORM ACT (1986).** The Tax Reform Act of 1986, passed under **Ronald Reagan**, was one of the most significant pieces of legislation of his presidency. The law simplified the **tax** code by phasing out deductions of consumer credit card interest and increasing personal and standard income tax deductions. The act also promoted home ownership by augmenting the deduction of mortgage interest from federal income taxes. Reagan had called for tax reform beginning in 1984. The bill that emerged in Congress in 1986 worried many Republicans and the business community, prompting the president to threaten to veto the bill if certain changes were not made. Reagan won those changes, and the bill was kept "revenue neutral" to avoid any tax increases.

**TERRORISM.** The term *terrorism* is traceable to the French Revolution (1789), when factions opposed to the monarchy used violence, fear, and intimidation to gain political power. Terrorism signifies violent acts perpetrated by groups in order to instill fear in the general population and coerce political authorities to cede to their demands. By a General Assembly resolution passed in 1999, the **United Nations** condemned terrorism as "criminal acts intended or calculated to provoke a state of terror in the general public," and found such acts unjustifiable "whatever the considerations of a political, philosophical, ideological, racial, ethnic, religious or other nature that may be invoked to justify them."

In the 1980s, the United States and its citizens were frequently the target of terrorism overseas. Muslim extremist groups were particularly angry at the United States' staunch support of the Jewish state of **Israel**, which groups like the **Palestinian Liberation Organization** and **Hezbollah** sought to destroy. The bombing of the Marine barracks in **Beirut, Lebanon**, in 1983 prompted President **Ronald Reagan** to issue **National Security Decision Directive (NSDD) 138** a year later. NSDD 138 strengthened counterterrorism efforts through a combination of intelligence programs and security measures undertaken domestically and abroad. In 1985 a radical militant Palestinian group linked to **Abu Abbas** nevertheless hijacked the Italian liner *Achille Lauro* and murdered a disabled Jewish American, **Leon Klinghoffer**.

Reagan took military action against **Libya** in 1986. He accused Libyan leader Colonel **Muhammar Qaddafi** of involvement in the bombing of the La Belle discotheque in West Berlin, which was frequented by U.S. service personnel. Reagan retaliated by launching raids on Tripoli and Benghazi (*see* OPERATION EL DORADO CANYON). In one of the most egregious acts of terrorism, Libyan **terrorist**s were suspected of planting a bomb aboard **Pan Am Flight 103**. The commercial aircraft exploded over **Lockerbie, Scotland**, in December 1988, killing 270 people, including all passengers and crew aboard and 11 residents of the town of Lockerbie.

Terrorism reached American soil on 11 September 2001 when 19 al-Qaeda terrorist operatives born in various countries of the Middle East hijacked four aircraft. Two of the aircraft were flown into the World Trade Center in New York City, another into the Pentagon in Washington, D.C., and the fourth crashed in Pennsylvania but was thought to be en route to the White House. The events of 11 September 2001 transformed the presidency of **George W. Bush**, who launched an indefinite campaign against terrorism at home and abroad that included the bombing and invasion of both **Afghanistan** and **Iraq**. *See also* UNITED NATIONS.

**TERRORIST.** A terrorist is anyone who engages in acts of **terrorism** or violent actions, individually or as a group, in order to achieve political goals. Common examples of terrorist acts include kidnapping, torturing, murdering and raping individuals, as well as bombing civilian or military targets (airplanes, ships, government offices, military bases). In the Middle East, many Islamic extremist groups justify terrorist acts by invoking an interpretation of the Koran that supports jihad, or holy war. During his two terms, **Ronald Reagan** actively sought to destroy terrorist networks that targeted Americans at home and abroad, and he took military action against **Libya** in 1986 (*see* OPERATION EL DORADO CANYON). Critics of Reagan, however, contend that American-backed anti-Communist insurgencies in **Angola** and Central America utilized terrorist acts that contradicted U.S. policy. The **United Nations** International Court of Justice found the United States guilty of supporting terrorism in **Nicaragua** by militarily and financially backing the **Contras**, but the United States refused to pay the fine. *See also* ABBAS, ABU; AFGHANISTAN; HAMAS; HEZBOLLAH; IRAQ; NATIONAL SECURITY DECISION DIRECTIVE (NSDD) 138; PALESTINIAN LIBERATION ORGANIZATION (PLO); PAN AM FLIGHT 103; QADDAFI, MUHAMMAR.

*TEXAS V. JOHNSON* **(1989).** In this landmark case the **Supreme Court**, by a 5–4 decision, struck down state laws that prohibited desecrating or burning the American flag. The case stemmed from Gregory Johnson's burning of a flag outside the Republican convention in Dallas, Texas, in 1984. Johnson, a Communist, was arrested and convicted of violating a Texas statute forbidding flag burning. Although Johnson's conviction was later overturned on appeal, the Texas appellate court did not address the broader constitutionality of the Texas law. The Supreme Court settled the question in the narrow decision, with the majority opinion contending that flag burning is a form of expressive conduct protected by the First Amendment. Two of President **Ronald Reagan**'s appointments to the Court—**Sandra Day O'Connor** and Chief Justice **William Rehnquist**—filed dissenting opinions. Justice **Antonin Scalia** joined the majority opinion, led by Justice William Brennan.

**THATCHER, MARGARET HILDA (1925– ).** Née Margaret Hilda Roberts and born in Grantham, Lincolnshire, England, Thatcher entered the UK Parliament in 1959 under the Conservative Party banner. She served as education minister in Edward Heath's Conservative government from 1970 to 1974, and became leader of the opposition from 1975 to 1979. She became prime minister in 1979, and won two subsequent elections in 1983 and 1987. Thatcher and President **Ronald Reagan** had a particularly close relationship. Both favored less government intervention in the economy, lower **taxes**, and a strong transatlantic alliance. Like Reagan, she also viewed the **Soviet Union** as a threat, and she was nicknamed the "Iron Lady" for her fiery, anti-Communist rhetoric. Thatcher presided over the successful 1982 **Falkland Islands War** with Argentina. In 1983 relations with Reagan became somewhat strained when the president ordered an invasion of the island of **Grenada**, a member of the British Commonwealth, to rescue American students. But Thatcher was fully supportive of Reagan's raid on **Libya** in 1986 when most other European leaders, including **François Mitterrand**, were not.

Thatcher's policies remain the subject of much controversy, from the economy and her stance on trade unions to the question of Northern Ireland. Thatcher was categorically opposed to a greater social and regulatory role for a centralized government in the European Community (now European Union). The issue of monetary union split Conservatives. Thatcher faced a leadership challenge and ultimately withdrew her candidacy as party leader. She was succeeded by John Major in November 1990. Thatcher was made a baroness in 1992 and a member of the House of Lords. She was also awarded the Order of Merit by Queen Elizabeth.

**THOMAS, CLARENCE (1948– ).** Born in a small town outside Savannah, Georgia, Thomas received a bachelor's degree from College of the Holy Cross, where he co-founded the school's Black Student Union. He earned his law degree from Yale University in 1974. He served as assistant attorney general of Missouri from 1974 to 1977, briefly entered corporate law with the Monsanto Corporation from 1977 to 1979, and served as a legislative assistant to Republican senator John Danforth from 1979 to 1981. A conservative skeptical of affirmative action, Thomas entered the administration of **Ronald Reagan** as assistant secretary for **civil rights** in the Department of Education, where he served from 1981 to 1982. He chaired the U.S.

Equal Employment Opportunity Commission (EEOC) from 1982 to 1990. President **George H. W. Bush** appointed Thomas to the U.S. Court of Appeals for the District of Columbia in 1990. A year later, Bush nominated him to replace retiring justice Thurgood Marshall on the **Supreme Court**.

To Bush's detractors, his replacement of Marshall, a famed civil rights advocate, with a conservative African American skeptical of government programs targeting minorities was disingenuous. Thomas's nomination galvanized the opposition of black groups around the nation, including the National Association for the Advancement of Colored Persons (NAACP) and the Urban League. Other groups worried about Thomas's potential opposition to **abortion** rights. His confirmation hearings before the Senate Judiciary Committee in late 1991 became a national **media** spectacle when allegations of sexual harassment by Thomas emerged from a leaked **Federal Bureau of Investigation (FBI)** report. Thomas's accuser, **Anita Hill**, was brought before the committee to testify about alleged incidents that took place when she and Thomas worked together at the EEOC. Although Hill's testimony and allegations were not corroborated, Thomas's confirmation was the closest in the 20th century for a Supreme Court justice. The Senate approved him by only two votes, 52–48, on 15 October 1991. Like fellow justice **Antonin Scalia**, Thomas is considered to be among the most conservative justices. He applies an originalist judicial philosophy guided by constitutional history and intent of the Framers.

**THORNBURGH, RICHARD LEWIS (1932– ).** A native of Pennsylvania, Thornburgh was educated at Yale and received a law degree from the University of Pittsburgh. Although he ran unsuccessfully for a Pennsylvania congressional seat in 1966, he became attorney general for western Pennsylvania in 1969, and was appointed assistant attorney general for the United States by President Gerald Ford in 1975. He was elected to two terms as governor of Pennsylvania from 1979 to 1987. He won acclaim for his handling of the nuclear plant accident at Three Mile Island, Pennsylvania, in the first year of his governorship. **Ronald Reagan** appointed Thornburgh attorney general in 1988 upon the resignation of **Edwin Meese**. Thornburgh continued in that position under President **George H. W. Bush** until

1991, at which time he left to run for the seat of the late Pennsylvania senator H. John Heinz III, who had died in an airplane crash that year. He was defeated by Democrat Harris Wofford. A founding member of the board of directors for the National Organization on Disability, Thornburgh was appointed to the review panel established by executives at CBS to investigate the news organization's problems in 2004.

**"THOUSAND POINTS OF LIGHT."** President **George H. W. Bush** used this phrase twice—once at his acceptance speech at the 1988 Republican nominating convention and again during his inaugural address in 1989. The phrase was aimed at encouraging voluntarism in lieu of greater governmental involvement in solving social problems. As he explained in his inaugural speech, "I have spoken of a thousand points of light, of all the community organizations that are spread like stars throughout the Nation, doing good. I will go to the people and the programs that are the brighter points of light, and I will ask every member of my government to become involved. The old ideas are new again because they are not old, they are timeless: duty, sacrifice, commitment, and a patriotism that finds its expression in taking part and pitching in." The phrase also spawned the Points of Light Foundation and Volunteer Center National Network, which coordinates volunteer workers around the United States. George H. W. Bush is honorary chairman of the organization.

**TIANANMEN SQUARE.** Built in the 15th century, Tiananmen Square is a large plaza in the center of Beijing, **China**. It was the site for student-led protests against the Communist government of the People's Republic of China (PRC) between 15 April 1989 and 4 June 1989. After a month of peaceful protest marches, the government declared martial law on 20 May, and troops were dispatched to put down the rebellion. Many of the events were captured by Western **media**, including the most famous footage of one protester who stood defiantly in front of an advancing tank for a half an hour. The army refused to shoot him, and he was pulled away by a bystander. Skirmishes between the army and protesters nevertheless resulted in an estimated death toll of between 400 and 3,000, with the injured numbering at least 7,000. The suppression of the protests sparked international condemnation of the PRC, whose leadership eventually prevented media coverage by Western networks. On 5 June, President **George H. W. Bush** announced sanctions on China that included an embargo of sales of weapons by the U.S. government or private corporations, in addition to a suspension of visits between American and Chinese governmental officials.

**TOWER COMMISSION.** On 26 November 1986, President **Ronald Reagan** mandated an independent investigation into the **Iran–Contra** scandal, headed by Senator **John Tower** and comprising former secretary of state Edmund Muskie and former **national security advisor Brent Scowcroft**. The commission hired 24 staff and conducted over 50 interviews. The final report, released on 27 February 1987, could not conclusively connect Reagan with the arms-for-hostages deal with Iran and the covert funding of the **Contras** in **Nicaragua**. Nonetheless, the report chastised Reagan for failing to control his national security staff and remaining too detached from its day-to-day operations. Reagan's lack of oversight arguably enabled Admiral **John Poindexter** and Colonel **Oliver North** to engage in the activities that violated the **Boland Amendment**, which Congress adopted to prohibit secret funding to the Contras. The release of the report prompted Reagan to make a televised speech to the nation on 4 March 1987, during which he accepted full responsibility for the scandal and promised better cooperation with Congress. The speech was followed by a reorganization of the **National Security Council**. Although Reagan weathered a drop in public approval, his acceptance of responsibility for the scandal put to rest any real threat of congressional impeachment. *See also* COLD WAR; ORTEGA SAAVEDRA, DANIEL.

**TOWER, JOHN GOODWIN (1925–1991).** A native of Houston, Texas, Tower was a **World War II** veteran and a graduate of Southwestern University (1948). He worked on President Dwight D. Eisenhower's 1956 reelection campaign in Texas, and later ran—unsuccessfully—as the Republican candidate against Lyndon Johnson for the U.S. Senate in 1960. But when Johnson resigned to run for vice president alongside John F. Kennedy, Tower won the special election and became the first Republican senator from Texas since

Reconstruction. Tower's career in the Senate focused on military affairs and modernization efforts until his retirement in 1985. President **Ronald Reagan** tapped him to investigate the events that led to the **Iran–Contra** scandal. The **Tower Commission** presented its report in February 1987. In 1989 President **George H. W. Bush** nominated Tower as secretary of defense. His confirmation hearings focused on allegations of womanizing and alcohol abuse. President Bush nevertheless stood by Tower, though the Senate ultimately rejected his nomination. Tower died in a plane crash in Georgia in 1991.

**TRANS WORLD AIRLINES (TWA) FLIGHT 847.** En route from Athens to Rome on 14 June 1985, the Boeing 727 was hijacked by two Middle Eastern **terrorist**s and forced to land in **Beirut, Lebanon**. In exchange for fuel, they allowed 19 passengers to leave the plane, and then ordered the pilot to fly to Algiers, Algeria. Another 20 passengers were released, and the plane returned to Beirut. The hijackers then beat Robert Stethem, a navy diver, fatally shot him in the head, and threw his body on the runway. At this point another 12 terrorists joined the two hijackers. The plane returned to Algiers, released another 65 passengers, and returned once again to Beirut. Eventually the remaining 48 passengers were released after a 17-day ordeal. One hijacker, Mohammed Homadi, was arrested in Germany and convicted of the murder of Stethem. The other perpetrators remain at large, with sizeable rewards offered by the U.S. government for their capture. *See also* TERRORISM.

**TRIDENT II MISSILES.** Designed to be launched from submarines, Trident II missiles were **intercontinental ballistic missiles (ICBMs)** armed with multiple nuclear warheads (multiple independently targetable reentry vehicles, or MIRVs). President **Ronald Reagan** advocated increasing the arsenal in the U.S. submarine fleet. The **Soviet Union** viewed the Trident II as a potential weapon of first strike, given the missile's accuracy. *See also* ARMS CONTROL; COLD WAR; DETERRENCE; INTERMEDIATE-RANGE NUCLEAR FORCES (INF) TREATY; MUTUALLY ASSURED DESTRUCTION (MAD).

**TRIPOLI, LIBYA.** *See* OPERATION EL DORADO CANYON.

**TUTU, DESMOND MPILO (1931– ).** A black South African and Anglican bishop, Tutu won the Nobel Peace Prize in 1984 for his peaceful opposition to **apartheid** in South Africa. He called for international sanctions against the white government to hasten political change. President Ronald Reagan vetoed a bill on **South Africa sanctions** in 1986, which Congress promptly overrode. *See* MANDELA, NELSON ROLIHLAHLA.

## – U –

**UNABOMBER.** *See* KACZYNSKI, THEODORE (TED).

**UNION OF SOVIET SOCIALIST REPUBLICS (USSR).** *See* SOVIET UNION.

**UNITED NATIONS.** Established on 24 October 1945, the United Nations (UN) is an international organization originally devoted to preventing conflicts between nations. Its mission has been expanded to include human rights monitoring and economic and democratic development. As of 2006, the organization now boasts a total membership of 191 countries. **China**, France, Russia, the United Kingdom, and the United States constitute the five nations with permanent membership on the Security Council. Any one of these countries can veto a resolution on such issues as the imposition of economic sanctions or military action.

The United States took a number of actions under the auspices of the United Nations during the presidencies of **Ronald Reagan** and **George H. W. Bush**. President Reagan agreed to send U.S. troops to Lebanon as part of a multinational peacekeeping force in August 1982. On 23 October 1983, a suicide bomber drove a car laden with explosives into the U.S. Marine barracks at the **Beirut** airport, killing 241 American service personnel. Reagan contemplated unilateral military action against the suspected **terrorist** perpetrators, but was dissuaded by Defense Secretary **Caspar Weinberger**.

Despite the Reagan administration's anti-terrorism stance against Middle Eastern groups and **Libya**, the United Nations International Court of Justice condemned the United States for supporting **terrorism** in Nicaragua. The court found that attacks on civilians and the Nicaraguan government by the anti-Communist **Contras**, who were backed by Reagan, constituted terrorism. The United States refused to recognize the decision, and did not pay the fine ordered by the General Assembly.

The United Nations played a critical role for President George H. W. Bush during the **Persian Gulf War**. When **Saddam Hussein** ordered Iraqi troops to invade **Kuwait** on 2 August 1990, the Security Council unanimously approved Resolution 660, condemning the invasion and calling for the restoration of the legitimate Kuwaiti government the very same day. On 29 November 1990, Resoluton 678 authorized member states to "use all necessary means to uphold and implement Resolution 660 and all subsequent relevant resolutions and to restore international peace and security in the area" by 15 January 1991. In the weeks before the deadline, Bush and the White House worked indefatigably to assemble an unprecedented multinational coalition of armed forces. When Hussein refused to comply with the resolution, the U.S.-led coalition began a successful military operation to liberate Kuwait (*see* OPERATION DESERT STORM).

A formal cease-fire between coalition troops and Hussein was signed on 9 April 1991. United Nations Resolution 687 mandated that Iraq would "accept the destruction, removal, or rendering harmless, under international supervision, of all nuclear, chemical and biological weapons and all stocks of agents and all related subsystems and components and all research, development, support and manufacturing facilities, as well as all ballistic missiles with a range greater than 150 kilometers and related major parts, and repair and production facilities." The United States and the United Kingdom subsequently imposed "no-fly zones" on Iraqi military aircraft in the northern and southern sections of Iraq, while United Nations weapons inspectors led teams to ensure Hussein's compliance with the conditions.

In March 2003, President **George W. Bush** launched a preemptive military attack against **Iraq**. Hussein had forced weapons inspectors out of the country in 2002. The United Nations subsequently adopted

Resolution 1441, which warned that Iraq would face "serious consequences" for failing to comply with its obligations under the 1991 cease-fire agreement. When Hussein continued to balk at allowing weapons inspectors to return to Iraq, Bush sought UN approval to take military action against Hussein's regime. He was unable to secure agreement, however. The United States and France disagreed on which types of action constituted "serious consequences." French President Jacques Chirac preferred economic sanctions, and vowed to veto any Security Council resolution on military action.

Bush subsequently arrayed a "coalition of the willing," including the United Kingdom, to preemptively invade Iraq. He contended that Hussein had weapons of mass destruction that he was planning to use against the United States and its allies, and posited links between Iraq and the al-Qaeda **terrorists** repsonsible for the 11 September 2001 attacks against New York and Washington, D.C. As of 2006, no weapons of mass destruction have been found in Iraq, and links between Hussein and al-Qaeda have not been substantiated. *See also* FOREIGN POLICY; KIRKPATRICK, JEANE DUANE JORDAN; REAGAN DOCTRINE.

**UNITED WE STAND AMERICA.** Business mogul and presidential candidate **H. Ross Perot** chose this slogan for his 1992 campaign against incumbent **George H. W. Bush**. Perot changed the name of his movement to the **Reform Party** by 1996.

**URUGUAY ROUND.** Named for the Punta del Este, Uruguay, location where meetings were first held, the Uruguay Round was a multilateral negotiation on the **General Agreement on Tariffs and Trade (GATT)** that began in September 1986. Ending in April 1994, the Uruguay Round replaced GATT with the World Trade Organization (WTO), which governs trade relations between member nations.

**USS *STARK*.** The USS *Stark* was deployed to the Middle East in the mid-1980s to keep the Persian Gulf open to shipping during the **Iran–Iraq War**. On 17 May 1987, the ship was hit by two missiles from an Iraqi fighter during the war. Thirty-seven of the crew were killed and another 21 were injured. The attack was considered the worst on a U.S. ship in peacetime to that point in history.

**USS *VINCENNES*.** On 3 July 1988, the USS *Vincennes* fired upon **Iran Air Flight 655**, an Airbus 300, while in the Strait of Hormuz off the coast of Iran. Two hundred and ninety passengers and crew died. The U.S. government contends that the *Vincennes* incorrectly identified the aircraft as an F-14 military fighter, and fired missiles when the aircraft refused to respond to radio contact. The aircraft had also deviated from its flight path, and Iranian military aircraft were in the area. The International Court of Justice condemned the attack as unlawful, but the United States has refused to apologize and contends that the blame remains with Iran. Nevertheless, the United States paid nearly $62 million to Iran to settle the case. *See also* KOREAN AIRLINES FLIGHT 007.

## – V –

**VELVET REVOLUTION.** The end of the Communist Party's rule in **Czechoslovakia** is frequently described as a "velvet revolution" for the lack of violence compared to other countries in Eastern Europe, such as Romania (*see* CEAUȘESCU, NICHOLAE). Between 16 November and 29 December 1989, demonstrations and strikes around the nation culminated in the resignation of the Communist Party government. **Alexander Dubček**, the leader of the 1958 uprising crushed by Soviet forces, was elected speaker of the federal legislature on 28 December. Dramatist and writer **Václav Havel** became president on 29 December. In June 1990, the country held its first democratic elections since 1946. *See also* BERLIN WALL; SINATRA DOCTRINE; WARSAW PACT.

**VERITY, CALVIN WILLIAM, JR. (1917– ).** As secretary of commerce between 1987 and 1989 under President **Ronald Reagan**, one of Verity's biggest accomplishments was the creation of the Office of Space Commerce, a predecessor to the Office of Space Commercialization. Born in Ohio and educated in economics at Yale, Verity served in the U.S. Navy in the Pacific during **World War II**. Following his military service, he returned to work at Armco, the steel corporation owned by his grandfather. Beginning in 1957, he held various executive positions in the company, becoming chairman of the board in 1971, and retired in 1982. Verity's relationship with President Ronald Reagan predated his appointment as commerce secretary; he had chaired the U.S. Chamber of Commerce from 1980 to 1981, as well as the president's task force on Private Sector Initiatives (1981). He was later appointed to the task force's advisory council. From 1979 to 1984 he cochaired the U.S.–USSR Trade Economic Council, an organization comprising business interests from both countries with the goal of promoting trade. *See also* SOVIET UNION.

**VETERANS AFFAIRS (DEPARTMENT OF).** The Department of Veterans Affairs Act of 1988 transformed the Veterans Administration, created in 1930, into a cabinet-level Department of Veterans Affairs. The legislation went into effect in March 1989 under President **George H. W. Bush**. The department oversees benefits, health care, and clinics for men and women who have served in the armed forces. *See also* DERWINSKI, EDWARD JOSEPH.

*VINCENNES*, **USS.** *See* USS *VINCENNES*.

**"VISION THING."** During the 1988 presidential campaign, **George H. W. Bush** commented that he did not have the "vision thing" when the **media** pressed him to articulate his worldview and future design for America if he won the White House. Instead, Bush focused on family, loyalty, and personal relationships he had cultivated throughout his career. Gerald Boyd of the *New York Times* summed up Bush's view as follows: "Portraying the 1988 election as a referendum on the future, he has avoided direct comment on how he will tackle present problems or how he regards the policies of the past" (19 May 1987). Bush's failure to paint a far-reaching vision of his future leadership or engage in dogmatic rhetoric was in keeping with his focus on the management of problems as they arose. Nevertheless, the phrase haunted Bush's term as critics charged that he failed to attack domestic or international problems with adequate speed, from aid to the former **Soviet Union** to **China**'s repression of dissidents and the domestic economic slowdown. *See also* BUDGET AGREEMENT (1990); CLINTON, WILLIAM JEFFERSON (BILL); TIANANMEN SQUARE.

**VOLCKER, PAUL ADOLPH (1927– ).** Born in Cape May, New Jersey, and a graduate of Princeton, Harvard, and the London School of Economics, Volcker was chairman of the **Federal Reserve System** under presidents **Jimmy Carter** and **Ronald Reagan** from 1979 to 1987. From 1969 to 1974, he was undersecretary for international monetary affairs in the Department of the Treasury. From 1975 to 1990, he served as president of the Federal Reserve Bank of New York. Volcker is generally credited with successfully controlling monetary policy as a means of lowering the high rates of inflation that dominated the last years of Carter's presidency and that contributed to the economic recession in Reagan's first term. Between 1981 and 1983, Volcker's emphasis on limiting the money supply reduced the inflation rate by more than 10 percent.

In April 2004, Volcker was appointed to head a **United Nations** investigation of Iraq's "oil for food" program, established after the **Persian Gulf War** to soften the blow of economic sanctions on Iraq's population. Volcker issued his final report in 2005, and reported widespread manipulation of the program by Iraq's dictator **Saddam Hussein** following **George W. Bush**'s invasion of the country in 2003.

**"VOODOO ECONOMICS."** During his bid for the Republican presidential nomination in 1980, **George H. W. Bush** referred disparagingly to **Ronald Reagan**'s economic policies as "voodoo economics." **Reaganomics**, which was based on supply-side theory, sought to create growth incentives in the economy through large **tax** cuts. Consumers and corporations were expected to reinvest savings in jobs, productivity would increase, and newly generated income would provide the federal government with sources of new revenue to offset deficits. The massive deficits of the 1980s, precipitated by large tax cuts combined with increased outlays for defense and entitlement programs, nevertheless caused many economists to question supply-side theory.

– W –

**WAITE, TERRY (1939– ).** A British author and humanitarian activist, Waite was chosen by the Archbishop of Canterbury as an envoy to

Lebanon in the wake of that country's civil war. Waite attempted to negotiate the release of four hostages. Instead, he was captured by the group Islamic Jihad and taken prisoner in February 1987. He was released in November 1991.

**WAŁĘSA, LECH (1943– ).** Born in Popowo, Poland, Wałęsa worked in the shipyards of Gdańsk beginning in the 1960s. Over the next decade he would face trials and spend time in prison for organizing workers and calling for strikes against the Communist regime in Poland. In 1980 he was elected to head the **Solidarity** trade union following national strikes precipitated by shipyard workers' protests. In 1981 Polish leader **Wojciech Jaruzelski** imposed martial law, and Wałęsa was detained by authorities in southeastern Poland for nearly a year. A Nobel Peace Prize winner in 1983, Wałęsa returned to work in the shipyards under the watchful eye of the state. He once again organized workers into Solidarity—though the leadership had fled to Brussels. In 1988 he called for yet another strike to force the government to give Solidarity legal status. Negotiations in 1989 yielded an agreement that morphed the labor union into a quasi political party. Solidarity contested in the elections that year, and won 48 percent of the vote (a majority of seats in the legislature was guaranteed to the Communist Party). By 1990 Wałęsa formed a larger coalition with Communists that paved the way for economic and political reform as Communist regimes in the **Warsaw Pact** began to crumble under Soviet leader **Mikhail Gorbachev**'s **"Sinatra Doctrine."** That year Wałęsa won the presidency, and presided over five years of substantial change as Poland transitioned to a market economy and a democratic framework of governance. His brusque leadership style nevertheless alienated many, and he lost his bid for reelection in 1995. *See also* BERLIN WALL.

**WALKER, JOHN ANTHONY (1937– ).** A native of Scranton, Pennsylvania, Walker was a career naval officer who worked as a communications specialist. From 1968 until his arrest by the **Federal Bureau of Investigation (FBI)** in 1985, he sold sensitive intelligence information to the **Soviet Union** and decoded scores of encrypted messages. He actively recruited other naval personnel and his own family into his spy ring, which was the most successful—and the most potentially damaging to U.S. intelligence—during the **Cold War**. Convicted of espionage, Walker is serving a life sentence in prison.

**WALL STREET.** *See* STOCK MARKET.

**WALSH, LAWRENCE (1912– ).** A graduate of Columbia Law School (1935), Walsh became a prosecutor in New York and worked for Governor Thomas Dewey. He was appointed to a federal district court for southern New York by President Dwight Eisenhower in 1954, but left the appointment three years later to work as deputy attorney general for the United States under William Rogers. He left the Eisenhower administration in 1960, and entered private practice in New York. President Richard M. Nixon appointed Walsh his personal representative at the Paris Peace Talks in 1969, which were aimed at ending the Vietnam War. Walsh returned to private practice, but was tapped by Congress in 1986 as **independent counsel** to investigate the **Iran–Contra** scandal. Walsh successfully won convictions for Colonel **Oliver L. North** and Admiral **John M. Poindexter**, but the convictions were overturned on appeal. In 1992 President **George H. W. Bush** pardoned Defense Secretary **Caspar Weinberger** and five others involved in the arms-for-hostages scandal, including former national security adviser **Robert McFarlane.**

**"WAR ON DRUGS."** President **George H. W. Bush** made illegal drug use and interdiction a priority in his inaugural address in 1989. The year before, Congress passed and President **Ronald Reagan** signed the Anti–Drug Abuse Act of 1988, which created the **Office of National Drug Control Policy** (ONDCP), to be housed within the **Executive Office of the President (EOP)**. Bush appointed **William J. Bennett** as the first "drug czar" to head the ONDCP, which is charged with stopping drug trafficking and use. *See also* ANDEAN INITIATIVE; DRUG TRAFFICKING; MARTINEZ, ROBERT (BOB).

*WARDS COVE V. ATONIO* **(1989).** *See* CIVIL RIGHTS; SUPREME COURT.

**WARSAW PACT.** Signed on 14 May 1955, the Warsaw Pact was the military alliance of Eastern European countries under the aegis of Soviet domination during the **Cold War**. The Warsaw Pact was aimed at countering the Western alliance of **North Atlantic Treaty Organization (NATO)** members. Member countries of the Warsaw Pact included Bulgaria, **Czechoslovakia**, East Germany, Hungary, Poland, and Romania. As with NATO signatories, the Warsaw Pact nations pledged to come to the aid of other member nations if attacked. The Warsaw Pact was formally dissolved on 1 July 1991 following the collapse of Communist regimes throughout Eastern Europe. *See also* BERLIN WALL; BREZHNEV, LEONID; BREZHNEV DOCTRINE; DETERRENCE; GORBACHEV, MIKHAIL SERGEYEVICH; INTERMEDIATE-RANGE NUCLEAR FORCES (INF) TREATY; MUTUALLY ASSURED DESTRUCTION (MAD); PERSHING II MISSILES; REAGAN DOCTRINE; SINATRA DOCTRINE; SS-20 MISSILES.

**WATKINS, JAMES D. (1927– ).** Born in California and a graduate of the United States Naval Academy and the Naval Postgraduate School (1958), Watkins served as chief of naval personnel, commander of the Sixth Fleet, vice chief of naval operations, and commander in chief of the Pacific Fleet. He was appointed chief of naval operations by President **Ronald Reagan** in 1982, and served in that position until 1986. Reagan appointed Watkins chairman of the Presidential Commission on the Human Immunodeficiency Virus (HIV) Epidemic (1987–88). President **George H. W. Bush** appointed him secretary of energy, and he served in the cabinet for the duration of Bush's term. Watkins's efforts were targeted on the development of a comprehensive national energy strategy, which culminated in the Energy Policy Act of 1992. *See also* ACQUIRED IMMUNE DEFICIENCY SYNDROME (AIDS).

**WATT, JAMES GAIUS (1938– ).** One of the most controversial members of President **Ronald Reagan**'s cabinet, the Wyoming native and secretary of the interior from 1981 to 1983 was reproached by **environment**al groups and activists for his conservative stances on land use and regulation. Watt won the attention of Reagan for his work as

president of the Mountain States Legal Foundation, which represented natural-resource corporations. The conservative group spearheaded lawsuits concerning environmental regulation, and championed legislation to force governments to compensate landowners for
the loss of property use due to regulatory requirements. Environmental groups severely criticized Watt as secretary of the interior for his
cutbacks to conservation funds and programs, sale of public lands to
private investors, decreased federal regulation on oil and mining, and
enthusiasm for new exploitation of oil and gas on federal lands. Despite intense interest-group activism by such groups as the Sierra
Club and the National Wildlife Federation, which called for Watt's
resignation in early 1981, it was Watt's own flippant comments that
led to his ultimate ouster. His remarks that a Senate advisory panel
was composed of "a black, a **woman**, two Jews and a cripple"
prompted the Senate to draft a bill calling for him to step down, but
he instead resigned in 1983. In 1996 he pleaded guilty to the charge
of attempting to influence a grand jury investigation dating to the
1980s, for which he was fined and received five years' probation.
Watt is author, with Doug Wead, of *Courage of a Conservative*
(1985).

**WEAVER, RANDALL (RANDY) (1948– ).** An Iowa native and
Green Beret during the Vietnam War, Weaver enrolled in college following three years of military service, but did not finish. His failure
to maintain steady employment prompted him and his wife, Vicki
Jordison, to move to a remote part of Idaho near Ruby Ridge, build a
cabin, and homeschool their children. Weaver became convinced that
the U.S. government was controlled by Zionists, and gravitated toward white-supremacist groups, notably the Aryan Nations. In 1992
the Bureau of Alcohol, Tobacco, and Firearms (ATF) put Weaver's
house under surveillance after he was caught selling illegal weapons.
While on a hunting excursion on his property, Weaver, his son Sam,
and a friend encountered ATF agents, precipitating a gun battle that
claimed the life of Sam. Weaver and his friend returned to the house
and began a standoff with federal agents that lasted 11 days. He surrendered on 31 August 1992, and faced murder and weapons charges,
against which he argued self-defense. He was acquitted of those
charges and eventually was awarded a $3.1 million settlement. The

Justice Department, which houses ATF, came under intense scrutiny by Congress, which reproached the actions of the federal agents.

**WEBSTER V. REPRODUCTIVE HEALTH SERVICES (1989).** This **Supreme Court** case took up the question of whether states could impose restrictions on **abortion**s. At issue was whether a Missouri law that restricted the use of state funds for abortions and abortion counseling contravened *Roe v. Wade* (1973), which guaranteed **women** the right to abortions. **Ronald Reagan**'s appointees **Sandra Day O'Connor** and **Antonin Scalia** wrote concurring opinions for the majority, arguing that state restrictions on the use of public funds for abortions did not present an "undue burden" on women, though Scalia expressed his disappointment that the high court was unwilling to use the Missouri case to overturn *Roe*.

**WEBSTER, WILLIAM HEDGCOCK (1924– ).** A native of Missouri and a navy veteran of **World War II**, Webster graduated with a law degree from Washington University in St. Louis (1949). He was a federal prosecutor for the Eastern District of Missouri in the early 1960s, and a member of the Missouri Board of Law Examiners from 1964 to 1969. He was appointed to the U.S. District Court for the Eastern District of Missouri in 1970 by President Richard Nixon. Three years later he was appointed to the U.S. Court of Appeals for the Eighth Circuit. He resigned as a judge in 1978 to become director of the **Federal Bureau of Investigation (FBI)**. In 1987 President **Ronald Reagan** appointed him to head the **Central Intelligence Agency** (CIA). Webster's appointment followed the death of his predecessor, **William Casey**, and the storm of controversy over **Iran–Contra**. Webster headed the CIA for the rest of Reagan's second term, and served under President **George H. W. Bush** until 1991. Upon his retirement he was awarded the Presidential Medal of Freedom, the Distinguished Intelligence Medal, and the National Security Medal. Webster returned to private law practice with the Washington, D.C., firm Milbank, Tweed. *See also* GATES, ROBERT MICHAEL.

**WEINBERGER, CASPAR WILLIARD (1917– ).** Weinberger served in **Ronald Reagan**'s White House as secretary of defense from 1982 to 1987, but his linkages to the president are traceable to his earlier political career in Republican politics in California. A graduate of Harvard Law School (1941), Weinberger served in the army in the Pacific during **World War II**, after which he worked under General Douglas MacArthur as a captain in intelligence. Returning to his native California, he won three successive elections to the California State Assembly (1952–56). After his unsuccessful bid for state attorney general in 1958, he became chair of the state Republican Party in 1962. He won the attention of Governor Reagan, who appointed him to head the Commission on California State Government Organization and Economy in 1967. The following year Weinberger was named state director of finance. He left Sacramento in 1970 to become chairman of the Federal Trade Commission. President Richard Nixon appointed him deputy director (1970–72) and then director of the White House **Office of Management and Budget** (formerly Bureau of the Budget). Weinberger also served briefly as secretary of Health, Education and Welfare under presidents Richard Nixon and Gerald Ford (1973–75). He left public service in the mid-1970s to become vice president and general counsel for the Bechtel Group in California.

As President Reagan's defense secretary, Weinberger was known for his staunch support for the **Strategic Defense Initiative (SDI)**, or "Star Wars," the president's plan to shield the United States from a nuclear attack by destroying incoming missiles from space. He also supported Reagan's plans to increase the United States' **deterrence** forces through the development and production of new **B1-B bombers** and the **Stealth Bomber**, as well as the deployment of **Trident II missiles** for submarines, **MX missiles**, and Airborne Warning and Control System **(AWACS)** on aircraft. Critics of the defense buildup were concerned that programs such as SDI undermined the 1972 **Anti–Ballistic Missile (ABM) Treaty** signed with the **Soviet Union**, and that other programs threatened to destabilize the doctrine of **Mutually Assured Destruction (MAD)** and give incentives for the Soviets to launch a preemptive nuclear strike.

Weinberger left office in November 1987 under a cloud due to his implication in the **Iran–Contra** scandal. He was indicted by **Lawrence Walsh,** the **independent counsel** investigating the affair, for obstruction of justice for failing to disclose to investigators his knowledge of arms sales to Iran. President **George H. W. Bush** granted Weinberger, as well as five other figures in the scandal, a free and unconditional pardon on 24 December 1992. Weinberger is author of *Fighting for Peace: Seven Critical Years in the Pentagon* (1990), *The Next War* (1998), and *Chain of Command* (2005). *See also* ARMS CONTROL; COLD WAR; REAGAN DOCTRINE.

**WILDER, DOUGLAS (1931– ).** Born in Richmond, Virginia, and the grandson of slaves, Wilder became the first African American elected to a governorship. He served as governor of Virginia from 1990 to 1994. A Bronze Star recipient for service in Korea, Wilder attended Howard University Law School and co-founded his own law firm before entering state politics in 1969. He rose to the position of lieutenant governor in 1989, and won the subsequent statewide election for the governorship. He successfully ran for the mayorship of Richmond, Virginia, in November 2004.

**WOMAN, WOMEN.** The presidencies of **Ronald Reagan** and **George H. W. Bush** were the backdrop to a number of developments—some precedent-setting—for women's role in politics. Reagan's appointment of **Sandra Day O'Connor** marked the first time a woman had served as a justice on the **Supreme Court**. That same year Reagan appointed influential conservative **Jeane Kirkpatrick** as ambassador to the **United Nations**. In 1984 **Geraldine Ferraro** became the first female vice-presidential candidate when **Walter Mondale** picked her as his running mate.

The 1980s and 1990s witnessed a growing divide between women who considered themselves traditionalists and feminists who sought greater political influence and equality. While **Nancy Reagan** served in her role as first lady by advocating a "just say no" policy toward drugs among America's youth, **Barbara Bush** took an active interest in reading and education. The traditional role these first ladies emphasized in the White House on noncontroversial policy issues and their accent on family values was reinforced by leading female conservatives such as Phyllis Schlafly, who opposes **abortion**, the Equal Rights Amendment, and feminist causes more broadly.

Discord over abortion politics intensified in the Reagan and Bush presidencies. Both presidents were "pro-life" and opposed to abortion. Reagan supported policies that curtailed U.S. support for international organizations providing abortions overseas. Bush vetoed a total of 10 bills because of provisions that eased restrictions on abortions. The Supreme Court also weighed in on the issue in two key cases, *Webster v. Reproductive Health Services* and *Planned Parenthood v. Casey*. Taken together, the two cases enabled states to place some restrictions on public funding of abortion, and revamped *Roe v. Wade*, which legalized abortion in 1973, by emphasizing the viability of a fetus outside the womb for the procedure to be considered constitutional.

Following the 1980 election, some observers noticed that men and women evidenced different voting patterns, with women often supporting Democratic candidates and Republicans supporting male candidates. Eleanor Smeal, a leader of the progressive National Organization for Women (NOW), titled this phenomenon the "gender gap." The distinctive pattern of voting between the sexes at the aggregate level surely masks microlevel differences in voting and policy preferences among men and women, but the phenomenon has remained visible through the 2004 presidential election.

The issue of sexual harassment of women took center stage during the Senate confirmation hearings of **Clarence Thomas**, whom George H. W. Bush nominated to the **Supreme Court** in 1991. One of Thomas's former colleagues, **Anita Hill**, testified that Thomas had made unwelcome advances toward her while they were working together at the Equal Employment Opportunity Commission (EEOC). Thomas denied the allegations, and was ultimately confirmed to the high court, but **media** coverage of the hearings brought the larger issue of workplace harassment of women to national attention.

The year 1992 is often billed as the "year of the woman." A record number of women—approximately 60 million—turned out at the polls. They helped to elect 24 new women members to the House of Representatives and five to the Senate. That year also emerged as the year of the "soccer moms"—women with whom Democratic presidential candidate **William Clinton**'s emphasis on health care reform and family leave resonated.

**WORLD WIDE WEB.** Launched in March 1989 and derived from a project by Briton Tim Berners-Lee, and later pioneered by CERN in Geneva, Switzerland, the World Wide Web began implementation a year later. The project was originally aimed at accessing library information located at different physical locations, and morphed into the Internet.

**WRIGHT, JAMES CLAUDE (JIM), JR. (1922– ).** A Fort Worth, Texas, native, Wright is a **World War II** veteran who was awarded a Distinguished Flying Cross as a combat pilot in the South Pacific. He got his start in Democratic politics as a representative to the Texas state legislature. He successfully ran for the U.S. House of Representatives in 1954, and was reelected from the 12th district of Texas 14 times. He served as majority leader from 1979 to 1987. He became Speaker of the House in 1988. Republican **Newt Gingrich** brought ethics charges against Wright in 1989. An investigation by the House Ethics Committee concluded that Wright had skirted congressional restrictions on outside income from a book deal and speaking engagements. He resigned from the Speakership in May 1989 and left Congress a month later, retiring from public life in Fort Worth.

**WYMAN, JANE (1914– ).** Née Sarah Jane Fulks, Wyman was a popular actress in the 1930s, 1940s, and 1950s. She was President **Ronald Reagan**'s first wife. The couple married in 1940 and divorced in 1948. Reagan's growing political activism was a contributing factor in the couple's breakup. She and Ronald Reagan appeared together in the film *Brother Rat* (1938) and its sequel, *Brother Rat and a Baby* (1940). Her prominent film roles include *The Lost Weekend* (1945), *The Yearling* (1946), *Stage Fright* (1950), *The Story of Will Rogers* (1952), and *Pollyanna* (1960). From 1955 to 1958 she was the host of the television show *Jane Wyman Presents*. She won an Oscar for Best Actress for her role in *Johnny Belinda* (1948).

## – Y –

**YELTSIN, BORIS NIKOLAYEVICH (1931– ).** Born in a rural village in the region of Sverdlovsk, Russia (then part of the **Soviet Union**), Yeltsin graduated college with a specialty in construction. He joined the Communist Party in 1961. He rose through the ranks, moving from party chief in his native Sverdlovsk to the Politburo to mayor of Moscow. A critic of **Mikhail Gorbachev**'s economic and political reforms, Yeltsin was removed from his post as head of the Moscow City Committee in 1987 and demoted. Two years later, amid much political turmoil, he was elected to the Congress of People's Deputies. He left the Communist Party when the Congress declared the Russian Soviet Federated Socialist Republic to be sovereign, setting the stage for the ultimate dissolution of the Soviet Union. Yeltsin won election to the presidency of the Russian Republic in June 1991. He successfully rallied opposition to a coup attempt against Gorbachev several months later, in August 1991, but Gorbachev's power had already reached a nadir. In December Yeltsin met with his Ukrainian and Belorussian counterparts. They effectively ended the Soviet Union and replaced it with a **Commonwealth of Independent States** (CIS). Gorbachev resigned on 24 December 1991.

Yeltsin enjoyed generally good relations with President **George H. W. Bush**. The two leaders declared an end to the **Cold War** in 1992. That same year, Yeltsin embarked on a series of economic reforms that proved painful for industries and consumers alike. Opposition to his leadership resulted in a failed impeachment. In retaliation, he illegally used his decree powers to disband the legislature in 1993. Despite his lack of popularity, Yeltsin won reelection in 1996 with the aid of business interests. He resigned on the last day of December 1999, enabling Vladimir Putin, his prime minister, to become acting president. Putin won the subsequent presidential election in March 2000. See also *GLASNOST; PERESTROIKA*.

**YEUTTER, CLAYTON KEITH (1930– ).** Yeutter served as U.S. trade representative during **Ronald Reagan**'s second term from 1985 to 1989. He was heavily involved in the **Uruguay Round** of the **General Agreement on Tariffs and Trade (GATT)** negotiations on the liberalization of international trade. He later served as secretary of agriculture for **George H. W. Bush** from 1989 to 1991. Yeutter was chairman of the Republican National Committee from 1991 to 1992.

**YOUNG, NEIL (1945– ).** Born in Toronto, Ontario, Canada, Young is a singer-songwriter who has been inducted into the Canadian Music Hall of Fame for his blend of folk, country, and rock music. With singers **Willie Nelson** and **John Mellencamp**, he co-founded the

1985 benefit concert known as **Farm Aid**, which was aimed at bringing public attention to the plight of farmers. *See also* AGRICULTURAL CREDIT ACT; BLOCK, JOHN RUSLING.

## – Z –

**ZEMIN, JIANG (1926– ).** Born in Yangzhou, **China**, Jiang joined the Communist Party following **World War II,** and pursued a degree in electrical engineering. In the 1950s he managed state factories. He worked at the Chinese embassy in Moscow for five years, returning to mainland China in 1960 to work in mechanical engineering in an automobile factor for nearly a decade. He became a governmental advisor in 1978, and worked as a vice-minister in trade and electronics matters until his election to the Chinese Communist Party's Central Committee in 1985. He was appointed mayor of Shanghai in 1985, and later became a member of the Politburo. Known as an economic reformer, he was appointed general secretary of the Communist Party in June 1989 following the military suppression of the **Tiananmen Square** protests. He continued to back economic reforms, but tightened restrictions on civil liberties. Observers suggest that his choice as general secretary was aimed at minimizing international repercussions following Tiananmen in light of his international relations experience and managerial background.

**ZERO OPTION.** The zero option was a negotiating position on intermediate-range nuclear forces in Europe adopted by the administration of **Ronald Reagan**. In 1984, under pressure from Western European allies whose publics were opposed to the deployment of short-range **Pershing II missiles** in West Germany, Reagan contended that he would cancel their deployment if the Soviets agreed to remove all **SS-20 missiles** targeting Western Europe. The position was rejected, as expected, by the **Soviet Union**. However, Reagan's stance was aimed at undercutting the protests against missile deployments in Europe and shifting some of the blame to the Soviets. By 1988 the Pershing II missiles were dismantled with the signing of the **Intermediate-Range Nuclear Forces (INF) Treaty** between the United States and Soviet Union. *See also* ARMS CONTROL.

# Appendix 1
## President Ronald Reagan and His Administration, 1981–89

### Presidential Election Results, 1980

|  | **Popular Votes** | **Electoral Votes** |
| --- | --- | --- |
| Ronald W. Reagan | 43,267,489 | 489 |
| James E. Carter Jr. | 34,964,583 | 49 |
| John B. Anderson | 5,588,014 | 0 |

### Presidential Election Results, 1984

|  | **Popular Votes** | **Electoral Votes** |
| --- | --- | --- |
| Ronald W. Reagan | 53,428,357 | 525 |
| Walter F. Mondale | 36,930,923 | 13 |

**Vice President:**
George H. W. Bush (1981–89)

### Cabinet

**Agriculture, Secretary of:**
John R. Block (1981–86)
Richard E. Lyng (1986–89)
**Attorney General:**
William French Smith (1981–85)
Edwin Meese III (1985–88)
Richard L. Thornburgh (1988–89)
**Commerce, Secretary of:**
Malcolm Baldrige (1981–87)
C. William Verity (1987–89)
**Defense, Secretary of:**
Caspar W. Weinberger (1981–87)
Frank C. Carlucci (1987–89)

**Education, Secretary of:**
Terrel H. Bell (1981–85)
William J. Bennett (1985–88)
Lauro F. Cavazos Jr. (1988–89)
**Energy, Secretary of:**
James B. Edwards (1981–82)
Donald P. Hodel (1982–85)
John S. Herrington (1985–89)
**Health and Human Services, Secretary of:**
Richard S. Schweiker (1981–83)
Margaret M. Heckler (1983–85)
Otis R. Bowen (1985–89)
**Housing and Urban Development, Secretary of:**
Samuel R. Pierce Jr. (1981–89)
**Interior, Secretary of the:**
James G. Watt (1981–83)
William P. Clark (1983–85)
Donald P. Hodel (1985–89)
**Labor, Secretary of:**
Raymond J. Donovan (1981–85)
William E. Brock (1985–87)
Ann Dore McLaughlin (1987–89)
**State, Secretary of:**
Alexander M. Haig Jr. (1981–82)
George P. Schultz (1982–89)
**Transportation, Secretary of:**
Andrew L. Lewis Jr. (1981–83)
Elizabeth H. Dole (1983–87)
James H. Burnley (1987–89)
**Treasury, Secretary of the:**
Donald T. Regan (1981–85)
James A. Baker III (1985–88)
Nicholas F. Brady (1988–89)

## Key White House Advisors and Staff

**Assistant to the President for Management and Administration and Director of the Office of Administration:**
John F. W. Rogers (1983–85)

**Assistant to the President for Cabinet Affairs:**
Craig L. Fuller (1982–85)
Alfred Kingon (1985–87)
Nancy Risque (1987–89)
**Chief of Staff:**
James A. Baker III (1981–85)
Donald T. Regan (1985–87)
Howard H. Baker Jr. (1987–88)
Kenneth Duberstein (1988–89)
Rex W. Scouten (1981–82)
**Assistant to the President and Director of Communications:**
Patrick J. Buchanan (1985–87)
**Counsel:**
Fred F. Fielding (1981–86)
Peter J. Wallison (1986–87)
Arthur B. Culvahouse Jr. (1987–89)
**Assistant to the President for Legislative Affairs:**
Max L. Friedersdorf (1981–82)
Kenneth M. Duberstein (1982–84)
M. B. Oglesby (1984–86)
William L. Ball III (1986–88)
**Press Secretary:**
James Scott Brady (1981–89)
**Assistant to the President and Principal Deputy Press Secretary:**
Larry M. Speakes (1984–87)
**U.S. Trade Representative:**
William E. Brock (1981–85)
Clayton K. Yeutter (1985–89)

## Other Key Advisors/Advisory Units

**Council of Economic Advisors, Chairman:**
Murray L. Weidenbaum (1981–83)
Martin Feldstein (1983–85)
Beryl W. Sprinkel (1985–88)
**Council of Economic Advisors, Members:**
Jerry L. Jordan (1982–83)
William A. Niskanen (1982–85)
William A. Poole (1983–85)

Thomas Gale Moore (1985–88)
Michael L. Mussa (1987–88)
**Council on Environmental Quality, Chairman**
Malcolm F. Baldwin, acting (1981–82)
A. Alan Hill (1982–88)
**Foreign Intelligence Advisory Board, Chairman**
Anne Armstrong (1982–89)
**National Security Council, Assistant to the President for National Security Affairs:**
Richard V. Allen (1981–82)
William P. Clark (1982–83)
Robert C. McFarlane (1983–85)
John Poindexter (1985–86)
Frank C. Carlucci (1986–87)
Colin Powell (1987–89)
**Office of Management and Budget, Director**
David A. Stockman (1981–86)
James C. Miller III (1986–88)

*Source:* www.AmericanPresident.org, Miller Center of Public Affairs, University of Virginia.

# Appendix 2
## Vetoes of Public Bills Cast by Ronald Reagan, 1981–89

### 97th Congress (1981–82)

H.J.RES.357. November 23, 1981. Continuing appropriations for FY-1982.

H.R.4353. December 30, 1981 (pocket veto). Bankruptcies bill.

S.1503. March 20, 1982. Presidential crude oil allocation power.

H.R.5118. June 1, 1982. Papago Tribe of Arizona.

H.R.5922. June 24, 1982. Supplemental appropriations for FY-1982.

H.R.6682. June 25, 1982. Supplemental appropriations for FY-1982.

* H.R.6198. July 8, 1982. Amending the manufacturing clause of the copyright law.

* H.R.6863. August 28, 1982. Supplemental appropriations for FY-1982.

H.R.1371. October 15, 1982. Amending Contract Disputes Act of 1978.

S.2577. October 22, 1982. Environmental research/development appropriations.

S.2623. January 3, 1983 (pocket veto). Tribally Controlled Community College Assistance Act.

H.R.7336. January 14, 1983 (pocket veto). Amending the Education Consolidation and Improvement Act of 1981.

H.R.9. January 14, 1983 (pocket veto). National Wilderness Preservation/Florida.

H.R.3963. January 14, 1983 (pocket veto). Drug services/federal offenders.

### 98th Congress (1983–84)

S.366. April 5, 1983. Mashantucket Pequot Indians.

S.973. June 18, 1983. Indian Self-Determination and Education Assistance Act.

H.R.3564. August 12, 1983. 1984 crop feed grain program.

H.J.RES.338. August 13, 1983. Correcting Public Law 98-63.

S.J.RES.149. August 23, 1983. Milk price supports.

* H.R.1062. October 19, 1983. Lane County, Oregon, public lands.

H.R.4042. November 30, 1983 (pocket veto). El Salvador military assistance.

* S.684. February 21, 1984. Water resources research.

S.2436. August 29, 1984. Corporation for Public Broadcasting.

S.1967. October 17, 1984 (pocket veto). Gros Venture and Assiniboine Indians.

S.1097. October 20, 1984 (pocket veto). NOAA/Commerce programs.

S.607. October 22, 1984. Amending the Communications Act of 1934.

S.2166. October 22, 1984. Indian Health Care Improvement Act.

H.R.6248. October 23, 1984 (pocket veto). Amending Omnibus Crime Bill.

H.R.5172. October 30, 1984 (pocket veto). National Bureau of Standards.

H.R.999. October 31, 1984. Indian lands.

S.2574. October 31, 1984 (pocket veto). Nurse Education Amendments of 1984.

H.R.5760. October 31, 1984 (pocket veto). Cocopah Indian Tribe of Arizona lands.

S.540. October 31, 1984 (pocket veto). Establishing National Institute of Arthritis.

H.R.5479. November 9, 1984 (pocket veto). Court proceedings/expenses.

## 99th Congress (1985–1986)

H.R.1096. March 6, 1985. Famine relief and recovery in Africa.

* H.R.2409. November 8, 1985. National Institutes of Health.

H.R.3036. November 15, 1985. Treasury, Postal Service appropriations.

H.R.1562. December 17, 1985. Textile and apparel industry.

H.R.1404. January 14, 1986. Eastern Shore of Virginia National Wildlife Refuge.

H.R.3384. January 17, 1986. Civil Service Retirement System.

H.R.2466. February 14, 1986. United States Coast Guard.

S.J.RES.316. May 21, 1986. Saudi Arabia defense sales.

H.R.3247. September 26, 1986. Amending the Native American Programs Act of 1974.

* H.R.4868. September 26, 1986. South Africa sanctions.

H.R.2787. October 7, 1986. Small Business Administration Pilot Programs.

H.J.RES.748. October 9, 1986. Continuing appropriations for FY-1987.

H.R.4175. October 28, 1986. Transportation appropriations.

H.R.5465. November 1, 1986. Energy conservation standards for appliances.

H.R.4961. November 4, 1986 (pocket veto). Independent Safety Board Act.

S.2057. November 5, 1986 (pocket veto). President's Council on Health Promotion.

S.1128. November 6, 1986 (pocket veto). Clean Water Act.

H.R.5495. November 14, 1986. NASA appropriations.

## 100th Congress (1987–88)

* H.R.1. January 30, 1987. Federal Water Pollution Control Act.

* H.R.2. March 27, 1987. Federal highways.

S.742. June 22, 1987. Fairness in broadcasting.

* S.557. March 16, 1988. Civil Rights Restoration Act of 1988.

H.R.3. May 24, 1988. Competitiveness of American industry.

H.R.4264. August 3, 1988. Defense appropriations for FY-1989.

H.R.1154. September 28, 1988. United States textile and apparel industries imports.

S.1259. October 11, 1988. Federal lands in the State of Arkansas.

H.R.2596. October 22, 1988 (pocket veto). Admiralty Island, Alaska, lands.

S.508. October 26, 1988 (pocket veto). Federal employees/prohibited personnel practices.

S.437. October 31, 1988 (pocket veto). Small Business Investment Act/loans.

H.R.3621. November 2, 1988. California lands.

S.2751. November 3, 1988 (pocket veto). Montana lands.

H.R.3966. November 5, 1988. FCC restrictions on broadcasters.

H.R.4833. November 5, 1988 (pocket veto). Nurse education.

H.R.4432. November 8, 1988 (pocket veto). Asian Americans and Pacific Islanders/Census.

S.1081. November 8, 1988 (pocket veto). National Nutrition Monitoring.

H.R.5043. November 25, 1988 (pocket veto). Post-employment activities.

H.R.5560. November 25, 1988 (pocket veto). Health Omnibus Programs Extension of 1988.

* Veto overridden (public law).

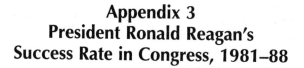

# Appendix 3
# President Ronald Reagan's
# Success Rate in Congress, 1981–88

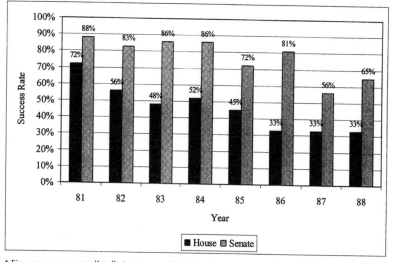

* Figures are percent roll-call victories on which President Reagan took a stand. Data are from *Congressional Quarterly Almanacs* (Washington, D.C.: CQ Press, 1981–88).

# Appendix 4
## President Ronald Reagan's
## Public Approval (%), 1981–88

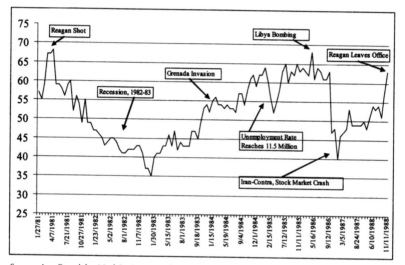

Source: Lyn Ragsdale, *Vital Statistics on the Presidency: Washington to Clinton* (Washington, D.C.: CQ Press, 1998).

# Appendix 5
## President Ronald Reagan's
## Monthly Approval Data (%), 1981–88

| Date | Approval | Date | Approval |
|------|----------|------|----------|
| 1/27/1981 | 57 | 7/25/1982 | 42 |
| 2/20/1981 | 55 | 8/1/1982 | 41 |
| 3/10/1981 | 59 | 8/15/1982 | 41 |
| 3/31/1981 | 67 | 8/29/1982 | 42 |
| 4/7/1981 | 67 | 9/19/1982 | 42 |
| 5/5/1981 | 68 | 10/17/1982 | 42 |
| 6/2/1981 | 59 | 11/7/1982 | 43 |
| 6/16/1981 | 59 | 11/21/1982 | 43 |
| 6/23/1981 | 58 | 12/21/1982 | 41 |
| 7/21/1981 | 56 | 1/16/1983 | 37 |
| 7/28/1981 | 59 | 1/25/1983 | 37 |
| 8/11/1981 | 60 | 1/30/1983 | 35 |
| 9/15/1981 | 52 | 2/27/1983 | 40 |
| 9/26/1981 | 56 | 3/13/1983 | 41 |
| 10/27/1981 | 54 | 4/17/1983 | 41 |
| 11/10/1981 | 49 | 5/1/1983 | 43 |
| 11/17/1981 | 55 | 5/15/1983 | 43 |
| 12/8/1981 | 49 | 5/22/1983 | 46 |
| 1/9/1982 | 49 | 6/12/1983 | 43 |
| 1/23/1982 | 47 | 6/26/1983 | 47 |
| 2/7/1982 | 47 | 7/24/1983 | 42 |
| 3/14/1982 | 46 | 8/1/1983 | 44 |
| 4/4/1982 | 45 | 8/7/1983 | 43 |
| 4/25/1982 | 43 | 8/14/1983 | 43 |
| 5/2/1982 | 44 | 8/21/1983 | 43 |
| 5/16/1982 | 45 | 9/11/1983 | 47 |
| 6/13/1982 | 45 | 9/18/1983 | 47 |
| 6/27/1982 | 44 | 10/10/1983 | 45 |

| Date | Approval | Date | Approval |
|---|---|---|---|
| 10/23/1983 | 49 | 11/11/1985 | 65 |
| 11/20/1983 | 53 | 12/6/1985 | 63 |
| 12/11/1983 | 54 | 1/10/1986 | 64 |
| 1/15/1984 | 52 | 3/7/1986 | 63 |
| 1/28/1984 | 55 | 4/11/1986 | 62 |
| 2/11/1984 | 56 | 5/16/1986 | 68 |
| 3/17/1984 | 54 | 6/6/1986 | 61 |
| 4/7/1984 | 54 | 6/9/1986 | 64 |
| 5/19/1984 | 53 | 7/11/1986 | 63 |
| 6/23/1984 | 54 | 8/8/1986 | 61 |
| 7/1/1984 | 53 | 9/12/1986 | 61 |
| 7/7/1984 | 53 | 10/24/1986 | 63 |
| 7/28/1984 | 52 | 12/4/1986 | 47 |
| 9/4/1984 | 57 | 1/16/1987 | 48 |
| 9/18/1984 | 57 | 2/27/1987 | 40 |
| 9/25/1984 | 54 | 3/5/1987 | 46 |
| 10/27/1984 | 58 | 3/14/1987 | 47 |
| 11/19/1984 | 61 | 4/10/1987 | 48 |
| 12/1/1984 | 62 | 6/8/1987 | 53 |
| 12/9/1984 | 59 | 7/10/1987 | 49 |
| 1/11/1985 | 62 | 8/24/1987 | 49 |
| 1/13/1985 | 62 | 12/4/1987 | 49 |
| 1/25/1985 | 64 | 1/22/1988 | 49 |
| 2/15/1985 | 60 | 3/9/1988 | 50 |
| 3/8/1985 | 56 | 5/13/1988 | 48 |
| 4/12/1985 | 52 | 6/10/1988 | 51 |
| 5/17/1985 | 55 | 7/15/1988 | 54 |
| 6/7/1985 | 58 | 8/19/1988 | 53 |
| 7/12/1985 | 63 | 9/25/1988 | 54 |
| 8/13/1985 | 65 | 10/21/1988 | 51 |
| 9/13/1985 | 60 | 11/11/1988 | 57 |
| 10/11/1985 | 63 | 12/27/1988 | 63 |
| 11/11/1985 | 62 | | |

*Source*: Lyn Ragsdale, *Vital Statistics on the Presidency: Washington to Clinton* (Washington, D.C.: CQ Press, 1998), pp. 209–14.

# Appendix 6
# President George H. W. Bush and
# His Administration, 1989–93

## Presidential Election Results (1988)

|  | Popular Votes | Electoral Votes |
|---|---|---|
| George H. W. Bush | 48,881,278 | 426 |
| Michael S. Dukakis | 41,805,374 | 111 |

## Presidential Election Results (1992)

|  | Popular Votes | Electoral Votes |
|---|---|---|
| William J. Clinton | 44,909,889 | 370 |
| George H. W. Bush | 39,104,545 | 168 |
| H. Ross Perot | 19,742,267 | 0 |

**Vice President:**
J. Danforth Quayle (1989–93)

## Cabinet

**Agriculture, Secretary of:**
Clayton K. Yeutter (1989–91)
Edward R. Madigan (1991–93)
**Attorney General:**
Richard L. Thornburgh (1989–91)
William P. Barr (1991–93)
**Commerce, Secretary of:**
Robert A. Mosbacher (1989–92)
Barbara Hackman Franklin (1992–93)
**Defense, Secretary of:**
Richard B. Cheney (1989–93)

**Education, Secretary of:**
  Lauro F. Cavazos Jr. (1989–91)
  Lamar Alexander (1991–93)
**Energy, Secretary of:**
  James D. Watkins (1989–93)
**Health and Human Services, Secretary of:**
  Louis Wade Sullivan (1989–93)
**Housing and Urban Development, Secretary of:**
  Jack French Kemp (1989–93)
**Interior, Secretary of the:**
  Manuel Lujan (1989–93)
**Labor, Secretary of:**
  Elizabeth Hanford Dole (1989–91)
  Lynn M. Martin (1991–93)
**State, Secretary of:**
  James A. Baker III (1989–92)
  Lawrence S. Eagleburger (1992–93)
**Transportation, Secretary of:**
  Samuel Knox Skinner (1989–92)
  Andrew H. Card Jr. (1992–93)
**Treasury, Secretary of the:**
  Nicholas F. Brady (1989–93)
**Veterans' Affairs, Secretary of:**
  Edward J. Derwinski (1989–91)


## Key White House Advisors and Staff

**Chief of Staff:**
  John H. Sununu (1989–91)
  Samuel K. Skinner (1991–92)
  James A. Baker III (1992–93)
**Deputy Chief of Staff:**
  Andrew H. Card Jr. (1989–92)
  W. Henson Moore (1992)
  Robert B. Zoellick (1992–93)
**Office of Communications, Director:**
  David F. Demarest Jr. (1989–92)
  Margaret DeBardeleben Tutwiler (1992–93)

**Counsel:**
C. Boyden Gray (1989–93)
**Press Secretary:**
Marlin Fitzwater (1989–93)
**Council on Environmental Quality, Chairman:**
A. Alan Hill (1989)
Michael R. Deland (1989–93)
**Foreign Intelligence Advisory Board, Chairman:**
Anne L. Armstrong (1989–90)
John G. Tower (1990–91)
Bobby Ray Inman (1991–93)
**Assistant to the President for Legislative Affairs:**
Frederick D. McClure (1989–92)
Nicholas E. Calio (1992–93)
**Office of National Drug Control Policy, Director:**
William J. Bennett (1989–91)
Robert Martinez (1991–93)
**National Security Council (NSC), Assistant to the President for National Security Affairs:**
Lt. Gen. Brent Scowcroft (1989–93) (retired, USAF)
**U.S. Trade Representative:**
AMB, Carla Anderson Hills (1989–93)

*Source:* www.AmericanPresident.org, Miller Center of Public Affairs, University of Virginia.

# Appendix 7
## Vetoes of Public Bills Cast by George H. W. Bush, 1989–93

### 101st Congress (1989–90)

H.R.2. June 13, 1989. Minimum wage.

S.J.RES.113. July 31, 1989. Japan FSX aircraft codevelopment.

H.J.RES.390. August 16, 1989 (pocket veto). Federal Deposit Insurance Corporation.

H.R.3026. October 27, 1989. District of Columbia appropriations.

H.R.2939. November 19, 1989. Appropriations for foreign operations.

H.R.3610. November 20, 1989. District of Columbia appropriations.

H.R.1231. November 21, 1989. Eastern Airlines dispute.

H.R.1487. November 21, 1989. Appropriations for FY-1990–91, Department of State.

H.R.2990. November 21, 1989. Labor, HHS, and Education appropriations.

H.R.2712. November 30, 1989. Chinese immigration.

H.R.2364. May 24, 1990. Rail Passenger Service Act (AMTRAK) appropriations.

H.R.20. June 15, 1990. Federal employee political participation.

H.R.770. June 29, 1990. Family leave.

H.R.4328. October 5, 1990. Textiles, apparel, and footwear imports.

H.J.RES.660. October 6, 1990. Continuing appropriations for FY-1991.

S.2104. October 22, 1990. Civil Rights Act of 1990.

H.R.4638. November 10, 1990 (pocket veto). Food, Drug and Cosmetic Act revisions.

H.R.4653 November 17, 1990 (pocket veto).

S.321. November 21, 1990 (pocket veto). Indian Preference Act.

S.2834. November 30, 1990 (pocket veto). Intelligence appropriations.

## 102nd Congress (1991–92)

H.R.2699. August 17, 1991. District of Columbia appropriations.

S.1722. October 11, 1991. Unemployment compensation benefits.

H.R.2707. November 19, 1991. Labor, HHS, and Education appropriations.

** S.1176. December 20, 1991 (pocket veto). Morris K. Udall Scholarship.

H.R.2212. March 2, 1992. China Most-Favored Nation Trade Status.

H.R.4210. March 20, 1992. Economic growth/tax relief.

S.3. May 9, 1992. Campaign finance reform.

S.2342. June 16, 1992. Mississippi Sioux Indians.

H.R.2507. June 23, 1992. National Institutes of Health.

S.250. July 2, 1992. National voter registration ("motor voter").

S.5. September 22, 1992. Family medical leave.

S.323. September 25, 1992. HHS/Abortion counseling.

H.R.5318. September 28, 1992. China Most-Favored Nation Status.

H.R.5517. September 30, 1992. District of Columbia appropriations.

* S.12. October 3, 1992. Cable television re-regulation.

S.3095. October 21, 1992 (pocket veto). Jena Band of Choctaws of Louisiana.

H.R.2859. October 27, 1992 (pocket veto). Lynn, Massachusetts, historical preservation.

H.R.5021. October 27, 1992 (pocket veto). New Jersey/Wild and Scenic Rivers Act.

H.R.5061. October 27, 1992 (pocket veto). Establish Dry Tortugas National Park, Florida.

H.R.5452. October 27, 1992 (pocket veto). Delaware River Port Authority.

H.R.2109. October 28, 1992 (pocket veto). Revere, Massachusetts/National Park System.

H.R.6185. October 30, 1992 (pocket veto). Federal Courts Study Committee.

H.R.6138. October 31, 1992 (pocket veto). Consolidated Farm and Rural Development Act.

S.3144. October 31, 1992 (pocket veto). Armed Forces/health care.

H.R.11. November 5, 1992 (pocket veto). Tax enterprise zones.

\* Veto overridden (public law).

\*\* The president neither signed nor returned this bill after Congress adjourned on November 27, 1991. The president and Congress disagreed on whether this bill ever became law. The bill was repassed as S. 2184, and became a public law on March 19, 1992.

# Appendix 8
## President George H. W. Bush's Success Rate in Congress, 1989–92

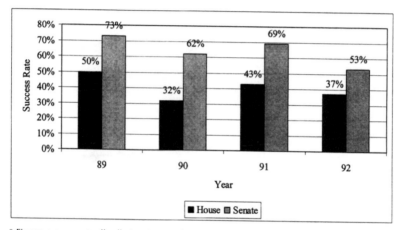

* Figures are percent roll-call victories on which President Bush took a stand. Data are from *Congressional Quarterly Almanacs* (Washington, D.C.: CQ Press, 1989–92).

# Appendix 9
## President George H. W. Bush's Public Approval (%), 1989–92

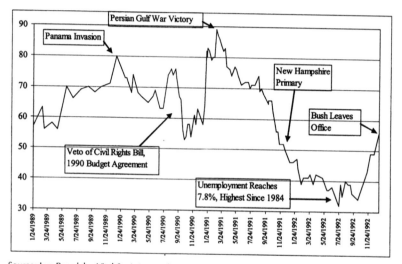

Source: Lyn Ragsdale, *Vital Statistics on the Presidency: Washington to Clinton* (Washington, D.C.: CQ Press, 1998).

# Appendix 10
## President George H. W. Bush's
## Monthly Approval Data (%), 1989–92

| Date | Approval | Date | Approval |
|------|----------|------|----------|
| 1/24/1989 | 57 | 9/10/1990 | 76 |
| 2/28/1989 | 63 | 9/14/1990 | 73 |
| 3/10/1989 | 56 | 9/27/1990 | 67 |
| 4/10/1989 | 58 | 10/3/1990 | 66 |
| 5/4/1989 | 56 | 10/11/1990 | 56 |
| 6/8/1989 | 70 | 10/18/1990 | 53 |
| 7/6/1989 | 66 | 10/25/1990 | 54 |
| 8/10/1989 | 69 | 11/1/1990 | 58 |
| 9/7/1989 | 70 | 11/8/1990 | 58 |
| 10/5/1989 | 68 | 11/15/1990 | 54 |
| 11/2/1989 | 70 | 11/29/1990 | 61 |
| 12/7/1989 | 71 | 12/6/1990 | 58 |
| 1/4/1990 | 80 | 12/13/1990 | 63 |
| 2/8/1990 | 73 | 1/3/1991 | 58 |
| 2/15/1990 | 73 | 1/11/1991 | 64 |
| 3/8/1990 | 68 | 1/17/1991 | 82 |
| 3/15/1990 | 74 | 1/19/1991 | 80 |
| 4/5/1990 | 68 | 1/23/1991 | 83 |
| 4/19/1990 | 67 | 1/30/1991 | 82 |
| 5/17/1990 | 65 | 2/7/1991 | 79 |
| 6/7/1990 | 67 | 2/14/1991 | 80 |
| 6/15/1990 | 69 | 2/21/1991 | 80 |
| 7/6/1990 | 63 | 2/28/1991 | 89 |
| 7/19/1990 | 63 | 3/7/1991 | 87 |
| 8/9/1990 | 74 | 3/14/1991 | 86 |
| 8/16/1990 | 75 | 3/21/1991 | 84 |
| 8/23/1990 | 76 | 3/28/1991 | 82 |
| 8/30/1990 | 74 | 4/4/1991 | 83 |

| Date | Approval | Date | Approval |
|------|----------|------|----------|
| 4/11/1991 | 77 | 1/3/1992 | 46 |
| 4/25/1991 | 76 | 1/16/1992 | 46 |
| 5/2/1991 | 74 | 1/31/1992 | 47 |
| 5/16/1991 | 77 | 2/6/1992 | 44 |
| 5/23/1991 | 76 | 2/19/1992 | 39 |
| 5/30/1991 | 74 | 2/28/1992 | 41 |
| 6/13/1991 | 71 | 3/11/1992 | 41 |
| 6/27/1991 | 72 | 3/20/1992 | 41 |
| 7/11/1991 | 72 | 3/26/1992 | 42 |
| 7/18/1991 | 70 | 4/9/1992 | 39 |
| 7/25/1991 | 71 | 4/20/1992 | 42 |
| 8/8/1991 | 71 | 5/18/1992 | 41 |
| 8/23/1991 | 74 | 6/4/1992 | 37 |
| 8/29/1991 | 69 | 6/12/1992 | 37 |
| 9/5/1991 | 70 | 6/26/1992 | 38 |
| 9/13/1991 | 68 | 7/24/1992 | 32 |
| 9/26/1991 | 66 | 7/31/1992 | 39 |
| 10/3/1991 | 65 | 8/8/1992 | 35 |
| 10/3/1991 | 66 | 8/21/1992 | 40 |
| 10/17/1991 | 66 | 8/31/1992 | 39 |
| 10/24/1991 | 62 | 9/11/1992 | 39 |
| 10/31/1991 | 59 | 9/17/1992 | 36 |
| 11/7/1991 | 56 | 10/12/1992 | 34 |
| 11/14/1991 | 56 | 11/20/1992 | 43 |
| 11/21/1991 | 52 | 12/4/1992 | 49 |
| 12/5/1991 | 52 | 12/18/1992 | 49 |
| 12/12/1991 | 50 | 1/8/1993 | 56 |

*Source:* Lyn Ragsdale, *Vital Statistics on the Presidency: Washington to Clinton* (Washington, D.C.: CQ Press, 1998).

# Bibliography

## CONTENTS

## INTRODUCTION

The politics of the Reagan–Bush era has spawned an extensive scholarly literature, even if—by historical standards—both presidencies are quite recent. The scholarship on Reagan's presidency is particularly comprehensive. While much research on Reagan was published in the 1980s, the end of the moratorium on archival records at the Ronald Reagan Presidential Library in 2001 and the president's death in 2004 have sparked a renewed interest in analysis of his long-term impact on American politics and society. Of particular note are the "second generation" scholarly evaluations of Reagan that have been undertaken in recent years. Historians and political scientists have redoubled efforts to place the 40th president's legacy within a broader perspective now that more than a decade and a half has passed since he left office.

George H. W. Bush's single term in office has not generated the same volume of academic coverage. The basis for future scholarship is quite promising, however, given the scope of changes in the global geopolitical landscape during his presidency. Historians and political scientists will continue to look to his term to better understand the fall of Communism and subsequent efforts at democratization in the former Soviet Union and Eastern Europe. Moreover, his conduct of foreign policy, international coalition-building skills, and management of the Persian Gulf War in 1991 undoubtedly contrast to his son's strategy for confronting Iraqi dictator Saddam Hussein in 2003. As more archival holdings are processed and now that the general moratorium on records at the George H. W. Bush Presidential Library expired in 2005, new material will surely tempt scholars from across subfields to begin reevaluating the 41st president's historical legacy.

The Reagan and Bush presidential libraries, administered by the National Archives and Records Administration, are, in fact, excellent places to commence research. The Reagan Library, situated atop a commanding hill in Simi Valley, California, not only boasts an impressive museum but also contains administration papers that have yet to be fully exploited. Finding aids and general information are available on the Internet at www.reaganlibrary.net and www.reagan.utexas.edu. Papers covering Reagan's two terms as governor of California are available at the California State Archives in Sacramento. More information is available on the Internet at www.ss.ca.gov/archives/archives_e.htm. Finally, the Bush Presidential Museum and Library on the campus of Texas A&M University in College Station, Texas, features state-of-the-art displays, such as troop movements during the Gulf War, that offer a unique perspective into the legacy of the 41st president. Researchers should consult finding aids available on the Internet at http://bushlibrary.tamu .edu.

The works cited in the selected bibliography that follows comprise those memoirs, scholarly books, and peer-reviewed articles in social sciences and history that analyze particular facets of the Reagan and

Bush presidencies—from administrative approaches to urban policy. Included in the repertoire are the most authoritative biographies as well as insightful critiques for each president. In addition, autobiographies and memoirs written by White House insiders are included.

Excellent biographies have been written for both presidents. The works of Lou Cannon, who spent a quarter century covering Ronald Reagan for the *Los Angeles Times* and *Washington Post*, are particularly noteworthy. His biographies *President Reagan: The Role of a Lifetime* (1991), *Reagan* (1982), and *Governor Reagan: His Rise to Power* (2003) are fair-minded and offer invaluable perspectives on the man, his politics, and his policies. Herbert Parmet's *George Bush: The Life of a Lone-Star Yankee* (1997) and Tom Wicker's *George Herbert Walker Bush* (2004) offer detailed accounts of Bush's life. John Robert Greene's *The Presidency of George Bush* (2000) provides solid, wide-ranging analysis of the president's term.

Both presidents' relations with the press and media have been examined in some detail by scholars and practitioners. Reagan was known for his command as a "Great Communicator," while Bush's performance is frequently regarded as substandard and "anti-rhetorical," to borrow from Mark Rozell. Robert Denton's *The Primetime Presidency of Ronald Reagan* (1988) evaluates Reagan's use of the media to enhance his image and leadership. Robert Dallek's *Reagan: The Politics of Symbolism* (1984) and William Ker Muir's *Bully Pulpit* (1992) similarly emphasize the centrality of Reagan's vision and communication skills in his leadership. Mark Hertsgaard's *On Bended Knee: The Press and the Reagan Presidency* (1988) uses extensive interviews to argue that the Reagan White House was able to transform the press into an advocate for the administration's policies. In *Hold On, Mr. President!* (1987), veteran television reporter Sam Donaldson recounts his experiences in covering the Carter and Reagan presidencies, and justifies his pointed, sometimes acerbic style. Marlin Fitzwater, who served as press secretary to both Reagan and Bush, describes his views of the press corps and relations with reporters who were sometimes antagonistic to the White House in *Call the Briefing!* (1995). Mark Rozell's *The Press and the Bush Presidency* (1996) is an impressive academic analysis of press coverage of Bush's term and the ways in which the media defined the president's leadership and style.

Many excellent insights into events and policies specific to each president may be gleaned from various books and journal articles. The selected bibliography covers Reagan's foreign policy and spans the following: the Strategic Defense Initiative ("Star Wars") and its impact on arms control and U.S.–Soviet relations; the invasion of Grenada; the Libyan air strikes, the bombing of the Marine barracks in Lebanon, and Middle East policy; support of counterrevolutionary insurgencies in Central America and Angola; and Iran–Contra. For Bush, the bibliography provides a guide to literature on foreign affairs including the invasion of Panama, the Persian Gulf War, and post–Cold War foreign policy. There is an extensive literature on the elections of 1980, 1984, and 1988. Finally, aspects of each president's administrative arrangements, congressional relations, budget and domestic policy, and regulatory approach are covered in the bibliography.

It is vital to mention notable works in history and political science for which the Reagan and Bush presidencies form a component of, or a "case study" in, larger endeavors to build comprehensive theories of the development of the modern presidency. These titles are *not* included in the selected bibliography but are important points of reference for the reader who wishes to place either or both presidents within a broader framework. Normative and empirical works treat one or both presidencies as a case that may be juxtaposed against others in order to gain perspective on presidential leadership and the role of the White House in the constitutional order over time. Richard Neustadt's *Presidential Power and the Modern Presidents* (New York: Free Press, 1991) remains one of the classic analyses and prescriptive works regarding the informal basis of presidential power. Stephen Skowronek's *The Politics Presidents Make: Leadership from John Adams to George Bush* (Cambridge, Mass.: Harvard University Press, 1993) seeks to reconcile the scholarly divide in studies that focus either on the "modern" presidency (post–Franklin D. Roosevelt) or his "pre-modern" predecessors. By constructing a theory of regime cycles, he shows how similar dynamics in broad political, economic, and societal developments traverse "political time" and enable a comparison of presidential leadership across not only decades but centuries. William E. Leuchtenburg, by contrast, shows how the indelible imprint Roosevelt left on the presidency influenced each of his successors as they attempted to emulate his leadership style and success in his *In the Shadow of FDR: From Harry Truman to Bill Clinton* (Ithaca, N.Y.: Cornell University Press, 1993).

Many scholars focus on presidents' seeming obsession with press relations, the use of the bully pulpit, and public opinion. Samuel Kernell's *Going Public: New Strategies of Presidential Leadership* (Washington, D.C.: Congressional Quarterly, 1997) is a remarkably in-depth examination of presidents' public activities. George C. Edwards's oeuvre entitled *On Deaf Ears: The Limits of the Bully Pulpit* (New Haven, Conn.: Yale University Press, 2003) represents a seminal attempt to study the *effects* of presidents' bids to mold public opinion. He concludes that despite chief executives' belief that they can shape the public's views, little evidence suggests they have been successful. Jeffrey C. Cohen examines a different facet of the presidency and public opinion. His book *Presidential Responsiveness and Public Policy-Making: The Public and the Policies That Presidents Choose* (Ann Arbor: University of Michigan Press, 1997) analyzes whether presidents lead public opinion or follow it.

A substantial literature has developed on presidents' relations with Congress. Quantitative approaches that examine the determinants of legislative success include George C. Edwards III, *At the Margins: Presidential Leadership of Congress* (New Haven, Conn.: Yale University Press, 1990), Jon R. Bond and Richard Fleisher, *The President in the Legislative Arena* (Chicago: University of Chicago Press, 1990), Richard S. Conley, *The Presidency, Congress, and Divided Government: A Postwar Assessment* (College Station: Texas A&M University Press, 2003), and Andrew Rudalevige, *Managing the President's Program: Presidential Leadership and Legislative Policy Formulation* (Princeton, N.J.: Princeton University Press, 2002). Paul C. Light's *The President's Agenda: Domestic Policy Choice from Kennedy to Clinton* (Baltimore, Md.: Johns Hopkins University Press, 1982) remains a foundational work. Mark A. Peterson's *Legislating Together: The White House and Capitol Hill from Eisenhower to Reagan* (Cambridge, Mass.: Harvard University Press, 1990) focuses on the determinants of presidential agenda success in Congress. Robert J. Spitzer's *The Presidential Veto: Touchstone of the American Presidency* (Albany: SUNY Press, 1988) and Richard A. Watson's *Presidential Vetoes and Public Policy* (Lawrence: University Press of Kansas, 1993) analyze the constitutional basis for the president's prerogative power and the impact of the veto on policy outcomes. Charles C. Cameron's *Veto Bargaining: Presidents and the Politics of Negative Power* (New York: Cambridge University Press, 2000) is a theory -rich and empirically sophisticated examination of the determinants of veto usage.

A growing literature has also begun to examine the unilateral powers of the presidency. Kenneth R. Mayer's *With the Stroke of a Pen: Executive Orders and Presidential Power* (Princeton, N.J.: Princeton University Press, 2001), Philip J. Cooper's *By Order of the President: The Use and Abuse of Executive Direct Action* (Lawrence: University Press of Kansas, 2002), and William G. Howell's *Power without Persuasion: The Politics of Direct Presidential Action* (Princeton, N.J.: Princeton University Press, 2003) offer excellent analyses of the politics and impacts of executive orders and independent decisions.

The Reagan and Bush presidencies are also covered in works that seek to understand the organizational imperatives of the White House. Stephen Hess's updated volume *Organizing the Presidency* (Washington, D.C.: Brookings, 2002) and John P. Burke's *The Institutional Presidency: Organizing and Managing the White House from FDR to Clinton* (Baltimore, Md.: Johns Hopkins University Press, 2000) are excellent starting points for examining staffing arrangements and models of advice. Similarly, James P. Pfiffner's *The Strategic Presidency: Hitting the Ground Running* (Lawrence: University Press of Kansas, 1996) and edited volume *The Managerial Presidency* (College Station: Texas A&M University Press, 1999) provide in-depth insight and advice on White House organization. *The White House World: Transitions, Organization, and Office Operations* (College Station: Texas A&M University Press, 2003), edited by Martha Joynt Kumar and Terry Sullivan, furnishes insider perspectives on the nexus between presidential transitions and staffing.

Finally, the authoritative works by Louis Fisher on the separation of powers and foreign policy should be noted. *Presidential War Power* (Lawrence: University Press of Kansas, 2004) covers the military conflicts under both Reagan and Bush, and sets them within a much longer historical frame of reference. Similarly, *Constitutional Conflicts between Congress and the President* (Lawrence: University Press of Kansas, 1997) assesses executive–legislative struggles over foreign and domestic affairs.

# THE REAGAN YEARS

## Administrative Presidency

Cohen, David B. "From the Fabulous Baker Boys to the Master of Disaster: The White House Chief of Staff in the Reagan and G. H. W. Bush Administrations." *Presidential Studies Quarterly* 32 (2002): 463–83.

Cohen, David. B., and George A. Krause. "Presidents, Chiefs of Staff, and White House Organizational Behavior: Survey Evidence from the Reagan and Bush Administrations." *Presidential Studies Quarterly* 30 (2000): 421–42.

Durant, Robert F. *The Administrative Presidency Revisited: Public Lands, the BLM, and the Reagan Revolution.* Albany, N.Y.: SUNY Press, 1992.

Golden, Marissa Martino. *What Motivates Bureaucrats? Politics and Administration During the Reagan Years.* New York: Columbia University Press, 2000.

Kessel, John H. "The Structures of the Reagan White House." *American Journal of Political Science* 28 (1984): 231–58.

Maranto, Robert. *Politics and Bureaucracy in the Modern Presidency: Careerists and Appointees in the Reagan Administration.* Westport, Conn.: Greenwood Press, 1993.

Martin, Janet M. "An Examination of Executive Branch Appointments in the Reagan Administration by Background and Gender." *Western Political Quarterly* 44 (1991): 173–84.

Nathan, Richard P. *The Administrative Presidency.* New York: Wiley, 1983.

Pious, Richard M. "Prerogative Power and the Reagan Presidency: A Review Essay." *Political Science Quarterly* 106 (1991): 499–510.

Rockman, Bert A. "Tightening the Reins: The Federal Executive and the Management Philosophy of the Reagan Presidency." *Presidential Studies Quarterly* 23 (1993): 103–14.

## Air Traffic Controller's Strike

Round, Michael A. *Grounded: Reagan and the PATCO Crash.* New York: Garland, 1999.

## Arms Control and Soviet Relations

Adelman, Kenneth. *The Great Universal Embrace: Arms Summitry—A Skeptic's Account.* New York: Simon and Schuster, 1989.

Busch, Andrew. "Ronald Reagan and the Defeat of the Soviet Empire." *Presidential Studies Quarterly* 27 (1997): 451–66.

Farnham, Barbara. "Reagan and the Gorbachev Revolution: Perceiving the End of Threat." *Political Science Quarterly* 116 (summer 2001): 225–52.

Hoekstra, Douglas J. "Presidential Beliefs and the Reagan Paradox." *Presidential Studies Quarterly* 27 (1997): 429–50.

Jackson, William D. "Soviet Reassessment of Ronald Reagan, 1985–88." *Political Science Quarterly* 113 (winter 1998–99): 617–44.

Krepon, Michael. *Arms Control in the Reagan Administration.* Lanham, Md.: University Press of America, 1989.

Leng, Russell J. "Reagan and the Russians: Crisis Bargaining Beliefs and the Historical Record." *American Political Science Review* 78 (1984): 338–55.

Loeb, Paul R. *Hope in Hard Times: America's Peace Movement and the Reagan Era.* Lexington, Mass.: Lexington Books, 1987.

Mandelbaum, Michael, and Strobe Talbot. *Reagan and Gorbachev.* New York: Vintage Books, 1987.

Scheer, Robert. *With Enough Shovels: Reagan, Bush, and Nuclear War.* New York: Random House, 1982.

Scott, Robert Travis. *Race for Security: Arms and Arms Control in the Reagan Years.* Lexington, Mass.: Lexington Books, 1987.

Shimko, Keith L. *Images and Arms Control: Perceptions of the Soviet Union in the Reagan Administration.* Ann Arbor: University of Michigan Press, 1991.

Talbott, Strobe. *Deadly Gambits: The Reagan Administration and the Stalemate in Nuclear Arms Control.* New York: Knopf, 1984.

Whelan, Joseph G. *Moscow Summit, 1988: Reagan and Gorbachev in Negotiation.* Boulder, Colo.: Westview Press, 1990.

## Assassination Attempt

Abrams, Herbert L. *The President Has Been Shot: Confusion, Disability, and the 25th Amendment in the Aftermath of the Attempted Assassination of Ronald Reagan.* New York: W. W. Norton, 1992.

Gantz, Walter. "The Diffusion of News About the Attempted Reagan Assassination." *Journal of Communication* 33 (1983): 56–66.

Mortensen, C. David. *Violence and Communication: Public Reactions to an Attempted Presidential Assassination.* Lanham, Md.: University Press of America, 1987.

## Autobiographies, Memoirs, and Selected Writings

Hannaford, Peter, ed. *The Quotable Reagan.* Washington, D.C.: Regnery, 1998.

Reagan, Ronald. *An American Life: The Autobiography.* New York: Simon and Schuster, 1990.

——. *The Official Ronald Wilson Reagan Quote Book*. St. Louis Park, Minn.: Chain-Pinkham Books, 1980.

——. *Where's the Rest of Me?* New York: Duell, Sloan and Pearce, 1965.

Skinner, Kiron K., Annelise Anderson, and Martin Anderson, eds. *Reagan, in His Own Hand: The Writings of Ronald Reagan That Reveal His Revolutionary Vision for America*. New York: Free Press, 2001.

Troxler, L. William, ed. *Along Wit's Trail: The Humor and Wisdom of Ronald Reagan*. New York: Holt, Rinehart, and Winston, 1984.

## Biographies

Cannon, Lou. *President Reagan: The Role of a Lifetime*. New York: Simon and Schuster, 1991.

——. *Reagan*. New York: Putnam, 1982.

Edwards, Anne. *Early Reagan*. New York: Morrow, 1987.

Noonan, Peggy. *When Character Was King: A Story of Ronald Reagan*. New York: Penguin Books, 2003.

Pemberton, William E. *Exit with Honor: The Life and Presidency of Ronald Reagan*. Armonk, N.Y.: M. E. Sharpe, 1997.

Smith, Hedrick. *Reagan: The Man, the President*. New York: Macmillan, 1980.

## Central America

Arnson, Cynthia J. *Crossroads: Congress, the Reagan Administration, and Central America*. New York: Pantheon, 1989.

Blanton, Shannon L. "Images in Conflict: The Case of Ronald Reagan and El Salvador." *International Studies Quarterly* 40 (1996): 23–44.

Brown, Jeremy M. *Explaining the Reagan Years in Central America: A World System Perspective*. Lanham, Md.: University Press of America, 1995.

Carothers, Thomas. *In the Name of Democracy: U.S. Policy Toward Latin America in the Reagan Years*. Berkeley: University of California Press, 1991.

Coleman, Kenneth M., and George C. Herring. *The Central American Crisis: Sources of Conflict and the Failure of U.S. Policy*. Wilmington, Del.: Scholarly Resources, 1985.

Hahn, Walter F., ed. *Central America and the Reagan Doctrine*. Lanham, Md.: University Press of America, 1987.

Hoover, Judith D. "Ronald Reagan's Failure to Secure Contra-Aid: A Post-Vietnam Shift in Foreign Policy Rhetoric." *Presidential Studies Quarterly* 24 (1994): 531–41.

Layton, Mike. *Easy Blood: Ronald Reagan's Proxy Wars in Central America*. Olympia, Wash.: DragonRed Publishers, 1997.

Lefeber, Walter. "The Reagan Administration and Revolutions in Central America." *Political Science Quarterly* 99 (1984): 1–25.

## Civil Rights

Amaker, Norman C. *Civil Rights and the Reagan Administration.* Washington, D.C.: Urban Institute Press, 1988.

Detlefsen, Robert R. "Affirmative Action and Business Deregulation: On the Reagan Administration's Failure to Revise Executive Order No. 11246." *Policy Studies Journal* 21 (1993): 556–64.

Detlefsen, Robert R., and Robert B. Hawkins. *Civil Rights under Reagan.* San Francisco: ICS Press, 1991.

Laham, Nicholas. *The Reagan Presidency and the Politics of Race: In Pursuit of Colorblind Justice and Limited Government.* Westport, Conn.: Praeger, 1998.

Shull, Steven A. *A Kinder, Gentler Racism? The Reagan–Bush Civil Rights Legacy.* Armonk, N.Y.: M. E. Sharpe, 1993.

## Comparative Perspectives

Abbott, Philip. "Leadership by Exemplar: Reagan's FDR and Thatcher's Churchill." *Presidential Studies Quarterly* 27 (1997): 186–206.

Adonis, Andrew, and Tim Hames, eds. *A Conservative Revolution? The Thatcher–Reagan Decade in Perspective.* New York: St. Martin's Press, 1994.

Clayton, Dorothy H., and Robert J. Thompson. "Reagan, Thatcher and Social Welfare: Typical and Nontypical Behavior for Presidents and Prime Ministers." *Presidential Studies Quarterly* (1989): 565–81.

Hoover, Kenneth R. "The Rise of Conservative Capitalism: Ideological Tensions within the Reagan and Thatcher Governments." *Comparative Studies in Society and History* 29 (1987): 245–68.

Kengor, Paul. "Comparing Presidents Reagan and Eisenhower." *Presidential Studies Quarterly.* 28 (1998): 366–93.

Krieger, Joel. *Reagan, Thatcher, and the Politics of Decline.* New York: Oxford University Press, 1992.

Pierson, Paul. *Dismantling the Welfare State? Reagan, Thatcher, and the Politics of Retrenchment.* New York: Cambridge University Press, 1994.

Royed, Terry J. "Testing the Mandate Model in Britain and the United States: Evidence from the Reagan and Thatcher Eras." *British Journal of Political Science* 26 (1996): 45–80.

Smith, Geoffrey. *Reagan and Thatcher.* London: Bodley Head, 1990.

Smithin, John N. *Macroeconomics after Thatcher and Reagan: The Conservative Revolution in Macroeconomic Policymaking.* Brookfield, Vt.: E. Elgar, 1990.

Yantek, Thom. "Polity and Economy under Extreme Economic Conditions: A Comparative Study of the Reagan and Thatcher Experiences." *American Journal of Political Science* 32 (1988): 196–216.

## Congressional Relations

Bartels, Larry M. "Constituency Opinion and Congressional Policy Making: The Reagan Defense Build Up." *American Political Science Review* 85 (1991): 457–74.

Bodnick, "'Going Public' Reconsidered: Reagan's 1981 Tax and Budget Cuts, and Revisionist Theories of Presidential Power." *Congress and the Presidency* 17 (1990): 13–28.

Collier, Kenneth E. "Behind the Bully Pulpit: The Reagan Administration and Congress." *Presidential Studies Quarterly* (1996): 805–15.

Conley, Richard S. "President Reagan, White House Lobbying, and Key Votes: A Reassessment." *White House Studies* 3 (2003): 131–55.

Fleisher, Richard, and Jon R. Bond. "Assessing Presidential Support in the House: Lessons from Reagan and Carter." *Journal of Politics* 45 (1983): 745–58.

Halpert, Leon. "Presidential Leadership of Congress: Evaluating President Reagan's Success in the House of Representatives." *Presidential Studies Quarterly* 21 (1991): 717–35.

Leloup, Lance T. "After the Blitz: Reagan and the U.S. Congressional Budget Process." *Legislative Studies Quarterly* 7 (1982): 321–39.

Ornstein, Norman J., ed. *President and Congress: Assessing Ronald Reagan's First Year*. Washington, D.C.: American Enterprise Institute for Public Policy Research, 1982.

Sinclair, Barbara. "Agenda Control and Policy Success: Ronald Reagan and the 97th House." *Legislative Studies Quarterly* 10 (1985): 291–314.

Sloan, John W. "Meeting the Leadership Challenges of the Modern Presidency: The Political Skills and Leadership of Ronald Reagan." *Presidential Studies Quarterly* 26 (1996): 795–804.

## Conservatives and Reagan

Edwards, Lee. *The Conservative Revolution: The Movement That Remade America*. New York: Free Press, 1999.

Hodgson, Godfrey. *The World Turned Right Side Up: A History of the Conservative Ascendancy in America*. Boston: Houghton Mifflin, 1996.

Hoeveler, J. David. *Watch on the Right: Conservative Intellectuals in the Reagan Era*. Madison: University of Wisconsin Press, 1991.

Reichley, A. James. "The Conservative Roots of the Nixon, Ford, and Reagan Administrations." *Political Science Quarterly* 96 (1981): 537–50.

Schneider, Gregory L. *Conservatism in America Since 1930: A Reader.* New York: New York University Press, 1999.

Schwab, Larry M. *The Illusion of a Conservative Reagan Revolution.* New Brunswick, N.J.: Transaction Publishers, 1991.

Weyrich, Paul. "The Reagan Revolution That Wasn't: Why Conservatives Have Achieved So Little." *Policy Review* (1987): 50–53.

## Domestic Policy

Palmer, John L., and Isabel V. Sawhill, eds. *The Reagan Record: An Assessment of America's Changing Domestic Priorities.* Cambridge, Mass.: Ballinger Publishers, 1984.

Sloan, John W. "The Reagan Presidency, Growing Inequality, and the American Dream." *Policy Studies Journal* 25 (fall 1997): 371–86.

Warshaw, Shirley Anne. "White House Control of Domestic Policy Making: The Reagan Years." *Public Administration Review* 56 (1995): 247–53.

## Economic Policy

Boskin, Michael J. *Reagan and the Economy: The Successes, Failures, and Unfinished Agenda.* San Francisco, Calif.: Institute for Contemporary Studies, 1987.

Campagna, Anthony. *The Economy in the Reagan Years: The Economic Consequences of the Reagan Administrations.* Westport, Conn.: Greenwood Press, 1994.

Durant, Robert F., Teresa Kluesner, and Jerome S. Legge Jr. "Domestic Programs, Budget Outlays, and the Reagan Revolution: A Test of Competing Theories in Four Policy Arenas." *Journal of Public Administration Research and Theory* 2 (1992): 369–86.

Friedman, Benjamin. *Day of Reckoning: The Consequences of American Economic Policy Under Reagan and After.* New York: Random House, 1988.

Gist, John R. "The Reagan Budget: A Significant Departure from the Past." *PS: Political Science and Politics* 14 (1981): 738–46.

Hulten, Charles R., and Isabel V. Sawhill. *The Legacy of Reaganomics: Prospects for Long-Term Growth.* Washington, D.C.: Urban Institute Press, 1984.

Kamlet, Mark S., David C. Mowery, and Tsai-Tsu Su. "Upsetting National Priorities? The Reagan Administration's Budgetary Strategy." *American Political Science Review* 82 (1988): 1293–1307.

Lowery, David. "The Keynesian and Political Determinants of Unbalanced Budgets: U.S. Fiscal Policy from Eisenhower to Reagan." *American Journal of Political Science* 29 (1985): 428–60.

Mills, Gregory B. *Deficit Dilemma: Budget Policy in the Reagan Era.* Washington, D.C.: Urban Institute Press, 1983.

Palmer, John L., and Isabel V. Sawhill. *The Reagan Experiment: An Examination of the Economic and Social Policies.* Lanham, Md.: University Press of America, 1982.

Porter, Roger B. "Economic Advice to the President: From Eisenhower to Reagan." *Political Science Quarterly* 98 (1983): 403–26.

Sloan, John W. *The Reagan Effect: Economics and Presidential Leadership.* Lawrence: University Press of Kansas, 1999.

Weidenbaum, Murray L. *Rendezvous with Reality: The American Economy After Reagan.* New York: Basic Books, 1988.

## Elections of 1980 and 1984

Broder, David. *Pursuit of the Presidency, 1980.* Edited by Richard Harwood. New York: Putnam, 1980.

Brudney, Jeffrey L., and Gary W. Copeland. "Evangelicals as a Political Force: Reagan and the 1980 Religious Vote." *Social Science Quarterly* 65 (1984): 1072–79.

Covington, Cary R., et al. "Shaping a Candidate's Image in the Press: Ronald Reagan and the 1980 Presidential Election." *Political Research Quarterly* 46 (1993): 783–98.

David, Paul T., and David H. Everson, eds. *Presidential Election and Transition, 1980–81.* Carbondale, Ill.: Southern Illinois University Press, 1983.

Germond, Jack W., and Jules Whitcover. *Blue Smoke and Mirrors: How Reagan Won and Why Carter Lost the Election of 1980.* New York: Viking, 1981.

Lanoue, David J. "One That Made a Difference: Cognitive Consistency, Political Knowledge, and the 1980 Presidential Debate." *Public Opinion Quarterly* 56 (1992): 168–84.

Laxalt, Paul. *The Nominating of a President: The Three Nominations of Ronald Reagan as Republican Candidate for the Presidency.* Reno, Nev.: Native Nevadan Publications, 1985.

Miller, Warren E. "A New Context for Presidential Politics: The Reagan Legacy." *Political Behavior* 9 (1987): 91–113.

Pomper, Gerald M., ed. *The Election of 1984: Reports and Interpretations.* Chatham, N.J.: Chatham House, 1985.

Ranney, Austin, ed. *The American Elections of 1980.* Washington, D.C.: American Enterprise Institute Press, 1981.

——. *The American Elections of 1984*. Durham, N.C.: Duke University Press, 1985.

Sandoz, Ellis, and Cecil V. Crabb Jr., eds. *A Tide of Discontent: The 1980 Elections and Their Meaning*. Washington, D.C.: Congressional Quarterly, 1981.

Schramm, Peter W., and Dennis J. Mahoney, eds. *The 1984 Election and the Future of American Politics*. Durham, N.C.: Carolina Academic Press, 1987.

Sick, Gary. *October Surprise: America's Hostages in Iran and the Election of Ronald Reagan*. New York: Times Books, 1991.

Sigelman, Lee, and Carol K. Sigelman. "Judgments of the Carter–Reagan Debate: The Eyes of the Beholders." *Public Opinion Quarterly* 48 (1984): 624–28.

## Environmental Policy

Kraft, Michael E., and Norman J. Vig. "Environmental Policy in the Reagan Presidency." *Political Science Quarterly* 99 (1984): 415–39.

Lash, Jonathan, with Katherine Gillman and David Sheridan. *A Season of Spoils: The Reagan Administration's Attack on the Environment*. New York: Pantheon, 1984.

Portney, Paul R. *Natural Resources and the Environment: The Reagan Approach*. Washington, D.C.: Urban Institute Press, 1984.

Shanley, Robert A. *Presidential Influence and Environmental Policy*. Westport, Conn.: Greenwood Press, 1992.

Smith, V. Kerry. *Environmental Policy Under Reagan's Executive Order: The Role of Cost-Benefit Analysis*. Chapel Hill, N.C.: University of North Carolina Press, 1984.

## Federalism

Conlan, Timothy J. *New Federalism: Intergovernmental Reform and Political Change from Nixon to Reagan*. Washington, D.C.: Brookings, 1988.

——. "The Politics of Federal Block Grants: From Nixon to Reagan." *Political Science Quarterly* 99 (1984): 247–70.

Nathan, Richard P. *The Consequences of the Cuts: The Effects of the Reagan Domestic Program on State and Local Governments*. Princeton, N.J.: Princeton University Press, 1983.

Nathan, Richard P., and Fred C. Doolittle. *Reagan and the States*. Princeton, N.J.: Princeton University Press, 1987.

Peterson, George E., and Carol W. Lewis. *Reagan and the Cities*. Washington, D.C.: Urban Institute Press, 1986.

Zuckert, Catherine H. "Reagan and That Unnamed Frenchman (De Tocqueville): On the Rationale for the New (Old) Federalism." *The Review of Politics* 45 (1983): 421–42.

## Film Career

Thomas, Tony. *Films of Ronald Reagan*. Secaucus, N.J.: Citadel Press, 1988.
Vaughn, Stephen. "Spies, National Security, and the 'Inertia Projector': The Secret Service Films of Ronald Reagan." *American Quarterly* 39 (1987): 355–80.
Vaughn, Stephen, et al. *Ronald Reagan in Hollywood: Movies and Politics*. New York: Cambridge University Press, 1994.

## Foreign and Defense Policy

Bell, Coral. *The Reagan Paradox: U.S. Foreign Policy in the 1980s*. New Brunswick, N.J.: Rutgers University Press, 1989.
Bostdorff, Denise M. "The Presidency and Promoted Crisis: Reagan, Grenada, and Issue Management." *Presidential Studies Quarterly* 21 (1991): 737–50.
Brown, James, and William Snyder, eds. *Defense Policy in the Reagan Administration*. Washington, D.C.: National Defense University Press, 1988.
Celmer, Marc A. *Terrorism, U.S. Strategy, and Reagan Policies*. New York: Greenwood Press, 1987.
Churba, Joseph. *The American Retreat: The Reagan Foreign and Defense Policy*. Chicago: Regnery Gateway, 1984.
Emerson, Steven. *Secret Warriors: Inside the Covert Military Operations of the Reagan Era*. New York: Putnam, 1988.
Fatton, Robert. "The Reagan Foreign Policy Toward South Africa: The Ideology of the New Cold War." *African Studies Review* 27 (1984): 57–82.
Fischer, Beth A. *The Reagan Reversal: Foreign Policy and the End of the Cold War*. Columbia: University of Missouri Press, 1997.
Goldstein, Walter. *Reagan's Leadership and the Atlantic Alliance: Views from Europe and America*. Washington, D.C.: Pergamon-Brassey, 1986.
Haass, Richard. *The Reagan Administration and Lebanon*. Pittsburgh: University of Pittsburgh Press, 1988.
Hall, David Locke. *The Reagan Wars: A Constitutional Perspective on War Powers and the Presidency*. Boulder, Colo.: Westview Press, 1991.
Hallenbeck, Ralph A. *Military Force as an Instrument of U.S. Foreign Policy: Intervention in Lebanon, August 1982–February 1984*. New York: Praeger, 1991.
Kernek, Sterling. *Foreign Policy in the Reagan Presidency: Nine Intimate Perspectives*. Edited by Kenneth W. Thompson. Lanham, Md.: University Press of America, 1993.

Lagon, Mark P. *The Reagan Doctrine: The Sources of American Conduct in the Cold War's Last Chapter.* New York: Praeger, 1994.

Livingston, Steven G. "The Politics of International Agenda-Setting: Reagan and North–South Relations." *International Studies Quarterly* 36 (1992): 313–29.

Luard, Evan. "Western Europe and the Reagan Doctrine." *International Affairs* (Royal Institute of International Affairs) 63 (1987): 563–74.

McFaul, Michael. "Rethinking the 'Reagan Doctrine' in Angola." *International Security* 14 (1989): 99–135.

Menges, Constantine C. *Inside the National Security Council: The True Story of the Making and Unmaking of Reagan's Foreign Policy.* New York: Simon and Schuster, 1988.

Morley, Morris H. *Crisis and Confrontation: Ronald Reagan's Foreign Policy.* Totowa, N.J.: Rowman and Littlefield, 1988.

Neier, Aryeh. "Human Rights in the Reagan Era: Acceptance in Principle." *Annals of the American Academy of Political and Social Science* 506, "Human Rights around the World" (November 1989): 30–41.

Novik, Nimrod. *Encounter with Reality: Reagan and the Middle East.* Boulder, Colo.: Westview Press, 1985.

Oye, Kenneth A., with Robert J. Lieber and Donald Rothchild. *Eagle Resurgent? The Reagan Era in American Foreign Policy.* Boston: Little, Brown, 1987.

Peck, Juliana S. *The Reagan Administration and the Palestinian Question: The First Thousand Days.* Washington, D.C.: Institute for Palestine Studies, 1984.

Rubner, Michael. "The Reagan Administration, the 1973 War Powers Resolution, and the Invasion of Grenada." *Political Science Quarterly* 100 (1985): 627–47.

Schmertz, Eric J., Natalie Datlof, and Alexej Ugrinsky, eds. *President Reagan and the World.* Westport, Conn.: Greenwood Press, 1997.

Schweitzer, Peter. *Victory: The Reagan Administration's Secret Strategy That Hastened the Collapse of the Soviet Union.* New York: Atlantic Monthly Press, 1994.

Scott, James M. *Deciding to Intervene: The Reagan Doctrine and American Foreign Policy.* Durham, N.C.: Duke University Press, 1996.

———. "Reagan's Doctrine? The Formulation of an American Foreign Policy Strategy." *Presidential Studies Quarterly* 26 (1996): 1047–61.

Stanik, Joseph T. *"Swift and Effective Retribution": The U.S. Sixth Fleet and the Confrontation with Qaddafi.* Washington, D.C.: Naval Historical Center, Government Printing Office, 1996.

Thornton, Richard C. *The Falkland Sting: Reagan, Thatcher, and Argentina's Bomb.* Washington, D.C.: Brassey's, 1998.

Wirls, Daniel. *Buildup: The Politics of Defense in the Reagan Era*. Ithaca, N.Y.: Cornell University Press, 1992.

Woodward, Bob. *Veil: The Secret Wars of the CIA, 1981–1987*. New York: Simon and Schuster, 1987.

*World Affairs* 153 (1990). Symposium: "The Neoconservatives and the Reagan Administration."

Yarbrough, Tinsley E. *The Reagan Administration and Human Rights*. New York: Praeger, 1985.

Zakaria, Fareed. "The Reagan Strategy of Containment." *Political Science Quarterly* 105 (1990): 373–95.

## General Perspectives

Barilleaux, Ryan J. *The Post-Modern Presidency: The Office after Ronald Reagan*. New York: Praeger, 1988.

Berman, Larry, ed. *Looking Back on the Reagan Presidency*. Baltimore, Md.: Johns Hopkins University Press, 1990.

Boaz, David, ed. *Assessing the Reagan Years*. Washington, D.C.: Cato Institute, 1988.

Boyer, Paul, ed. *Reagan as President: Contemporary Views of the Man, His Politics, and His Policies*. Chicago: Ivan R. Dee, 1990.

Brownlee, W. Elliot, and Hugh Davis Graham eds. *The Reagan Presidency: Pragmatic Conservatism and Its Legacies*. Lawrence: University Press of Kansas, 2003.

Conley, Richard S., ed. *Reassessing the Reagan Presidency*. Lanham, Md.: University Press of America, 2003.

D'Souza, Dinesh. *Ronald Reagan: How an Ordinary Man Became an Extraordinary Leader*. New York: Free Press, 1997.

Evans, Rowland, and Robert Novak. *The Reagan Revolution*. New York: Dutton, 1981.

Greenstein, Fred I. "Ronald Reagan—Another Hidden-Hand Ike?" *PS: Political Science and Politics* 23 (1990): 7–13.

Greenstein, Fred I., ed. *The Reagan Presidency: An Early Assessment*. Baltimore, Md.: Johns Hopkins University Press, 1983.

Hill, Dilys M., with Raymond A. Moore and Phil Williams. *The Reagan Presidency: An Incomplete Revolution?* New York: St. Martin's Press, 1990.

Hoeveler, J. David. *Watch on the Right: Conservative Intellectuals in the Reagan Era*. Madison: University of Wisconsin Press, 1991.

Hogan, Joseph, ed. *The Reagan Years: The Record in Presidential Leadership*. New York: Manchester University Press, 1990.

Johnson, Haynes. *Sleepwalking Through History: America in the Reagan Years*. New York: Anchor Books, 1992.

Jones, Charles O. *The Reagan Legacy: Promise and Performance*. Chatham, N.J.: Chatham House, 1988.

Mervin, David. *Ronald Reagan and the American Presidency*. New York: Longman, 1990.

Palmer, John L., ed. *Perspectives on the Reagan Years*. Washington, D.C.: Urban Institute Press, 1988.

Rockman, Bert A. "What Didn't We Know and Should We Forget It? Political Science and the Reagan Presidency." *Polity* 21 (summer 1989): 777–92.

Salamon, Lester M., and Michael S. Lund, eds. *The Reagan Presidency and the Governing of America*. Washington, D.C.: Urban Institute Press, 1985.

Schaller, Michael. *Reckoning with Reagan: America and Its President in the 1980s*. New York: Oxford University Press, 1992.

Schwab, Larry M. *The Illusion of a Conservative Reagan Revolution*. New Brunswick, N.J.: Transaction Publishers, 1991.

White, F. Clifton, and William J. Gill. *Why Reagan Won: A Narrative History of the Conservative Movement, 1964–1981*. Chicago: Regnery, 1981.

White, John Kenneth. *The New Politics of Old Values*. Lanham, Md.: University Press of America, 1998.

———. "How Should Political Science Judge Ronald Reagan?" *Polity* 22 (summer 1990): 701–15.

Williams, Walter. *Mismanaging America: The Rise of the Anti-Analytic Presidency*. Lawrence: University Press of Kansas, 1990.

## Governorship of California

Biggart, Nicole. W., and Gary G. Hamilton. "The Power of Obedience" [Study of the Gubernatorial Administrations of Ronald Reagan and Jerry Brown]. *Administrative Science Quarterly* 29 (1984): 540-49.

Cannon, Lou. *Governor Reagan: His Rise to Power*. New York: Public Affairs, 2003.

Dallek, Robert. *The Right Moment: Ronald Reagan's First Victory and the Decisive Turning Point in American Politics*. New York: Oxford University Press, 2004.

Gable, Richard W. *California in the Reagan Years: Trends in the Economy and Public Service*. Berkeley: University of California Institute of Government, 1979.

Hamilton, Gary G., and Nicole Woolsey Biggart. *Governor Reagan, Governor Brown: A Sociology of Executive Power*. New York: Columbia University Press, 1984.

## Insider Accounts

Bell, Terrell. *The Thirteenth Man: A Reagan Cabinet Memoir*. New York: Free Press, 1988.

Deaver, Michael K. *A Different Drummer: My Thirty Years with Ronald Reagan.* New York: Harper Collins, 2001.

Haig, Alexander M. *Caveat: Reagan, Realism, and Foreign Policy.* New York: Simon and Schuster, 1984.

Kirkpatrick, Jeane J. *The Reagan Doctrine and U.S. Foreign Policy.* Washington, D.C.: Heritage Foundation, 1985.

Ledeen, Michael A. *Perilous Statecraft: An Insider's Account of the Iran–Contra Affair.* New York: Scribner, 1988.

McFarlane, Robert. *Special Trust: Inside the Reagan White House.* New York: Caddell and Davies, 1994.

Meese, Edwin. *With Reagan: The Inside Story.* Washington, D.C.: Regnery, Gateway, 1992.

Moynihan, Daniel Patrick. *Came the Revolution: Argument in the Reagan Era.* New York: Harcourt Brace Jovanovich, 1988.

Niskanen, William A. *Reaganomics: An Insider's Account of the Policies and the People.* New York: Oxford University Press, 1988.

Noonan, Peggy. *What I Saw at the Revolution: A Political Life in the Reagan Era.* New York: Random House, 1990.

Regan, Donald T. *For the Record: From Wall Street to Washington.* San Diego, Calif.: Harcourt Brace Jovanovich, 1988.

Roberts, Paul Craig. *The Supply-Side Revolution: An Insider's Account of Policymaking in Washington.* Cambridge, Mass.: Harvard University Press, 1984.

Shultz, George P. *Turmoil and Triumph: My Years as Secretary of State.* New York: Scribner's, 1993.

Smith, William French. *Law and Justice in the Reagan Administration: The Memoirs of an Attorney General.* Stanford, Calif.: Hoover Institution Press, 1991.

Speakes, Larry. *Speaking Out: The Reagan Presidency from Inside the White House.* New York: Scribner, 1988.

Stockman, David A. *The Triumph of Politics: Why the Reagan Revolution Failed.* New York: Harper and Row, 1986.

Thompson, Kenneth W. *Leadership in the Reagan Presidency: Seven Intimate Perspectives.* Lanham, Md.: Madison Books, 1992.

Weinberger, Caspar. *Fighting for Peace: Seven Critical Years in the Pentagon.* New York: Warner Books, 1990.

## Interest Groups

Peterson, Mark A. "The Presidency and Organized Interests: White House Patterns of Interest Group Liaison." *American Political Science Review* 86 (1992): 612–25.

## Iran–Contra

Brody, Richard A., and Catherine R. Shapiro. "Policy Failure and Public Support: The Iran–Contra Affair and Public Assessment of President Reagan." *Political Behavior* 11 (1989): 353–69.

Busby, Robert. *Reagan and the Iran–Contra Affair: The Politics of Presidential Recovery*. New York: St. Martin's Press, 1999.

Draper, Theodore. *A Very Thin Line: The Iran–Contra Affairs*. New York: Hill and Wang, 1991.

Hicks, D. Bruce. "Presidential Foreign Policy Prerogative after the Iran–Contra Affair: A Review Essay." *Presidential Studies Quarterly* 26 (1996): 962–77.

Marshall, Jonathan, Peter Dale Scott, and Jane Hunter. *The Iran–Contra Connection: Secret Teams and Covert Operations in the Reagan Era*. Boston, Mass.: South End Press, 1987.

Mayer, Jane, and Doyle McManus. *Landslide: The Unmaking of the President, 1984–88*. New York: Houghton Mifflin, 1989.

Sobel, Richard. "Contra Aid Fundamentals: Exploring the Intricacies and the Issues." *Political Science Quarterly* 110 (summer 1995): 287–306.

Tower, John. *The Tower Commission Report: The Full Text of the President's Special Review Board*. New York: Bantam Books, 1987.

Traeger, Oliver, ed. *The Iran–Contra Arms Scandal: Foreign Policy Disaster*. New York: Facts on File, 1988.

Walsh, Lawrence E. *Firewall: The Iran–Contra Conspiracy and Cover-Up*. New York: Norton, 1997.

## Nicaragua

Americas Watch Committee. *Human Rights in Nicaragua: Reagan, Rhetoric, and Reality*. New York: Americas Watch Committee, 1985.

Burns, E. Bradford. *At War in Nicaragua: The Reagan Doctrine and the Politics of Nostalgia*. New York: Harper and Row, 1987.

Guttman, Roy. *Banana Diplomacy: The Making of American Policy in Nicaragua, 1981–1987*. New York: Simon and Schuster, 1988.

Kornbluh, Peter. *Nicaragua, the Price of Intervention: Reagan's Wars Against the Sandinistas*. Washington, D.C.: Institute for Policy Studies, 1987.

Scott, James M. "Interbranch Rivalry and the Reagan Doctrine in Nicaragua." *Political Science Quarterly* 112 (1997): 237–60.

Siegel, Daniel, and Tom Spaulding. *Outcast Among Allies: The International Costs of Reagan's War Against Nicaragua*. Washington, D.C.: Institute for Policy Studies, 1985.

Walker, Thomas W. *Reagan vs. the Sandinistas: The Undeclared War on Nicaragua*. Boulder, Colo.: Westview Press, 1987.

## Press Relations

Denton, Robert E., Jr. *The Primetime Presidency of Ronald Reagan: The Era of the Television Presidency*. New York: Praeger, 1988.

Donaldson, Sam. *Hold On, Mr. President!* New York: Random House, 1987.

Fitzwater, Marlin. *Call the Briefing! Bush and Reagan, Sam and Helen: A Decade with Presidents and the Press*. New York: Times Books, 1995.

Hertsgaard, Mark. *On Bended Knee: The Press and the Reagan Presidency*. New York: Farrar, Straus, Giroux, 1988.


## Public Opinion

Citrin, Jack, et al. "Presidential Leadership and the Resurgence of Trust in Government." *British Journal of Political Science* 16 (1986): 431–53.

Gilboa, Eytan. "Effects of Televised Presidential Addresses on Public Opinion: President Reagan and Terrorism in the Middle East." *Presidential Studies Quarterly* 20 (1990): 43–53.

Gilens, Martin. "Gender and Support for Reagan: A Comprehensive Model of Presidential Approval." *American Journal of Political Science* 32 (1988): 19–49.

Goodman, John L. *Public Opinion During the Reagan Administration: National Issues, Private Concerns*. Lanham, Md.: University Press of America, 1984.

Mondak, Jeffrey J. "Source Cues and Policy Approval: The Cognitive Dynamics of Public Support for the Reagan Agenda." *American Journal of Political Science* 37 (1993): 186–212.

Ostrom, Charles W. J., et al. "The Man in the Teflon Suit? The Environmental Connection, Political Drama, and Popular Support in the Reagan Presidency." *Public Opinion Quarterly* 53 (1989): 353–87.

Rosenblatt, Alan J. "Aggressive Foreign Policy Marketing: Public Response to Reagan's 1983 Address on Lebanon and Grenada." *Political Behavior* 20 (1998): 225–40.

Sigelman, Lee. "Disarming the Opposition: The President, the Public, and the INF Treaty." *Public Opinion Quarterly* 54 (1990): 37–47.

Sigelman, Lee, and Kathleen Knight. "Expectation/Disillusion and Presidential Popularity: The Reagan Experience." *Public Opinion Quarterly* 49 (1985): 209–13.

Wilcox, Clyde, and Dee Allsop. "Economic and Foreign Policy as Sources of Reagan Support." *Western Political Quarterly* 44 (1991): 941–58.


## Regulatory Politics and Reform

Eads, George C. *The Reagan Regulatory Strategy: An Assessment*. Washington, D.C.: Urban Institute Press, 1984.

Eads, George C., and Michael Fix. *Relief or Reform? Reagan's Regulatory Dilemma*. Washington, D.C.: Urban Institute Press, 1984.

Friedman, Barry D. *Regulation in the Reagan–Bush Era: The Eruption of Presidential Influence*. Pittsburgh: University of Pittsburgh Press, 1995.

Goodman, Marshall R., and Margaret T. Wrightson. *Managing Regulatory Reform: The Reagan Strategy and Its Impact*. New York: Praeger, 1987.

## Rhetoric, Speeches, and Addresses

Arca, Emil, and Gregory J. Pamel. *Triumph of the American Spirit: The Presidential Speeches of Ronald Reagan*. Detroit, Mich.: National Reproductions Corp, 1984.

Dallek, Robert. *Ronald Reagan: The Politics of Symbolism*. Cambridge, Mass.: Harvard University Press, 1984.

Houck, Davis W., and Amos Kiewe, eds. *Actor, Ideologue, Politician: The Public Speeches of Ronald Reagan*. Westport, Conn.: Greenwood Press, 1993.

Israel, Fred I., ed. *Ronald Reagan's Weekly Radio Addresses: The President Speaks to America*. Wilmington, Del.: Scholarly Resources Inc., 1987.

Kiewe, Amos, and Davis W. Houck. *A Shining City on a Hill: Ronald Reagan's Economic Rhetoric, 1951–1989*. New York: Praeger, 1991.

Moen, Matthew C. "Ronald Reagan and the Social Issues: Rhetorical Support for the Christian Right." *Social Science Journal* 27 (1990): 199–207.

———. "The Political Agenda of Ronald Reagan: A Content Analysis of the State of the Union Messages." *Presidential Studies Quarterly* 18 (1988): 775–85.

Muir, William Ker. *Bully Pulpit: The Presidential Leadership of Ronald Reagan*. San Francisco: ICS Press, 1992.

*Presidential Studies Quarterly*. "The Bully Pulpit and the Reagan Presidency." Special symposium, Volume 25 (winter 1995).

Reagan, Ronald. *A Time for Choosing: The Speeches of Ronald Reagan, 1961–1982*. New York: Regnery, 1983.

Rimmerman, Craig A. *Presidency by Plebiscite: The Reagan–Bush Era in Institutional Perspective*. Boulder, Colo.: Westview Press, 1993.

Rowland, Robert C., and John M. Jones. "'Until Next Week': The Saturday Radio Addresses of Ronald Reagan." *Presidential Studies Quarterly* 32 (2002): 84–106.

Stuckey, Mary E. *Getting into the Game: The Pre-Presidential Rhetoric of Ronald Reagan*. New York: Praeger, 1989.

———. *Playing the Game: The Presidential Rhetoric of Ronald Reagan*. New York: Praeger, 1990.

Weiler, Michael, and W. Barnett Pearce. *Reagan and Public Discourse in America* (Studies in Rhetoric and Communication). Tuscaloosa: University of Alabama Press, 1992.

Welch, Reed L. "Was Reagan Really a Great Communicator? The Influence of Televised Addresses on Public Opinion." *Presidential Studies Quarterly* 33 (2003): 853–76.

## Strategic Defense Initiative (SDI)

Bjork, Rebecca. *The Strategic Defense Initiative: Symbolic Containment of the Nuclear Threat*. Albany: SUNY Press, 1992.

Boffey, Philip M. *Claiming the Heavens: The New York Times Complete Guide to the Star Wars Debate*. New York: Times Books, 1988.

Dallmeyer, Dorinda G., ed. *Strategic Defense Initiative: New Perspectives on Deterrence*. Boulder, Colo.: Westview Press, 1986.

Drell, Sidney, Philip J. Farley, and David Holloway. *The Reagan Strategic Defense Initiative: A Technical, Political, and Arms Control Assessment*. Cambridge, Mass.: Ballinger, 1985.

Drell, Sidney D., Philip J. Farley, and David Holloway. "Preserving the ABM Treaty: A Critique of the Reagan Strategic Defense Initiative." *International Security* 9 (1984): 51–91.

Fitzgerald, Frances. *Way Out There in the Blue: Reagan, Star Wars, and the End of the Cold War*. New York: Simon and Schuster, 2000.

Lakoff, Sanford, and Herbert F. York. *A Shield in Space? Technology, Politics, and the Strategic Defense Initiative*. Berkeley: University of California Press, 1989.

Snyder, Craig, ed. *The Strategic Defense Debate: Can Star Wars Make Us Safe?* Philadelphia: University of Pennsylvania Press, 1986.

## Supreme Court

Davis, Sue. "The Supreme Court: Rehnquist's or Reagan's?" *Western Political Quarterly* 44 (1991): 87–99.

Gimpel, James G., and Robin M. Wolpert. "Rationalizing Support and Opposition to Supreme Court Nominations: The Role of Credentials." *Polity* 28 (1995): 67–82.

Hodder-Williams, Richard. "The Strange Story of Judge Robert Bork and a Vacancy on the United States Supreme Court." *Political Studies* 36 (1988): 613–37.

## Welfare Politics and Policy

O'Connor, John. "U.S. Social Welfare Policy: The Reagan Record and Its Legacy." *Journal of Social Policy* 27 (1998): 37–61.

Piven, Frances Fox, and Richard A. Cloward. *The New Class War: Reagan's Attack on the Welfare State and Its Consequences*. New York: Pantheon Books, 1982.


## THE BUSH YEARS

### Administrative Presidency

Cohen, David B. "From the Fabulous Baker Boys to the Master of Disaster: The White House Chief of Staff in the Reagan and G. H. W. Bush Administrations." *Presidential Studies Quarterly* 32 (2002): 463–83.

Cohen, David. B., and George A. Krause. "Presidents, Chiefs of Staff, and White House Organizational Behavior: Survey Evidence from the Reagan and Bush Administrations." *Presidential Studies Quarterly* 30 (2000): 421–42.

Crane, Edward H. "Bush and His Cabinet: A First-Year Report Card." *Policy Review* 51 (1990): 30–39.

Laffin, Martin. "The President and the Subcontractors: The Role of Top Level Policy Entrepreneurs in the Bush Administration." *Presidential Studies Quarterly* 26 (spring 1996): 550–66.

Michaels, Judith E. "A View from the Top: Reflections of the Bush Presidential Appointees." *Public Administration Review* 55 (1995): 273–83.

Mullins, Kerry, and Aaron Wildavsky. "The Procedural Presidency of George Bush." *Society* 28 (1991): 49–59.

Pfiffner, James P. "Establishing the Bush Presidency." *Public Administration Review* 50 (1990): 64–73.

Tiefer, Charles. *The Semi-Sovereign Presidency: The Bush Administration's Strategy for Governing Without Congress*. Boulder, Colo.: Westview Press, 1994.

Williams, Walter. "George Bush and Executive Branch Policymaking Competence." *Policy Studies Journal* 21 (1993): 700–717.


### Autobiographies and Memoirs

Bush, George H. W. *Looking Forward: An Autobiography*. Garden City, N.J.: Doubleday, 1987.

———. *All the Best, George Bush: My Life in Letters and Other Writings*. New York: Scribner, 1999.

Bush, George H. W. *George Bush in His Own Words*. New York: Scribner, 2001.

Bush, George H. W., and Brent Scowcroft. *A World Transformed*. New York: Knopf, 1998.

## Biographies

Parmet, Herbert S. *George Bush: The Life of a Lone-Star Yankee*. New York: Scribner, 1997.

Stinnett, Robert B. *George Bush: His World War II Years*. New York: McMillan, 1992.

Wicker, Tom. *George Herbert Walker Bush*. New York: Lipper/Viking, 2004.

## Budget Politics

Eastland, Terry. "Bush's Fatal Attraction: Anatomy of the Budget Fiasco." *Policy Review* 60 (1992): 20–24.

Pious, Richard M. "The Limits of Rational Choice: Bush and Clinton Budget Summitry." *Presidential Studies Quarterly* 29 (September 1999): 617–37.

## Central and Latin America Policy

Leogrande, William M. "From Reagan to Bush: The Transition in U.S. Policy Towards Central America." *Journal of Latin American Studies* 22 (1990): 595–621.

## China Policy

Schaefer, Donald D. A. "U.S. Foreign Policies of Presidents Bush and Clinton: The Influence of China's Most Favored Nation Status Upon Human Rights Issues." *Social Sciences Journal* 35 (1998): 407–21.

Skidmore, David, and William Gates. "After Tiananmen: The Struggle over U.S. Policy Toward China in the Bush Administration." *Presidential Studies Quarterly* 27 (1997): 514–39.

## Civil Rights

Shull, Steven A. *A Kinder, Gentler Racism? The Reagan–Bush Civil Rights Legacy*. Armonk, N.Y.: M. E. Sharpe, 1993.

## Clarence Thomas Appointment

Gimpel, James G., and Robin M. Wolpert. "Rationalizing Support and Opposition to Supreme Court Nominations: The Role of Credentials." *Polity* 28 (1995): 67–82.

Massaro, John. "President Bush's Management of the Thomas Nomination: Four Years, Several Books, Two Videos Later (And Still More to Come!)." *Presidential Studies Quarterly* 26 (summer 1996): 816–27.

Shefter, Martin. "Institutional Conflict over Presidential Appointments: The Case of Clarence Thomas." *PS: Political Science and Politics* 25 (December 1992): 676–79.

## Congressional Relations

Conley, Richard S. "George Bush and the 102nd Congress: The Impact of Public and Private Veto Threats on Policy Outcomes." *Presidential Studies Quarterly* 33 (December 2003): 730–50.
———. "A Revisionist View of George Bush and Congress, 1989: Congressional Support, 'Veto Strength,' and Legislative Strategy." *White House Studies* 2 (winter 2002): 359–74.
Fleisher, Richard, and Jon R. Bond. "Assessing Presidential Support in the House II: Lessons from George Bush." *American Journal of Political Science* 36 (1992): 525–41.
Joslyn, Mark R. "Institutional Change and House Support: Assessing George Bush in the Postreform Era." *American Politics Quarterly* 23 (1995): 62–80.
Spitzer, Robert J. "Presidential Prerogative Power: The Case of the Bush Administration and Legislative Power." *PS: Political Science and Politics* 24 (1991): 38–42.
Wittkopf, Eugene R., and James M. McCormick. "Congress, the President, and the End of the Cold War: Has Anything Changed?" *Journal of Conflict Resolution* 42 (1998): 440–66.

## Domestic Policy

Himmelfarb, Richard, and Rosanna Perotti, eds. *Principle over Politics? The Domestic Policy of the George H. W. Bush Presidency.* Westport, Conn.: Praeger, 2004.

## Elections of 1988 and 1992

Abramowitz, Alan I., and Jeffrey A. Segal. "Beyond Willie Horton and the Pledge of the Allegiance: National Issues in the 1988 Elections." *Legislative Studies Quarterly* 15 (1990): 565–80.
Alvarez, R. Michael, and Jonathan Nagler. "Economics, Issues and the Perot Candidacy: Voter Choice in the 1992 Election." *American Journal of Political Science* 39 (1995): 714–44.
Bolce, Louis, Gerald De Maio, and Douglas Muzzio. "The 1992 Republican 'Tent': No Blacks Walked In." *Political Science Quarterly* 108 (1993): 255–70.

Denton, Robert E., Jr., ed. *The 1992 Presidential Campaign: A Communication Perspective*. Westport, Conn.: Praeger, 1994.

Doherty, Kathryn M., and James G. Gimpel. "Candidate Character vs. the Economy in the 1992 Election." *Political Behavior* 19 (1997): 177–96.

Drew, Elizabeth. *Election Journal: Political Events of 1987–1988*. New York: William Morrow and Company, 1988.

Germond, Jack W., and Jules Witcover. *Whose Broad Stripes and Bright Stars? The Trivial Pursuit of the Presidency, 1988*. New York: Warner Books, 1989.

Gopoian, J. David. "Images and Issues in the 1988 Presidential Election." *Journal of Politics* 55 (1993): 151–66.

Hetherington, Marc J. "The Media's Role in Forming Voters' National Economic Evaluations in 1992." *American Journal of Political Science* 40 (1995): 372–95.

Kenney, Patrick J., and Tom W. Rice. "The Psychology of Political Momentum." *Political Research Quarterly* 47 (December 1994): 923–38.

Lacy, Dean, and Barry C. Burden. "The Vote-Stealing and Turnout Effects of Ross Perot in the 1992 U.S. Presidential Election." *American Journal of Political Science* 43 (1999): 233–55.

Lichter, Robert S., Daniel Amundson, and Richard Noyes. *The Video Campaign: Network Coverage of the 1988 Primaries*. Washington, D.C.: American Enterprise Institute, 1988.

Lieske, Joel. "Cultural Issues and Images in the 1988 Presidential Campaign: Why the Democrats Lost Again!" *PS: Political Science and Politics* 24 (1991): 180–87.

McCann, James A. "Electoral Choices and Core Value Change: The 1992 Presidential Campaign." *American Journal of Political Science* 41 (1997): 564–83.

Mendelberg, Tali. "Executing Hortons: Racial Crime in the 1988 Presidential Campaign." *The Public Opinion Quarterly* 61 (spring 1997): 134–57.

Morrison, Donald, ed. *The Winning of the White House, 1988*. New York: Time Incorporated, 1988.

Norquist, Grover. "The Unmaking of the President: Why George Bush Lost." *Policy Review* 63 (1993): 10–17.

Ornstein, Norman J. "Foreign Policy and the 1992 Election." *Foreign Affairs* 71 (1992): 1–15.

Sapiro, Virginia, and Pamela Johnston Conover. "The Variable Gender Basis of Electoral Politics: Gender and Context in the 1992 U.S. Election." *British Journal of Political Science* 27 (1997): 497–523.

Shanks, J. Merril, and Warren E. Miller. "Partisanship, Policy and Performance: The Reagan Legacy in the 1988 Election." *British Journal of Political Science* 21 (1991): 129–97.

Stone, Walter J., and Ronald B. Rapoport. "It's Perot Stupid! The Legacy of the 1992 Perot Movement in the Major-Party System, 1994–2000." *PS: Political Science and Politics* 34 (2001): 49–58.

Sullivan, John L., Amy Fried, and Mary G. Dietz. "Patriotism, Politics, and the Presidential Election of 1988." *American Journal of Political Science* 36 (1992): 200–234.

Timmerman, David M. "1992 Presidential Candidate Films: The Contrasting Narrative of George Bush and Bill Clinton." *Presidential Studies Quarterly* 26 (1996): 364–73.

Waterman, Richard W. "Storm Clouds on the Political Horizon: George Bush at the Dawn of the 1992 Presidential Election." *Presidential Studies Quarterly* 26 (1996): 337–49.

## Foreign Policy

Beschloss, Michael R. *At the Highest Levels: The Inside Story of the End of the Cold War.* Boston: Little, Brown, 1993.

Blumenthal, Sidney. *Pledging Allegiance: The Last Campaign of the Cold War.* New York: Harper Collins, 1990.

Cohen, David B. "From START to START II: Dynamism and Pragmatism in the Bush Administration's Nuclear Weapon Policies." *Presidential Studies Quarterly* 27 (summer 1997): 412–28.

Halberstam, David. *War in a Time of Peace: Bush, Clinton, and the Generals.* New York: Scribner, 2001.

Nixon, Richard M. "American Foreign Policy: The Bush Agenda." *Foreign Affairs* 68 (1989): 199–219.

Petersen, Paul E. "The President's Dominance in Foreign Policy Making." *Political Science Quarterly* 109 (summer 1994): 215–34.

Rose, Richard. *The Postmodern President: George Bush Meets the World*, second edition. Chatham, N.J.: Chatham House Publishers, 1991.

Schlesinger, James R. "Quest For a Post–Cold War Foreign Policy." *Foreign Affairs* 72 (1993): 17–28.

## General Perspectives

Barilleaux, Ryan J., and Mark J. Rozell. *Power and Prudence: The Presidency of George H. W. Bush.* College Station: Texas A&M University Press, 2004.

Barilleaux, Ryan J., and Mary E. Stuckey, eds. *Leadership and the Bush Presidency: Prudence or Drift in an Era of Change?* New York: Praeger, 1992.

Campbell, Colin, and Bert A. Rockman, eds. *The Bush Presidency: First Appraisals.* Chatham, N.J.: Chatham House Publishers, 1991.

Duffy, Michael. *Marching in Place: The Status Quo Presidency of George Bush.* New York: Simon and Schuster, 1992.

Feldman, Leslie D., and Rosanna Perotti, eds. *Honor and Loyalty: Inside the Politics of the George H. W. Bush White House.* Westport, Conn.: Greenwood Press, 2002,. Prepared under the auspices of Hofstra University Contributions in Political Science, Number 394.

Green, Fitzhugh. *George Bush: An Intimate Portrait.* New York: Hippocrene Books, 1989.

Greene, John Robert. *The Presidency of George Bush.* Lawrence: University Press of Kansas, 2000.

King, Nicholas. *George Bush: A Biography.* New York: Dodd, Mead and Company, 1980.

## Insider Accounts

Baker, James A., III. *The Politics of Diplomacy: Revolution, War, and Peace, 1989–1992.* New York: G. P. Putnam's Sons, 1995.

Kolb, Charles. *White House Daze: The Unmaking of Domestic Policy in the Bush Years.* New York: Free Press, 1994.

Podhoretz, John. *Hell of a Ride: Backstage at the White House Follies, 1989–1993.* New York: Simon and Schuster, 1993.

## Leadership

Hammer, Dean C. "The Oakeshottian President: George Bush and the Politics of the Present." *Presidential Studies Quarterly* 25 (spring 1995): 301–14.

Rozell, Mark J. "In Reagan's Shadow: Bush's Antirhetorical Presidency." *Presidential Studies Quarterly* 28 (winter 1998): 127–38.

Thompson, Kenneth W., ed. *The Bush Presidency: Ten Intimate Perspectives of George Bush.* Lanham, Md.: University Press of America.

Wead, Doug. *Interviews with George Bush—Man of Integrity.* Eugene, Oreg.: Harvest House Publishers, 1988.

## Panama Invasion

Dinges, John. *Our Man in Panama: How General Noriega Used the United States—and Made Missions in Drugs and Arms.* New York: Random House, 1990.

Flanagan, Gen. Edward. *Battle Panama: Inside Operation Just Cause.* New York: Brassey's, 1993.

Gilboa, Eytan. "The Panama Invasion Revisited: Lessons for the Use of Force in the Post Cold War Era." *Political Science Quarterly* 110 (1995): 539–62.

Kempe, Frederick. *Divorcing the Dictator: America's Bungled Affair with Noriega*. New York: Putnam's Sons, 1990.

## Persian Gulf War and Operation Desert Storm

Allen, Barbara, Paula O'Loughlin, Amy Jasperson, and John L. Sullivan. "The Media and the Gulf War: Framing, Priming, and the Spiral of Silence." *Polity* 27 (1994): 255–84.

Crabb, Cecil V., and Kevin Mulcahy. "George Bush's Management Style and Operation Desert Storm." *Presidential Studies Quarterly* 25 (1995): 251–65.

Decosse, David E. *Bush, Was It Just? Reflections on the Morality of the Persian Gulf War.* New York: Doubleday, 1992.

Hess, Gary R. *Presidential Decisions for War: Korea, Vietnam, and the Persian Gulf*. Baltimore, Md.: Johns Hopkins University Press, 2001.

Hybel, Alex Roberto. *Power over Rationality: The Bush Administration and the Gulf Crisis*. Albany: SUNY Press, 1993.

Jentleson, Bruce W. *With Friends Like These: Reagan, Bush, and Saddam, 1982–1990*. New York: W.W. Norton.

Nacos, Brigitte Lebens. "Presidential Leadership during the Persian Gulf Conflict." *Presidential Studies Quarterly* 24 (summer 1994): 543–61.

Northcutt, Susan Stoudinger. "An Analysis of Bush's War Speech." *International Social Science Review* 67 (1992): 123–29.

Pan, Zhongdang, and Gerald M. Kosicki. "Voters' Reasoning Processes and Media Influences during the Persian Gulf War." *Political Behavior* 16 (1994): 117–56.

Renshon, Stanley A., ed. *The Political Psychology of the Gulf War: Leaders, Publics, and the Process of Conflict*. Pittsburgh: University of Pittsburgh Press, 1993.

Sifry, Micah L., and Christopher Cerf, eds. *The Gulf War Reader: History, Documents, Opinions*. New York: Times Books, 1991.

Smith, Hedrick, ed. *The Media and the Gulf War*. Washington, D.C.: Seven Locks Press, 1992.

Smith, Jean Edward. *George Bush's War*. New York: H. Holt, 1992.

Whicker, Marcia Lynn, James P. Pfiffner, and Raymond A. Moore, eds. *The Presidency and the Persian Gulf War*. Westport, Conn.: Praeger, 1993.

Wilz, John Edward. "The Making of Mr. Bush's War: A Failure to Learn From History?" *Presidential Studies Quarterly* 25 (summer 1995): 533–54.

Woodward, Bob. *The Commanders*. New York: Simon and Schuster, 1991.

## Press Relations

Fitzwater, Marlin. *Call the Briefing! Bush and Reagan, Sam and Helen: A Decade with Presidents and the Press*. New York: Times Books, 1995.

Groeling, Tim, and Samuel Kernell. "Is Network News Coverage of the President Biased?" *Journal of Politics* 60 (November 1998): 1063–87.

Rozell, Mark J. *The Press and the Bush Presidency*. Westport, Conn.: Praeger, 1996.

## Public Opinion

Brace, Paul, and Barbara Hinckley. "George Bush and the Costs of High Popularity: A General Model with Current Application." *PS: Political Science and Politics* 26 (1993): 501–6.

Clarke, Harold D., Jonathan Rapkin, and Marianne C. Stewart. "A President out of Work: A Note on the Political Economy of Presidential Approval in the Bush Years." *British Journal of Political Science* 24 (October 1994): 535–48.

Krosnick, John A., and Laura A. Brannon. "The Impact of the Gulf War on the Ingredients of Presidential Evaluations: Multidimensional Effects of Political Involvement." *American Political Science Review* 87 (1993): 963–75.

Murray, Shoon Kathleen, and Peter Howard. "Variation in White House Polling Operations: Carter to Clinton." *The Public Opinion Quarterly* 66 (winter 2002): 527–58.

Norrander, Barbara, and Clyde Wilcox. "Rallying Around the Flag and Partisan Change: The Case of the Persian Gulf War." *Political Research Quarterly* 46 (1993): 759–70.

Parker, Suzanne L. "Toward an Understanding of 'Rally' Effects: Public Opinion in the Persian Gulf War." *Public Opinion Quarterly* 59 (1995): 526–46.

## Urban Policy

Rich, Michael J. "Riot and Reason: Crafting an Urban Policy Response." *Publius* 23 (1993): 115–24.

# About the Author

**Richard S. Conley** was born in 1967 in southern California. He attended the University of California, Irvine, from 1985 to 1989, and majored in political science. Following several years in the private sector, he returned to graduate school and earned a masters degree from McGill University in Montréal, Canada, in 1993. He moved to Washington, D.C., that year, where he worked in international affairs for the Federal Aviation Administration and later for the Department of Housing and Urban Affairs as a research assistant. He completed his dissertation and Ph.D. in political science at the University of Maryland (College Park) in 1998. His dissertation, which focused on presidential–congressional relations in the post–World War II era during periods of divided government, won the Department of Government and Politics' Dillon Award.

Dr. Conley took up an appointment as an assistant professor in political science at the University of Florida in 1998. He subsequently earned tenure and was promoted to associate professor in 2004. Dr. Conley routinely teaches courses in American politics, and is a specialist on the U.S. presidency and executive–legislative relations. He also has an interest in comparative politics, and has taught courses on comparative executives and legislatures, as well as Canadian and French politics, both in Florida and for the university's summer study-abroad programs in France.

Dr. Conley is author of *The Presidency, Congress, and Divided Government* (2002), and editor of *Reassessing the Reagan Presidency* (2003) and *Transforming the American Polity: The Presidency of George W. Bush and the War on Terrorism* (2005). His numerous articles on American and comparative politics have appeared in *American Politics Research*, *Comparative Political Studies*, *Congress and the*

*Presidency*, *Political Research Quarterly*, *Political Science Quarterly*, *Politics and Policy*, *Presidential Studies Quarterly*, and *White House Studies*. He is currently working on a book that places the legacy of President George W. Bush in comparative perspective with his Republican predecessors since Eisenhower.